R.A. Arnold

Social Politics

R.A. Arnold

Social Politics

ISBN/EAN: 9783337070595

Printed in Europe, USA, Canada, Australia, Japan

Cover: Foto ©Suzi / pixelio.de

More available books at **www.hansebooks.com**

BY

ARTHUR ARNOLD.

LONDON:

C. KEGAN PAUL AND CO., 1, Paternoster Square.

1878.

CONTENTS.

NOTE.

I have to thank Mr. James Knowles, Mr. John Morley, Mr. A. Strahan, Mr. W. Allingham and Messrs. Longmans, for permission to make use of so much of the material of this volume as has appeared in the 'Nineteenth Century,' the 'Fortnightly Review,' the 'Contemporary Review,' and 'Fraser's Magazine.'

I.

THE BUSINESS OF DISESTABLISHMENT.

IT does not appear probable that Disestablishment—which is attended and followed by Disendowment as the substance by the shadow—will ever be proposed by a Conservative Government. Educators as audacious and ingenious as any that exist will no doubt arise. But this would seem to be a task beyond their powers. And when in time to come, in days which I trust are yet remote, sorrowing admirers and sincere political friends are seeking an epitaph for their departed chief, it is by no means unlikely that Lord Beaconsfield's monument may be graven with the words in which he denounced Disestablishment in 1868 : 'If government is not divine, it is nothing.' That the government of Ireland, which, in the meaning of these words, has ceased to be divine, and is merely ducal, is far less onerous and more secure than it was ten years ago, is a fact which would shake the faith of many in the dogma that the salvation of a State rests in the principle of Establishment. But admitting improvement in Ireland, the Conservative party would point to the divinity which hedges the supreme Government in Whitehall, which blossoms in the offices of a Chaplain-General, of Queen Anne's Bounty, and of the Ecclesiastical Commission.

On the other hand, Churchmen whose religious devotion and sincerity are unquestionable—men who have a firm, wide hold on the domestic side of the Conservative party—declare that not only is there no divinity in this association of Church

B

and State, but that the divine character of the Church demands
separation.   The Ritualist pleas are plaintive and pointed.
To the average mind of the Conservative party, the bench
of bishops is an element in the State which secures the divinity
of Government, and redeems it, as Lord Beaconsfield says,
from nothingness.   But to Mr. Mackonochie and his friends
'it is a grievous scandal that the chief pastor and typical
representative of the lowly Carpenter of Galilee should be,
in an earthly kingdom, simply by reason of his spiritual office,
the highest peer not of royal blood.'[1] To the Dissenters, the
Church Establishment is a continual offence, a standing injustice, compelling them to wear a badge of nonconformity.
These parties, with the aid and it may be under the direction,
of politicians who believe that 'if government is not human
it is nothing,' will probably in time accomplish this great work.
The Disestablishment and Disendowment of the Churches of
England and Scotland, 'as by law established,' will be effected.
But those who will take some trouble to study the magnitude
and method of the business will be the most likely to avoid the
error of assuming that it is an easy matter,—that for this part
of the United Kingdom we have merely to write 'England'
in place of 'Ireland' in a copy of the Act of 1869.

At the end of April, 1878, 'the Representative Body of the
Church of Ireland' issued a report, in which they recognise
'good grounds for hope' that they will be able to place 'the
new arrangements of the Church upon a solid and durable
basis.' Never, in any one of their reports, have the Church
Body complained of Disestablishment; they have mentioned
'evils brought about by Disendowment.'   But where Disestablishment is most due, there must Disendowment involve most
difficulty.   Undoubtedly the Church Body have had to contend
with many and grave disadvantages. Sympathisers and opponents
must alike admit that they have wrought a promise of success
out of circumstances which for obvious reasons presented

[1] *Nineteenth Century*, June, 1877.

formidable obstacles. The material assistance they have received from England has not been liberal, nor equal to their hopes. Nor can it be said that the great absentee landlords have, except in a few cases, extended adequate encouragement. Perhaps some English Churchmen have not relished the spectacle of unity, and of successful co-operation on the part of the laity, which have been exhibited in Ireland. However this may be, it is certain that the prophecies of Lord Beaconsfield have not been accomplished. In the debate upon the Irish Church Bill, he committed himself definitely to the statement that ' no permanent endowment could accrue from the scheme,'[1] and in the same speech he said 'it is not only possible but highly probable—that in a certain number of years, probably in the ten years which the right hon. gentleman [Mr. Gladstone] fixes upon, the Irish Protestant Church will not have a shilling of property.'[2] That this was 'heedless rhetoric' we shall see when we glance at the solid investments of the Irish Church Body. It had relation of course to the possibility of a similar process in England, a prospect upon which Lord Beaconsfield then threw out many warnings.

Regarding the business of Disestablishment, what is the difference between the undertaking in Ireland and in England ? According to the present First Minister of the Crown, the argument which was decisive in Ireland may be used with reference to England. Lord Beaconsfield said : 'I ask you, How can you meet the question of England ? Let not honourable members around me say, There are millions and millions in England who are members of the Established Church. That does not answer the stern conclusion from the census returns, viz. : that in England the majority of the people are not members of the Church.'[3] When Mr. Gladstone foreshadowed the Disestablishment of the Church of Ireland,

---

[1] *House of Commons Debates*, March 18, 1869.
[2] *House of Commons Debates*, April 3, 1868.
[3] *Ibid.*

he said that it implied abolition of the Ecclesiastical Courts ; the cessation of ecclesiastical jurisdiction; that the ecclesiastical laws in Ireland would no longer bind by any authority as law; that the rights of peerage would lapse on the part of the bishops, and that all ecclesiastical corporations would be dissolved. Lord Beaconsfield said that Disestablishment was a policy which would ' dangerously touch even the tenure of the Crown.'[1] At present, the Sovereign is by law a member of the Church of England. The admixture of clerical patronage with highest judicial duties in the Lord Chancellor has rendered his office subject to the same restriction. That the coronation is an ecclesiastical function performed in an ecclesiastical building is a matter of custom and ceremony, and nothing more. If it appeared more seemly that the Sovereign should solemnly assume the crown in Buckingham Palace, or in the House of Lords, there would be no difficulty in the matter. The coronation is merely a ceremony: the Sovereign's authority is as full before as after that solemnity. Perhaps it would not be incorrect to regard the coronation as peculiarly investing the Sovereign with the title and dignity of Supreme Governor of the Church ; and that is a title which, upon the enactment of Disestablishment, must be laid aside. The Sovereign in that capacity, as nominator of the bishops and patron of ecclesiastical offices and benefices, is in fact one of those ecclesiastical corporations which would be dissolved. This is what occurred with regard to Ireland. But diminution of the Sovereign's ecclesiastical authority, such as was made by the Irish Church Act of 1869, is a very different matter from the extinction of that authority, which would be the consequence of Disestablishment in England. When that is accomplished there must be no act on the part of Government implying the existence of any ' national' Church. The religion of the Sovereign would then be a separate matter, concerning the nation just as much, or as little, as the nation pleased.

[1] *House of Commons Debates,* April 3, 1868.

Whoever takes in hand the business of Disestablishment in England, will have to encounter much language of a similar character with that which I have quoted from the lips of Lord Beaconsfield. In no part of the subject, perhaps, will error be more common than in regard to the relations between the Church and the Crown. In the 'Practical Suggestions relative to Disestablishment of the Church of England,' issued in 1877 by the Liberation Society, there are suggestions which appear to be misleading upon this point. At the conclusion of these 'Suggestions' it is stated that the most important of the matters, which, though popularly associated with Disestablishment, have no necessary connection with it, is 'the succession to the Crown under what is known as the Act of Settlement.' The 'suggestion' is 'that the exclusion of members of the Roman Catholic Church from the throne of Great Britain, is a political question quite as much as an ecclesiastical question, and must be dealt with on its own merits. It was left untouched when the Irish Establishment was abolished, and may in like manner be left untouched when those of England and Scotland are also disestablished.' In the first place, I may say that 'the Act of Settlement' is hardly a correct expression, inasmuch as there are two Acts of Settlement directly affecting the matter. The rule of James II. and the Revolution, as it is called, of 1688, had convinced the English Parliament of the impolicy of placing a Roman Catholic on the throne; and, resolving 'that it is inconsistent with the safety and welfaire of this Protestant Kingdome, to be governed by a popish prince, or by any king or queene marrying a Papist,' the legislature declared that persons who should either be themselves members of the Church of Rome, or should marry a Papist, should be incapable of holding the crown, which in any such case of incapacity, should descend to the nearest Protestant in the line of succession. This, I admit, is 'a political quite as much as an ecclesiastical question,' but that Act (1 William and Mary, c. 2) was, upon the death of Mary without issue, followed by another

Act of Settlement (12 and 13 William III., c. 2), which, preserving all the limitations of the former Act, provided that all future Sovereigns must be members of the communion of the Church of England as by law established.

An Act of Disestablishment would directly affect this latter Act of Settlement. But it would touch it only so far as to render the words affected obsolete. Upon the next demise of the Crown such an obligation as is here expressed could not then be enforced upon the Queen's successor. In any Act of Disestablishment it would be necessary to insert a saving clause of the same character as Section 69 of the Irish Church Act, which is as follows :—

> In all enactments, deeds, or other documents in which mention is made of the United Church of England and Ireland, the enactments and provisions relating thereto shall be read distributively in respect of the Church of England and the Church of Ireland, but, as to the last mentioned Church, subject to the provisions of this Act.

That clause covers the coronation oath, and a clause of a like character would deal with the corresponding obligations of the Crown touching the Church of England. The Act of Settlement must be so far amended by the same process that the words 'as by law established,' having reference to the Church of England, must cease, upon the Act of Disestablishment, to have operation or authority. It may be held unnecessary to repeal the provision for communion on the part of the Sovereign with the Church of England. But whether the Church of England is or is not disestablished, a positive change must be made in the coronation oath upon the demise of the Crown. Her present Majesty, upon her coronation, took oath to 'maintain and preserve inviolably the settlement of the United Church of England and Ireland, and the doctrine, worship, discipline, and government thereof, as by law established within England and Ireland,' and to 'preserve to the bishops and clergy of England and Ireland, and to the churches there committed to their charge, all such rights and privileges as do or shall appertain unto them or any of them.' That oath cannot be administered in its entirety to Her Majesty's successor, because the legislative union of the Churches has been dissolved by section 2 of the Irish Church Act, which declared that 'on and after the first day of January, 1871, the said Union created by Act of Parliament between the Churches of England and Ireland shall be dissolved,' and because by the same section it has been enacted that 'the said Church of Ireland shall cease to be established by law.' Her Majesty's obligation under the oath was probably held by her responsible advisers to be subject to the prior obligation she accepted on the same occasion. In the Coronation Service, before the Sovereign entered into the pledge which I have quoted, a promise of far greater gravity and importance was recorded. The Sovereign was required 'solemnly' to 'promise and swear to govern the people of this United Kingdom of Great Britain and Ireland, and the dominions thereto belonging, according to the statutes in Parliament agreed on, and the respective laws and customs of the same.' This, which is the first part of the coronation oath, rules the remainder. The monarch swears to govern according to parliamentary law and custom, which certainly involves royal assent to a measure of Disestablishment carried by a large majority in a Parliament elected with special reference to that object, and introduced by Ministers enjoying the confidence of the Crown as well as of that majority.

The personality, the personal conscience and the private religious conviction of the Sovereign were not held to be involved in these oaths. This may be clearly shown by comparing the oath concerning the Anglican Church with the oath having reference to the Established (Presbyterian) Church of Scotland. In the Treaty of Union, the 'Act for securing the Church of England as by law established,' maintained those words which I have quoted from the coronation oath, and which in the language of that oath were held to imply (for England), 'the true profession of the Gospel and the Protestant reformed religion, established by law.' By the Scotch oath, the Sovereign makes a precisely similar declaration concerning a religion which abhors episcopacy. At the Union it was provided, in order to prevent unseemly jarring of these oaths, that 'the security of the Church of Scotland' should be promised and sworn, 'not at the coronation.' But the Scots had another motive for avoiding the coronation. That is a ceremony not necessary to the authority of the Sovereign. They therefore obtained 'security' upon accession. According to the terms by which England and Scotland were united in the Kingdom of Great Britain, the Sovereign is required to 'swear and subscribe,' upon 'his or her accession to the crown,' that 'the settlement of the true Protestant religion,'—that is, the Presbyterian Church of Scotland—shall, 'as established,' be maintained inviolably. On this point, however, and on all such matters, the Sovereign is not immediately affected by Disestablishment. The difficulties of Disestablishment would be enhanced if the Sovereign had at once to undergo a civil coronation, or even, to accept a revised oath.

These are times in which the conscientious scruples of princes meet with consideration, and the absence of such scruples with contempt, and if the acts of princes are made, even in appearance, subject to ecclesiastical sanction, it would become more difficult to accept the true position of a constitutional Sovereign. Any needless meddling with real or even with fanciful attributes of the Sovereign, would of course be avoided by those who desired an Act of Disestablishment. They would not vainly perplex themselves with the meaning of terms and titles. They would not inquire whether the Sovereign did or did not rule 'by the grace of God.' There was a time, if I remember rightly, when the mysterious title, 'Defender of the Faith,' was omitted upon a certain issue of coins. Lord Russell was then in the position now occupied by Lord Beaconsfield. Clamour arose for the restoration of 'F. D.' upon the coinage. Yet who can tell what 'Fidei Defensor' means, and who will contend that words of this sort, which have no definite meaning, must be affected by Disestablishment? We may write of them in that tone of uncertainty which John Byrom assumed at a Jacobite dinner-party:—

> ' God bless the King! God bless the Faith's Defender!
> God bless—no harm in blessing—the Pretender!
> Who the Pretender is, and who the King,
> God bless us all! that's quite another thing.'

Lord Beaconsfield is, or was, of opinion that we have religious equality in England,—that as touching equality, Establishment is nothing. The Prime Minister has defined ' religious equality ' to be that condition in which ' a man has complete and perfect enjoyment of his religion, and can uphold and vindicate his religious privileges in the courts of law.'[1] But it may be asked, Is equality possible between a Church which is made political and other Churches which remain non-political? for this is the meaning which in another speech Lord Beaconsfield has annexed to Establishment. He said in the debate on the Irish Church Bill, that what he understood by the union of Church and State was an arrangement ' which renders the State religious,' and which ' renders the Church political.'[2] It would be difficult to set up religious inequality by a more audacious argument. Disestablishment is in truth the dissolution of a fiction founded upon fact. There was a time—there were centuries—when the Church was co-extensive with the nation. All acts of authority had religious sanction, because the Church and the people were one and the same body. Dissent in those days was a crime and misdemeanour against the general law. The union of Church and State is a different matter when diversity of religious belief becomes established as one of the great facts of national life.

We may judge pretty well how Establishment gained and how it waned, by a glance at the Toleration Act, one of the early legislative fruits of the reign of William and Mary. It

---

[1] *House of Commons Debates*, May 22, 1868.
[2] *House of Commons Debates*, March 18, 1869.

was then that Nonconformity ceased to be illegal, and when, by
the fact that Dissent was no longer held criminal, the nation
gave proof that it was not of one mind in matters of religion,—
that, indeed, the Church was no longer co-extensive with the
nation—the principle of Establishment began to lose force.
Before the passing of the Toleration Act there were statutes
in operation which ordered attendance at the services of the
Church of England, with threat of severe penalties upon conviction of neglect.   But especially were these statutes directed
to the prevention of attendance at 'conventicles'; and the
feeling of that time, even though it had been kindled into what
was then regarded as Liberalism by the revolution of the
preceding year (1688) did not permit the repeal of these
obnoxious statutes.   The Toleration Act, the Magna Charta of
Dissent, merely provided that these Establishmental laws should
not be construed to extend to any person who should testify
his loyalty by taking the oaths of supremacy and allegiance
and his Protestantism by subscribing the declaration against
transubstantiation.   The rift in the basis of Establishment
began when the Toleration Act relaxed the severe laws of
that period.   Even then the Church made every Dissenting
minister put his hand to all except a few of the Thirty-nine
Articles.   But this could not be done with the Quaker, who
would swear to nothing, and he was let off upon making profession of his faith 'in the divinity of the Son and of the Holy
Ghost, and in the inspiration of the Old and New Testaments.'[1]
'Such,' Macaulay adds, 'were the terms upon which the Protestant Dissenters of England were for the first time permitted
by law to worship God according to their own conscience,' and it
may be taken for certain that any measure for Disestablishment
will display, as the historian says did the Toleration Act,
'the peculiar vices, and the peculiar excellences, of English
legislation.   To think nothing of symmetry and much of
convenience; never to renounce an anomaly merely because

---

[1] Macaulay, *Hist. of England*, ch. xi.

it is an anomaly; never to innovate except when some grievance is felt; never to innovate except so far as to get rid of a grievance; never to lay down any proposition of wider extent than the particular case for which it is necessary to provide; these are the rules which have, from the age of John to the age of Victoria, generally guided the deliberations of our two hundred and fifty Parliaments.' [1]

The consolation which Macaulay applied to this mixture of vices and excellences, that 'it would not be easy to name another country in which there has been so little retrogression,' is hardly admissible with regard to Disestablishment. There are arguments favourable to the maintenance of Establishment. One may adduce the control of the clergy by the State, and the reduction, if not the disappearance, of lay authority, which, in his opinion, would in time follow upon Disestablishment; another may dilate upon the blessings of an universal provision of religious offices, with no sectarian limitation. But no one appears to suppose that religious Establishments will be a feature of new communities,—that the rising nations of the New World will establish and endow an episcopalian or any other Church. There can be no retrogression in regard to a policy which lost its logical foundation at the birth of religious liberty.

Disestablishment would include the abolition of the bench of bishops. They must then quit the House of Lords. But, on the other hand, not the bishops only, but all the clergy, must be rendered eligible for seats in either House of Parliament. Their exclusion is justified now on the ground of their 'political' connection with the State. That is Lord Beaconsfield's word. By another authority the clergy have been called 'a branch of the Civil Service,' and the members of that service are, as everybody knows, disqualified for places in Parliament. The State would cease to recognise anything like indelibility in the Orders of the Church. If a bishop, upon compounding,

[1] Macaulay, *Hist. of England*, ch. xi.

or otherwise receiving compensation for the loss of his official
position in the State, thought proper to invest the money and
his energies in secular pursuits, and gained in civil life the
suffrages of some borough, he would, on his name being returned
in the writ, be entitled to take his place in the House of
Commons.   Men who have acted with distinction as Nonconformist ministers are now in Parliament, and a clergyman
of the disestablished Church would of course be free to take
the same position.

There has been a time in the history of many nations when
the clergy occupied all the higher offices of State, and held a
large personal share of influence in every assembly.   Any one
who, with competent knowledge, examines the ruins of the
ancient Theatre of Dionysius beside the Acropolis of Athens,
will note that in Byzantine days the first circle of seats was
allotted to ecclesiastics.   If we may judge from the inscriptions
upon those ruined chairs of white marble, the chief seats
belonged almost exclusively to hierarchs, and it was pretty
much the same in England.   Buckle has pointed out that 'in
early and barbarous periods' one half of the House of Lords
consisted of spiritual peers ; that by the beginning of the eighth
century the proportion had dwindled to one-eighth ; and that in
the middle of the nineteenth century it had shrunk to one-
fourteenth.   It has continued to shrink, and is now even less
than the last proportion mentioned by Buckle.   In the Middle
Ages, not a few clergy sat in the House of Commons. Then
for centuries they were excluded by custom, which was broken
by the Rev. Horne Tooke, whose unwelcome presence as
M.P. for Old Sarum led to the passing of the 41 George III.,
c. 63, which excluded ordained clergymen from Parliament.

We can well conceive England without an Act of Uniformity ; beneficed clergy without *ex-officio* powers in matters
of local government ; Convocation free to speak and free to
act, subject to such obligations as the laity controlling the
funds of the disestablished Church thought fit to impose ;

we can imagine all this as following upon Disestablishment, and for the rest let us learn what we can by looking fully and fairly at the Irish case. It will bear and will reward inspection. The success has been very great. Parliament lent a helping hand. Mr. Gladstone's Irish Church Bill was no unkindly measure. The corporations, sole and aggregate, which composed the dignified and beneficed ranks of that Church were not scattered carelessly to the winds of heaven, shorn of their glebes and tithes. Every facility was given for preserving the life of the Church. It was at the invitation, almost, we may say, at the bidding, of Parliament that the Representative Church Body arose and became incorporated in place of the Church as by law established. On the passing of the Act, all property belonging to the Ecclesiastical Commissioners for Ireland was transferred to the specially appointed Commissioners of Church Temporalities in Ireland and on the day of Disestablishment (1st January, 1871) all Church property passed into the same hands. To those Commissioners the clergy had then to look for their incomes, and other Church officers for their emoluments and compensations.

In all this the interests of the, as yet, unborn Body were carefully regarded. The clergy were induced to commute their incomes in order that the commutation money, and with it the superintendence of their interests, might be passed on to the Church Body. The income of each benefice was taken as an annuity at 3½ per cent., to which a bonus of 12 per cent. (on the ground of the superior longevity of the clergy, and of the cost of superintendence) was added. There were several inducements to commutation. (1) By commuting, their pecuniary interest was transferred to the Church Body ; professional loyalty and duty were therefore enlisted. (2) The bonus of 12 per cent. was added when three-fourths of the clergy in any diocese had signified their readiness to commute. (3) There could be no compounding without commutation. By all three of these means the establishment of the Church Body was promoted. Every one who wished well to the Episcopal Church in the future urged the clergy to commute, and this policy was so successful that at the end of 1871, the first year of Disestablishment, the Church Body were able to report that 'commutation has been generally adopted.' In every diocese more than the requisite three-fourths of the clergy had intimated willingness; in fact, only about 300 cases remained 'to complete the whole list of annuitants.'

When the Temporalities Commissioners commuted an income, the annuity was calculated at 3½ per cent. Thus, supposing an incumbent was forty years of age, the Church Body received for every £10 of his income the sum of £160 2s. 8d. To this was added a bonus of 12 per cent., making a total sum of nearly £180. The Church Body have found no difficulty in obtaining suitable investment for their funds at nearly 4½ per cent. In the report for 1878, giving a statement of their finances made up to the 31st December, 1877, we find the following account of their investments :—

	Cost.			Income.		
	£	s.	d.	£	s.	d.
£2,717.216 Railway Debenture and Preference Stock	2,908,751	3	5	128,746	8	6
Mortgages on Land at 4¼ per cent. .	1,119,864	18	1	47,594	5	2
Mortgages on Land at 4½ per cent. .	2,368,679	16	10	106,590	12	0
Sundries per donors for various trusts	55,605	9	5	2,342	14	5
	£6,452,901	7	9	£285,274	0	1

It will be seen from the above statement that the average rate of interest obtained upon these six millions and a half is £4 8s. 6d. per cent., which is 18s. 6d. per cent. more than the cost to the Church Body of the annuities. This addition is superadded upon the bonus of 12 per cent. The total amount of annuities payable to the clergy of all ranks, when the Church Body commenced their career, did not exceed £460,000 per annum, a charge less than 8 per cent. upon the above investment of capital. The Church Body were therefore liable to suffer a diminution of their funds in the first year equal to 4 per cent. This liability would diminish as the annuities became extinguished by death among the clergy, and, with reference to the provision of incomes for the successors of expired annuitants, would be liable to new and perhaps enhanced charges. To meet this claim upon their capital the Church Body have had assistance from four sources. (1) Subscriptions and donations, which appear to have been liberal, from the resident Protestant gentry; to display notable refusals on the part of absentee landlords; and to have been unsympathetic, in a degree almost scandalous, on the side of the wealthy clergy and laity of the Church of England. The Church Body, in their report for 1875, call attention to 'the limited amount of assistance received from many quarters, where more liberal contributions might have been expected, and the refusal of all aid from many absentee landed proprietors.' But from all sources these donations and subscriptions have substantially met the drain upon the capital of the Church Body. The annual totals have been as follow :—

	£	s.	d.		£	s.	d.
1870	229,753	14	2	1874	257,021	2	1
1871	214,709	8	4	1875	218,499	3	8
1872	248,445	1	8	1876	212,095	7	7
1873	230,179	11	0	1877	197,739	6	7

Considering the poverty of Ireland and the feebleness of zeal in many rural parishes, these figures appear to me very remarkable. Surely, no stronger tribute to the energy engendered by religious dependence on voluntary aid has ever been afforded. In their report for 1878, the Church Body view the decline of the total with wise apprehension. They say the receipts up to and including 1874, 'were swelled by the payment of the last instalment of the large donations which were promised by many liberal contributors when the Church was disendowed in 1869, and the payment of which was spread over a period of five years. The continued decrease of the total amount of contributions during the last three years is certainly discouraging. The experience of other voluntary Churches had led many persons to expect that, year by year, as the various wants of the Church became more widely known, and the claims of our poorer brethren upon our sympathy and aid were more clearly realised, there would be a steady augmentation in the contribution to the funds from which alone these wants could be supplied.   In the Free Church of Scotland, for example, the total contributions to the General Sustentation Fund, which in the year 1844 were only £68,704 14s. 8d., have shown a steady and progressive annual increase (with only two or three insignificant exceptions) until, in the year ending May, 1877, they amounted to £172,641 18s. 3d., being an increase of nearly threefold in a period of little more than thirty years.'

The Church Body would doubtless have made this complaint with better effect, and with larger promise of result, had they been entirely dependent upon voluntary aid. But Mr. Gladstone put them in quite a different position.   I have touched only one source of income.   The Church Body have (2) derived profit from dealings with glebe houses and glebe lands.   (3) The Church Body have largely reduced the amount of annuities chargeable upon their funds by composition, or compounding with the clergy.   The general body of the clergy obtained advantage through the system of compounding, because, by the extinction of annuities on payment of two-thirds of the com-mutation money, the diocesan fund was enlarged by the remaining third.   And there was very legitimate scope for compounding on the indisputable ground that the Irish Church was over-manned with clergy.   No one will say that composi-tion has been limited to those whose services were in excess of the labours required by the Church.   But there was an excess. The rule in regard to composition has been that the money left in the hands of the Representative Body is passed to the credit of the diocese ; and this is fair and prudent, because the reason that the Church Body have been able to reduce the number of clergy in any diocese is owing to the scarcity of members of the Church, which is a cause of local difficulty in providing contributions to the Sustentation Fund.

The reduction in the number of clergy has been the most legitimate and beneficial operation of the arrangement as to compounding. The sanction of the Bishop or of the Diocesan Council was not necessary in making application. Commutation would not have been so readily or generally adopted, and the Church Body thus firmly founded, had there been any restriction as to compounding; the only conditions imposed by the resolutions of the Church Body upon compounding were that the 'life shall be insurable at ordinary rates at the time of composition,' and it was provided 'that the right of composition shall, in any case, where the clergyman applying has not, previous to his application, served in the ministry of the Church of Ireland, at any time, for a period of three years, be subject to the discretion of the Representative Body, who shall be at liberty to postpone his composition until he shall have completed that period of service'; and it was stated that 'the Representative Body were induced to adopt these resolutions by the debates in the Convention, from which it appeared that if the right of compounding were not conceded, general commutation would be impossible.' Many an 'ecclesiastical person,' conscious of talents which would ensure employment in England, if not in Ireland, looked with no dislike upon the whole process, because he had in prospect the sale of his position for the sum to be obtained on compounding, to which would be added freedom to seek another income. The rule for compounding was this,—the operation being limited of course to those who had commuted: 'Every person of the age of sixty-five and upwards may receive two-thirds of his commutation money, including the twelve per cent. bonus; and that for persons of lower ages a nineteenth part of the whole commutation money shall be deducted for every year below sixty-five.'

I have already given an example of the value of an annuity of £10 upon the scale of commutation; I will now give an example of the value of a similar annuity upon composition. For every £10 of annuity, the compounding applicant, at the

C

age of forty, has received £69 14s. 11d. In this case the sum remaining in the hands of the Church Body, for the benefit of the diocese in which the composition was effected, would exceed £100. But by their fifteenth resolution the Church Body specially reserved 'the power of considering propositions from individual ecclesiastical persons, with reference to both commuting and compounding, and of granting more favourable terms.' The cases of this sort have not been numerous. A tabular statement of the details of composition was issued in 1875, from which it appeared that out of a total of 753 compounders there had been 154 special cases. Many of these special cases were in some way remarkable ; I will, however, only refer to that which is most notable, the case of the only bishop who has compounded. The Bishop of Derry was, at the time of general commutation, about forty years of age. The commutation sum of the net annual value of his episcopal income, amounting to £6,847 12s. 5d., together with the bonus of 12 per cent., was £111,367 19s. 1d. That was the amount paid by the Temporalities Commissioners to the Church Body as the commuted value of the Bishop of Derry's income. From the general report of 1875 we learn that the Bishop of Derry has compounded, and in the statement from the Sustentation Committee we find the following notice : 'That by the very liberal and judicious disposition of his annuity by the Bishop of Derry, a sufficient provision has been made to secure to his successor a permanent income of £2,000 a year.' There is another reference to the matter in the report for the preceding year (1874). There the Representative Body state that 'for future Bishops of Derry, by means of an arrangement made between the Representative Body and the Bishop on his compounding, in which his lordship makes a large sacrifice of income during his life, there has been secured for that See an income of £2,000 per annum.'

Now, what was that arrangement? On the general rule of compounding, the Bishop of Derry would have been entitled to a sum between £45,000 and £50,000, and the Church Body would have retained upwards of £60,000 for the permanent endowment of the See of Derry, a sum which at 4 per cent. would have produced £2,400 a year. I am told that the Church Body have retained £50,000 (which is confirmed by their statement as to £2,000 a year), and upon his compounding have handed over £61,000 to Dr. Alexander, who of course retains in addition the £2,000 a year so long as he is Bishop of Derry. It is difficult to comprehend the process of reasoning by which the Sustentation Committee were led to distinguish this transaction as 'very liberal.' But it is impossible to look through the reports of the Representative Body of the Church of Ireland without feeling increased confidence in the virtues and the efficiency of self-government. Hasty deduction from what has taken place in Ireland might produce one signal error,—the supposing that harmony of opinion within the Church Body would be similarly manifested under like circumstances in England. The Establishment in Ireland was always essentially and uniformly Protestant, because it was confronted in the greater number of parishes by a majority of Roman Catholics. That constitutes a very important and material difference. On the other hand, the financial points which presented most difficulty in Ireland, and which have been so far surmounted only by the aid which Parliament gave in the institution of the Church Body and by unremitting and most arduous labour on the part of zealous members and friends of the Church, would occur in England amid circumstances of a precisely opposite character.

The annals of the Irish Church Body more than vindicate Mr. Gladstone's legislation. They encourage a similar policy in the larger island. Not only are the Irish Church Body so far successful that their latest utterance breathes 'an expression of deep thankfulness,' but so acclimatised are Churchmen to altered circumstances that they speak even of 'drawbacks' with self-gratulation. 'There are,' say they, 'drawbacks in-

herent in every voluntary system; and some press with increased force in a country like Ireland, where, in many places,
the members of the Church are few in number and widely
scattered in remote country localities.' Of their practical
good sense in dealing with the burial question, and of the
valuable uses of adversity, we have evidence in the recommendation that where 'parishes have expressed their inability to
keep the burial-grounds in proper repair . . . the burial-ground
should be transferred to the Guardians of the Poor Law Union
in which such burial-ground is situated.' These annals give
encouragement especially to those of the Church laity who
are desirous of possessing a reasonable Church policy, and
for themselves an effective control. To the clergy they speak
volumes—of profitable dealing with the funds of the Establishment. To the laity they exhibit the most succesful chapter
of lay co-operation which the history of religion has hitherto.
afforded. To all they declare that success is born of difficulty
in religious as well as in secular matters. Their lesson is
plain and simple, and their influence irresistible. The framers
of the Irish Church Act did not desire to lay in ruins the
organisation which they sought to detach from official connection with the State. Mr. Gladstone did his work with care
and even solicitude for the Disestablished Church. It is not
to be expected that bishops who have lost their rights of
peerage will be just critics, but a Church is not made for, nor
is it composed of, bishops. There can be no doubt whatever
that throughout the ranks of Protestant laity in Ireland there
is profound satisfaction with their success. To many members
of the Church of England the records of the Irish Church Body
will be an incentive to speedy action. We may suppose they
have to some extent inspired the 'Practical Suggestions' which
I am about to examine.[1] It is open to any one to suggest how,
if the Church of England is to be disestablished, the work shall be

---

[1] *Practical Suggestions relative to the Disestablishment and Disendowment of the
Church of England.* Published by the Society for the Liberation of Religion from
State Patronage and Control.

accomplished. But it is not possible to doubt, that when governmental action is in view, this that has been done in Ireland will be regarded as a precedent of the utmost importance. There will be a tendency now and from henceforth in the Liberal party to avoid the lines upon which the work was undertaken in Ireland. But will that party be prepared and will it be able, when the time of action arrives, to stand out against, and to defeat, propositions which by their liberality would paralyse the main body of resistance?

A matter of the highest importance in the business of Disestablishment is whether or not the State should, as it did in Ireland, promote by Act of Parliament the reorganisation of the Church. The institution of a Church Body in this way appears from one side to be in direct contravention of the principle of religious equality. On the other hand it has been said that this is but just compensation to the laity for interference with their rights as Churchmen. I should hesitate to affirm so positively as do these 'Practical Suggestions' that only the bishops, clergy, and church officers, together with the owners of advowsons and next presentations, will be entitled to compensation. That is quite true so far as money is concerned. But the Church in its widest and most proper meaning —the clergy and laity, the congregations, separate in parishes and districts, and aggregate as to the whole, would seem to have a strong equitable claim to the consideration of Parliament. Yet the institution of a Church Body on the Irish plan cannot be conceded without to a certain extent invalidating the plea to satisfy which Disestablishment is effected. There would be a great desire for the constitution by authority of such a body into whose treasury the commutation capital should be passed, and this desire would be expressed by the most liberal and valuable section of the Church. Co-operation between the parties in the Church might be found impossible if it were not fostered by Parliament in the Act of Disestablishment. But if Parliament is called upon to provide religious equality it must forbear from undertaking to prevent religious dissension. For Parliament to institute or indicate the formation of a Church Body is an encouragement, if not a direction, that the Protestant Episcopal Church in England should continue one and undivided. Such legislation involves direct interference with the internal politics of a religious community, and is therefore in opposition to the principle of religious equality. But it is just because such a proceeding would be the most likely to compose differences within the Church, to draw together and to hold in compact the warring parties of the Establishment—it is because the institution of a Church Body would seem the surest way to reinvest the laity with some of that authority which must be lost upon Disestablishment by the repeal of the Act of Uniformity and the renunciation of Parliamentary control—it is for these reasons that the introduction of the germs of a Church Body into any Act of Disestablishment would be urged by that large and influential, because so moderate, section of the Church which is possessed of such vast power in Parliament. And perhaps I may safely predict that if, when the time of Disestablishment arrives, an organisation is not formed upon the lines of the Irish model, it will not be that Parliament is disposed to abstract justice in the matter of religious equality, but because the strife of parties within the Church will have assumed such proportions that it would be preposterous on the part of the Legislature to assume to bind opinions in a bond, the mention of which would be resented as an affront by those spiritualists of the Church who, like Mr. Mackonochie, repudiate all association with the temporalities of State authority and control.

The formation of a Church Body under the patronage of Parliament ought certainly to be resisted by those who advocate Disestablishment for the sake of religious equality. But of course it would be the duty of Parliament to remove every legal impediment from the way of all who desired to promote such organisation upon an independent basis. There are obvious reasons why in this matter the Irish precedent should not be followed in England. The Church of England possesses far greater vitality, and power, and wealth ; and in England the release of the clergy from their connection with the State could under no circumstances present to them the opportunity, upon compounding and cutting, of offering their services to a more wealthy Church. The English clergy would have no inducement to reciprocate the compliment which has been paid to their position by the disestablished and compounding clergy of the Church of Ireland.

For the clergy, the terms laid down in the ' Practical Suggestions ' are, it may be said, more advantageous than those of the Irish Church Act. In Ireland, the State in a measure tied the clergy to the Church Body. Their compensation was made conditional. The ' Practical Suggestions ' propose, in language which is more true to the principle of Disestablishment, that there should be no conditions imposed on the clergy—that they should not be passed on from service in connection with the State to service in connection with a Church Body. The ' Suggestions ' of the Liberation Society indicate that ' the State should deal only with the individuals concerned, and not with any body acting on behalf of the members of the Disestablished Church, or with any ecclesiastical corporation which has been dissolved by the Act of Disestablishment.' The clergy have much cause to prefer this method, and for that reason the laity may be expected to dislike it. Substituting ' England ' for ' Ireland,' we may say of the former what Mr. Gladstone said of the latter in 1869: 'We presume that during the interval which the Bill will create after the disabilities are removed, the bishops, clergy, and laity of the Church of England will proceed to constitute for themselves, in the same manner as other religious communities have done, something in the nature of a governing body.' Now it is obvious that the power of the clergy, and their influence in moulding the constitution and rules of this body, will be considerable if they deal solely with the State in regard to their official claims, and are able to approach this body as independent members of the Church. Is it not very obvious that their pecuniary interests would lie in the same direction; because as their dealing with the State would have no reference to the continuance of their duties, they would be free to enter into new arrangements with their congregations or with a Church Body? And assuming that the clergy have a claim to be dealt with in this manner directly by the State, there can be no question that such a method, if fairly carried out, would render the surplus at the disposal of Parliament larger than if the Irish plan were adopted.

The compensation of the clergy, calculated upon the scale applied to 'other branches of the Civil Service,' would amount to a smaller sum than the commutations upon the Irish method. We may see this by an example. I take the first person, of the age of forty, whose name appears in the lengthy list[1] of those who, having been in the Civil Service, have received compensation upon the abolition of the office·in respect of which their salary was paid. The name is that of a gentleman in the Home Office who had served continuously from the age of seventeen, and whose salary at retirement was £525 a year. His office was abolished in 1871, and a retiring allowance of £447 was granted, which, after five months, was commuted into a capital sum of £3,898 15s. 9d., a composition which was paid for the extinction of the annuity. Now, if this gentleman had been a clergyman in the Disestablished Church of Ireland, though he had held his benefice, valued at £525, but a single month, his commutation money, payable to the Church Body, calculated, according to the Act, at the rate of about £180 for every £10 of the annuity, would have amounted to more than £9,000. The charge of a case of this sort upon the funds of the Disestablished Church would therefore be less than half that which was paid in Ireland, if the State dealt directly and solely with the clergyman and compensated him upon the plan

[1] *Financial Reform Almanack*, 1877.

adopted in the Civil Service. The Liberation Society have, we may presume, an eye to this advantage in their 'Practical Suggestions.' Their 'Suggestions' on this head are not extravagant. It would be impossible to deal with the clergy upon less liberal terms than are adopted in the Civil Service. And if compensation were carried out in this form it must be conducted upon the intelligible principle of regard for the practice in departments of State. The 'suggestion,' therefore, of the Bishops' Resignation Act is not admissible. It is clear that bishops over sixty years of age could, according to the general practice in the Civil Service, claim their full salary upon compulsory retirement.

Regarding the State as interested in the amount of the surplus remaining after the satisfaction of all claims upon the property of the Establishment, and looking at the matter from that point of view, we may say that the largest gain in adopting the method of the 'Practical Suggestions' rather than that of the Irish Church Act, would be in the compensation paid to the beneficed clergy. There would be a corresponding gain in dealing with curates of the 'permanent' and of the 'unattached' class, whose stipends, under the provisions of the Irish Church Act, were dealt with upon the same terms as the incomes of the parochial clergy. In Ireland, 'temporary' curates received a gratuity, which could not exceed £200 if they had not completed eight years' service, and could in no case exceed £600. But a great part of the advantage of dealing directly and only with the clergy would lie in the matter of what are called 'private endowments.' What are those endowments which must be reserved in their entirety exclusively for Church purposes? In reply to this question—one of such vast importance in the business of Disestablishment—it is found necessary to assign a date. In proposing the Irish Church Bill, Mr. Gladstone took 1660, the year of the restoration of the Stuarts, as the date at which he would ask Parliament 'to distinguish private and public endowments, because,' he said, 'we

know historically that a man at any rate knew what he was
doing, and the fair presumption arises that if he gave his money
to the Church it was for the support of that form of religion to
which it is now applied.'[1]   He took that date because he held
that up to that time there had been no declared supremacy
obtained either by Episcopacy or Presbyterianism in their continual struggles and inextricable entanglement; because not till
then did Protestant Episcopacy emerge from the conflict as the
Established religion of Ireland.   But it does not appear to me
that justice is done to the importance of union with the State
by such a remote limitation.   If we consider what was the
condition of Ireland at that period; how the country had
recently been soaked with the blood of its inhabitants in the
fights of the Cromwellian conquest; how the landowners had
been ruthlessly dispossessed and their properties forfeited by
the rudest processes—by acts which Charles the Second was
obliged for his own security to condone—when we read in the
preamble of the Irish Act of Settlement, passed about the
period from which Mr. Gladstone claimed endowments as the
private property of the Church of Ireland, 'that Almighty God
had given His Majesty, by and through his English Protestant
subjects, absolute victory and conquest over the Irish Popish
rebels and enemies, so that they, their lives, liberties, and estates
were at His Majesty's disposition by the laws of the kingdom,'[2]
we can hardly feel quite sure, upon a dissolution of the union
between Church and State in Ireland, that 'we know historically
that a man knew what he was doing,' we are somewhat doubtful
as to the title of the Irish Church Body to exclude endowments of
that date from the general fund applied in the first place to the
compensation of clerical and other claims, and, as to the surplus,
'to be appropriated mainly to the relief of unavoidable calamity
and suffering'[3] in Ireland.

As to England, who shall fix this date?   There was no Day

[1] *House of Commons Debates*, March 1, 1869.   [2] 14 & 15 Car. II. c. 2.
[3] Irish Church Act, 1869, sect. 68.

of Reformation. From 1528 to 1688 the battle of Protestantism was undecided. Many would say that the Church of England as by law established dates from November 1534, the time at which the 26 Henry VIII. c. 1—the Act of Supremacy—was passed. But the 'Anglicana Ecclesia,' which was established by that famous statute, of which Henry was to 'be taken, accepted, and reputed the only supreme Head in earth,' needed another Act of Establishment in five-and-twenty years. It had been burnt to ashes in the fires of the Marian persecutions. It was set up again by Elizabeth's Act of Uniformity (1 Elizabeth, c. 2). Episcopacy fell in Cromwell's time, and was restored under Charles the Second. But why go on? The history of these changes could not be closed even by reference to 1688. I am disposed to think, using Mr. Gladstone's words again, that we can safely assume that a man 'knew what he was doing' only when he is alive to tell us that the property which he gave to the Church in union with the State is to be held solely for and by the Church when that connection is dissolved. Beyond a comparatively short period, I do not think it a 'fair presumption that if he gave his money to the Church it was for the support,' in a manner different from earlier endowments, of the Church disunited from the State. I might indeed suggest a precedent which would curtail within brief limits this question of private endowments—one taken from the very period of the Reformation. At that time the Roman Catholic clergy were prone, in evasion of the Mortmain Act, to induce persons to leave estates 'to provide a priest for ever to sing for their souls.' But by the 23 Henry VIII. c. 10 it was declared that twenty years was long enough to sing a soul out of purgatory. It was enacted that 'after twenty years the lands were to relapse to the service of the living, and sinners were expected in equity to bear the consequence in their own persons of such offences as remained after that time unexpiated.'[1] The 'Practical Suggestions' of the Liberation Society

---

[1] Froude, *History of England*, vol. i. ch. 4.

appear to me to be not inequitable upon this important matter. They propose that any endowment given by a person 'living at' the date of Disestablishment' could be reclaimed by him, subject to the rights of the holder of the benefice, and that, as to endowments created by voluntary subscriptions, these should be the property of the congregations—or, if it pleased the congregations, the property of the Church Body—where such endowments have been created 'since the date of the first of the Church Building Acts (1818).' With reference then to this —which is one of the most important points in the business of Disestablishment—the date proposed is, as regards personal endowments, the existence of the donor, and, as regards endowments by subscription, the year 1818.

The mention of the congregations as the recipients of these endowments carries us to the consideration of their position— that of the laity of the Church as affected by Disestablishment. When Mr. Gladstone introduced the Irish Church Bill, he made what appears to be an untenable distinction between 'the Church' and 'its members.' He said : 'What the Church will receive under the plan of the Government I will endeavour to separate from what its members will receive. No doubt its members will receive compensation, and the congregations of the Church have a very real interest, if not a vested interest, in those compensations.' Technically and historically, there is no Church apart from its members, and from any Government contemplating an Act of Disestablishment the lay members of the Church have an undoubted right to inquire how they and their religious interests are to be dealt with. In the first place, subject to the consequences of the date fixed upon with reference to private endowments, they have an evident claim to the churches for the uses of their public worship and for other offices of their religion. In some of these churches the claim of the State, irrespective of religious denomination, is immeasurably greater than that of the congregation. Westminster Abbey, for example, must always remain the property of the

State. The congregation is of all creeds; it is gathered from no particular area, and besides, the building has other and distinctly national uses. It is a national mausoleum; it is stored with historical traditions of State ceremony, and it may be desirable to use it as long as it endures for such purposes, with or without the services of the Church, as Parliament may appoint. The same may be said of St. Paul's Cathedral, and of all cathedral churches, as well as of some other churches, throughout the kingdom. These are not parochial buildings; they are related to large areas; in a peculiar sense they belong to the nation, and it would be part of the business of Disestablishment to retain these ancient monuments for the nation.

The 'Practical Suggestions' propose that all ancient churches (*i.e.* churches built before 1818) 'should be vested in a parochial board to be elected by the ratepayers, which board should have power to deal with them for the general benefit of the parishioners in such ways as it may determine.' I should regard this as a mischievous proposal if it was designed to erect another and a special local authority. There is a tendency to multiply elections which needs to be checked. Upon the occurrence of Disestablishment, the proposal would seem to be acceptable if it provided for handing over the church to the local authority where an elected body existed, having jurisdiction within an area conterminous with that to which the church belonged in the parochial system. Churches erected after 1818, at the sole cost of any person living at the date of Disestablishment, would, in the same manner as endowments, on his application, be vested in him or in such persons as he may appoint. Modern churches built by subscription, and endowments created by subscription, would be offered to the congregations, with reversion, in case of refusal, to the local authority, and churches (all subject to the above-mentioned date) built in part by public funds would be handed over, charged with that expenditure. It is important to bear in mind the result of these provisions. In the case of the Irish Church, the date 1660 having been taken, private endowments were commuted into a sum of £500,000, which was handed over to the Church Body, and to that Body were conveyed all the fabrics required for the service of the Church.

The adoption of the ' Suggestions ' I have now noticed would produce three important results. (1) The State would have no hand in erecting, nor any dealings with, a Church Body. (2) The compensation for private endowments would be confined to personal donors and to congregations, and be subject to the date of the first of the Church Building Acts (1818), and (3) much greater freedom of action would belong to the laity and the clergy in the formation and in the resolutions of a Church Body. The plea of the English laity for the institution of a Church Body in the Act of Disestablishment could not be so strong as that of their co-religionists in Ireland. There the Church people are few; they are scattered and in some places sparse; their wealth is comparatively small, and of the wealthy class not a few, and these the richest, are absentees who have disclaimed all interest in the future of the Church. There the independent formation of a Church Body might have been doubtful, and success, such as has been achieved, would have been impossible without the assistance of the State. Here there can be no doubt as to the formation of a Church Body; the gravest question will be—and it would be for Churchmen only to decide—whether they could unite in one Church Body. Here the Church people are not scattered ; they are numerous, influential, and abounding in wealth. Suppose the Irish precedent were followed so far that, upon Disestablishment, Conventions of the Church were called to determine the formation of the Church Body. Is it conceivable that the laity would obtain so much power as if they had, at the time of convention, the churches and the private endowments in their hands? In order to secure the due representation of the laity, Mr. Gladstone made Her Majesty's Government the judge of the representative character of the Church Body. There would be peculiar difficulties in adopting that course in England. It would be right and proper to leave that matter to the clergy and laity to be settled among themselves. But Parliament may be expected to favour any plan which would insure to the laity their just weight of influence, and it is a merit of these ' Practical Suggestions' that they do contain strong guarantees upon that subject.

The business of Disestablishment would include dealings with parsonage houses, glebe lands, tithe rent-charges, with the claims for compensation from Church and parochial officers, with the plate and furniture of churches. But, when the main lines of operation are laid down, none of these matters present serious difficulty. There would be interests in the lands and houses to be paid for out of the proceeds of sale, and if the tithe rent-charges were sold to the owners of the lands in respect of which they are payable, at the price which was set upon the Irish tithes, such a douceur might do something to mollify opposition. There can be but few English landowners who would not think it an advantage to make their acres tithe free by payment of twenty-two and a half years' purchase of the rent-charge. Mr. Disraeli said that 'a reason why he was greatly opposed to the confiscation (that was Mr. Disraeli's word for disendowment) of Church property was because he invariably observed that when Church property is confiscated, it is always given to the landed proprietors.'[1] Well, if this matter should come before Parliament in Lord Beaconsfield's time, he will have the remedy in his own hands, so far as the tithe rent-charge is concerned. Strange to say, the Liberation Society, in their 'Practical Suggestions,' assent to the Irish figure of twenty-two and a half years' purchase. It was a low figure in Ireland, but it would look much lower in England, where the price of such securities is substantially higher. Lord Beaconsfield may prefer thirty years' purchase, and if he is followed by the landed gentry, I shall say that not only has he educated them above the level of self-interest, but that in selling the State tithes at a

---

[1] *House of Commons Debates,* March 18, 1869.

just price, he has rendered a signal service to the material interests of the community.

Before passing to consider and examine what is the wealth of the Church of England and what are the claims upon that fund which must be computed and discharged before the surplus can become available for such purposes as Parliament may direct, it will be well to recapitulate and to review the business of Disestablishment, touching only the more important heads of procedure. There would be first, suspension of appointments in the Church under existing conditions; then would follow the surrender by the Crown of all rights of patronage, and the nomination of commissioners into whose hands would pass the property of the Ecclesiastical Commission. These commissioners would proceed, in the interval before the fixed date of Disestablishment, to ascertain the net yearly incomes of all persons affected by the Act, including the yearly incomes of curates: the salaries of Church lay officers, including clerks and sextons, together with the amount of compensation to be paid to lay patrons. There must be repeal of all laws prohibiting the holding of assemblies, synods, and conventions. A date must be fixed upon which the Church of England would cease to be established by law; at which all Church property would be vested in the Temporalities Commissioners, tithe rent-charge absolutely, the rest subject to life interests; at which date there would be dissolution of all ecclesiastical corporations and lapse of all the bishops' rights of peerage; at which compensation would be payable to all ecclesiastical persons, including curates and lay officers; at which there would be abolition of Ecclesiastical Courts and jurisdiction, and of ecclesiastical law, except as relating to matrimonial affairs. After that date there would remain the completion of the payments by way of compensation; the commissioners would receive and entertain applications for churches from parochial bodies, and also for the purchase or letting of parsonages. They would make over such private endowments as could be claimed; they would sell

Church lands to the tenants who chose to claim pre-emption. They would sell tithe rent-charges to owners, and in every other possible way would convert into money the property vested in them, so that at the end of the term, having discharged all claims, they would be able to present the surplus for the disposal of Parliament.

To what sum would that surplus amount? No one, who has looked closely into this part of the subject, will answer the question with confidence amounting to anything like certainty, in the absence of further and more authentic information than is at present attainable. Those commissioners above referred to must make their investigation and report before the figures upon this subject can assume anything like an unalterable character. But from the general accuracy of Mr. Gladstone's forecast in the case of the Irish Church, it would seem possible to indicate by trustworthy, if not precise, figures the broad outlines of the larger undertaking. It must be remembered that the Irish Church Bill was materially changed to the advantage of the clergy after Mr. Gladstone made his introductory statement. He estimated the capitalised value of the property of the Irish Church at about £16,000,000, having previously set the income at £700,000. The compensation to the 'incumbents of all kinds in the Church—bishops, dignitaries, and parochial clergy,—he placed at £4,900,000. The total amount of commutation agreed upon to the end of July, 1874, excluding the 12 per cent. bonus subsequently obtained from Parliament, was rather more than £5,000,000. The curates, partly owing to subsequent changes in the Bill, have cost more than double the amount of Mr. Gladstone's estimate. Still, if we take his highest summary of cost, which was £9,000,000, we shall probably be not far from the actual result of this great transaction. And if there has been throughout as much care and economy on the part of the Temporalities Commissioners, as there has been manifested by the Church Body, it may well be thought that in the end they will be able to present accounts to Parliament showing a surplus of

D

something more than £7,000,000, which would verify Mr. Gladstone's statement that 'the sum at the disposal of Parliament will not be less than between £7,000,000 and £8,000,000.'

With regard to the income and the capitalised value of Church property in England, I shall occasionally refer to, though I shall not rely upon, the report which Mr. Frederick Martin has lately prepared at the request of the Executive Committee of the Liberation Society.[1] There are now (including St. Alban's) twenty-nine episcopal sees in the Church of England and Wales, the archbishops' and bishops' incomes being fixed by law and having no relation whatever to their separate estates. But in proceeding to assess the value of property devoted to Church purposes, we must take first the landed property of the archbishops and bishops. And for this we cannot do better than go to the New Domesday Books. From those ponderous volumes we gather that the archbishops and bishops directly hold land to the extent of 30,233 acres, of which the gross estimated rental is £40,854. I have, in the article which follows this, and which is entitled 'The Abuses of a Landed Gentry,' dealt with those books in connection with another class and the returns concerning this large episcopal property are not, more satisfactory than in regard to the landed gentry. The metropolitan area is not included and all such woods and mines as were not rateable when the lists were compiled, are also excluded. These are matters which we must bear in mind as affecting the statement of all the parcels of Church property. This £40,854 derived from the rental of separate estates is barely sufficient to pay one-fourth of the fixed salaries of the bishops, whose revenues, supervised by the Ecclesiastical Commission, are made up with income from various sources—fines on renewals of leases, tithes, and dues of many kinds. But in estimating the property of the Church we take first these separate estates, and to those we must add the episcopal resi-

[1] *The Property and Revenues of the English Church Establishment.* By Frederick Martin, author of the *Statesman's Year Book.*

dences, thirty-one in number. These palaces are moderately valued at £400 each, that is £12,400 a year, which sum, added to the salaries of the twenty-nine bishops (amounting together to £156,600), makes the annual episcopal charge upon the Church revenues amount to £169,000.

The second item of Church property is that which belongs to deans and chapters, who appear as owners of land in the New Domesday Books to the extent of 68,838 acres, the gross estimated rental of that area being £136,488. The official residences of the members of decanal and capitular establishments may probably be estimated, without serious error, at £50,000 a year. As in the case of the bishops, that area and value are exclusive of London, of mines, of woods and waste land, and equally as in the case of their ecclesiastical superiors it would be erroneous to suppose that this represents the whole property devoted to the payment of deans and chapters, whose salaries alone amount, for deans, of whom there are twenty-nine, to £43,972, and for canons, of whom there are one hundred and thirty-four, to £125,194.

When we have in view the claims upon Church property, we shall have to estimate the number of the parochial clergy. At this moment we are concerned with their income and the sources from whence it is obtained. Pew-rents are not property in the meaning of our present inquiry, nor are voluntary payments of any sort. Practically we may confine our attention to the value of tithes, of glebe or parsonage houses, and of glebe or Church lands. Briefly as to tithes, I shall take the estimate placed, by authority of the Local Government Board, in the preface to the New Domesday Books, which is £5,000,000. The whole of this vast sum is not paid to the parochial clergy ; it is, however, all Church property. From Parliamentary Returns with reference to the operations of the Tithe Commissioners, it would seem reasonable to assume that about one-fifth is held by lay impropriators. We may take the annual value of the tithes at £4,000,000. It is impossible, without fresh inquiry, to make a correct statement as to the number and value of the glebe or parsonage houses. We know, also from the preface to the New Domesday Books, that, exclusive of London, there are about 15,000 parishes in England and Wales. Mr. Martin believes that 'the number of churches in existence may be estimated at about 16,000, probably rather under than over this number.' I should be inclined to think that, including the metropolitan area, the number was nearer 20,000. There are few parishes in England and Wales without a church, and there are certainly more than a few parishes which contain ten or even more churches. But it is quite evident that there is not a glebe-house in every parish. Mr. Martin, after a careful examination of diocesan calendars, believes 'it be may said, roughly speaking, that there are about 10,000 glebe-houses in England and Wales.' He thinks it would not be an over-statement to compute the annual value of these glebe-houses and their curtilages at £1,000,000. However, I prefer the sum he takes—£750,000—as more accurate. As to the glebe-lands, he is not so near the mark. For information on this head he has also turned to the diocesan calendars, and it is difficult to know how one can do better. Yet it is clear that those compilations exhibit a very incomplete statement of glebe-lands, and that the lands indicated are for the most part the smallest in extent. For example, in the calendar for Worcester, the total area of glebe-lands attached to 234 benefices is 3,983 acres, an average of seventeen acres for each. Mr. Martin's final calculation is an average of fifteen acres for 10,000 benefices. That is not a large estimate. I have examined the New Domesday Books, which, however, are not very instructive. The glebe-lands are not distinguishable, because, with very few exceptions, these lands are returned as belonging to the individual clergymen, who are in fact only holders during good behaviour. The largest number of incumbents returned as incumbents is contained in the list of owners within the county of Huntingdon. In Hertford only three incumbents are returned by the title of their ecclesiastical office, in Bucks only five, in the great county of Lancaster only seven. In Huntingdon there are forty-four rectors and vicars so returned. The aggregate area of their glebe-lands is 4,414 acres, and the gross estimated rental £7,979. This gives 100 acres for each incumbent, with a yearly value of £181. The three Hertfordshire incumbents have an average of 22½ acres, which must be greatly under the general average in that county. In Bucks the average is the same, 22½ acres, and in Lancaster it is 26½ acres. Deducting the extent of ground occupied by the glebe-houses, it would seem that twenty acres for each of 10,000 benefices must be a very moderate estimate. It is less than one-fifth of the lands of the Huntingdonshire incumbents. In the smaller areas the value of the land is much larger. If we consider that the glebe-lands amount only to 200,000 acres, we may safely estimate the annual value at £400,000, which is less per acre than the declared value of the probably less valuable lands held by deans and chapters.

In the English counties, and in most of the Welsh counties, there are lands held by churchwardens for ecclesiastical purposes. In Yorkshire more than 1,500 acres of highly valuable land are returned as so held in the New Domesday Books. From an examination of those Books it appears that 250 acres would be a low average to assume for each of the forty counties of England. Adding only 500 acres for churchwardens' lands in Wales, we have 10,500 acres, the annual value of which will probably be very much understated at £21,000.

The Governors of Queen Anne's Bounty have a considerable revenue. Mr. Martin sets their net income at £34,000. That may be, I am inclined to think, an excessive estimate. In the early years of this century the Governors received large donations not only from Parliament, but from private individuals. Their current income from private donations forms, of course, no part of Church property in the meaning of our present inquiry. If we take the net income at £30,000, we must place the same valuation upon it as upon the tithes. When I proceed to indicate the claims which, upon an Act of Disestablishment, would be made upon Church property, I shall feel compelled to glance at the thoroughly Parliamentary character of this corporation and also of the Ecclesiastical Commission. The Ecclesiastical Commissioners are returned ⁚n the New Domesday Books as owners in England and Wales of 149,882 acres of land, of which the gross estimated rental is £311,207. This statement completes the roll of the lands of the Church. As the compilers of the New Domesday Books admit great omissions, it is of necessity very imperfect. Such as it is, let us recapitulate the quantities and values :—

	Acres.	Rental.
Lands of Bishops	30,233	£40,854
„ „ Deans and Chapters . .	68,838	136,488
Glebe Lands	200,000	400,000
Lands of Churchwardens, etc. . .	10,500	21,000
„ „ Ecclesiastical Commissioners .	149,882	311,207
For Woods, Mines, Waste Lands, and Property in Metropolitan Area, omitted from New Domesday Books[11] .	36,593	361,860
	496,046	£1,271,409

Mr. Martin estimates the lands belonging to the Church at 1,000,000 acres. I do not find any firm support for this statement, nor any good reason to believe that half that extent would not be a more accurate estimate.

Reverting to the Ecclesiastical Commissioners in the general survey of Church property, I have in the above statement included only a portion of their income—that derived from ownership of lands. The latest 'Revenue Account' contains the following entries : 'Rental of estates vested in the Commissioners,

[11] The compilers of the New Domesday Books estimate in their preface that the extent of land *omitted* from those volumes is not less than 2,781,063 acres, and that the gross estimated rental of the property omitted is £32.501,412. I have considered that the property of the Church in this omitted area and value would bear the same proportion which the recorded area of their lands bears to the sum of all the lands in the New Domesday Books—the value being taken at £27,501,412 in consequence of a deduction of £5,000,000 being allowed for tithes.

£733,423.' 'Dividends and interest on investments, chiefly Government securities, £97,424.' To some extent, the unrecorded landed property of the Commissioners is included in the last item of the above tabular account. But that can be true concerning only a small portion of their income, because it will be seen that the 'rental of estates vested in the Commissioners' exceeds, by the very large sum of £422,218, the income from their lands in the New Domesday Books. Their income, excluding all but the two entries just mentioned, is £830,847. We shall surely be making abundant allowance for the considerations I have indicated in taking their disposable revenue at £700,000.

Our survey of the revenues of the Church is now complete. Mr. Martin has added £1,000,000 on account of the voluntary aid given for the building and repairing of churches, etc. But that is clearly an error. I see no reason to dispute the assertion that such a sum has been given annually for the last thirty-five years, nor have I the slightest doubt that it would be doubled if the needs of the Church required such expenditure. My present concern is to ascertain what would be the amount of the fund at the disposal of the State in the event of Disendowment, and I will now proceed to summarise the revenue according to the foregoing calculations. With regard to the capitalised value, I am of course aware that the subjoined estimate is very moderate. This property is certainly worth, and might be expected to sell for, at least thirty years' purchase instead of twenty-five years' purchase, the basis upon which the calculations have been made for land, tithes, etc.; the houses of bishops, dignitaries, and clergy being calculated at twenty years' purchase of the supposed net annual value.

	Revenues.	Capitalised Value.
Bishops' Estates . . .	£40,854	£1,021,350
„ Palaces . . .	12,400	248,000
Deans' and Chapters' Estates .	136,488	3,412,200
„ „ Residences, etc.	50,000	1,000,000
Tithes	4,000,000	100,000,000
Glebe Houses . . .	750,000	15,000,000

	Revenues.	Capitalised Value.
Glebe Lands	400,000	10,000,000
Churchwardens', etc., Lands .	21,000	525,000
Queen Anne's Bounty . .	30,000	750,000
Ecclesiastical Commissioners .	700,000	17,500,000
Property omitted from New Domes-day Books . . .	361,860	9,046,500
	£6,502,602	£158,503,050

Accepting all responsibility for these figures, I submit them with some confidence. From this estimate it appears that we have to deal with a revenue of £6,500,000, and a capitalised value amounting to £158,500,000. It remains for us to consider what are the claims upon this property which in any Act of Disestablishment would be admitted by Parliament.

I have already laid down the principles upon which I propose to make out this account. The State would deal directly with the clergy and lay officers of the Church, compensating them for the abolition of their offices where these are held in connection with, and by authority of, the State. I doubt if this plan could reasonably be made less costly, so far as the bishops and dignitaries of the Church are concerned, than the Irish plan of commuting their incomes in connection with a Church Body. There are twenty-nine bishops (including archbishops) and one hundred and forty-three dignitaries connected with cathedral establishments. They are, for the most part, men long past middle age. Their influence and their character would claim for them the highest consideration. Taking the average of their salaries, these one hundred and seventy-two dignitaries of the Church each receive about £2,000 a year. In the Civil Service, upon compulsory retirement, men of the age of most of the bishops and dignitaries, and of such distinguished service, would receive full pay, and, upon commutation of their pensions, would obtain from nine to eleven years' purchase. It would probably not be safe to take less than ten years' purchase of the average salary, which would amount to £20,000 for each, making a total claim of £3,440,000.

There has been no official numbering of the clergy since 1831. Then the roll of the beneficed clergy appeared, from the report of the Commission appointed to inquire into the Ecclesiastical Revenues of England and Wales, to have been 10,718, and their average income £303. Gross inequality then prevailed in the value of benefices. There were 'livings' with annual incomes of less than £10, and the scale mounted to the golden rectory of Doddington with more than £7,000 a year. In 1831 there were 1,006 curates employed by resident incumbents, and 4,224 curates employed by non-resident incumbents. The stipends of the first class of curates averaged £86, and those of the latter class £79. But that report will soon be half a century out of date. The present materials for calculation are the *Clergy List* and Crockford's *Clerical Directory*, which appear to have been tested and scrutinised with extraordinary care by the Rev. Canon Ashwell in preparing the statement which he laid before the Select Committee upon the Public Worship Bill in 1875. The following tabular statement as to the number of the clergy of the Church of England has been drawn from Canon Ashwell's figures :—

Church Dignitaries	172
Incumbents holding benefices . .	13,300
Curates	5,765
Total of Clergy serving in churches .	19,237
Schoolmasters and Teachers . . .	709
Chaplains, Inspectors, etc. . . .	465
Fellows of Universities, Missionaries, etc. .	434
Unattached Clergy . . .	3,893
Other Clergy	5,501
Total . .	23,738

I believe that the general accuracy of these figures is unquestionable. The next point to determine is the average income of the beneficed clergy. In the *Financial Reform Almanack* for the year 1877 there is a carefully prepared table entitled 'Classifi-

cation of Benefices.' It is a compilation from the *Clergy List.*
This table shows that there are in England and Wales 13,257
benefices, the aggregate value being £4,261,033, which gives an
average of £321 for each living. The number of benefices in
this statement is very close to that given by Canon Ashwell.
We may take it, without risk of serious error, that there are
13,300 beneficed clergy with incomes averaging £320 a year.
To what compensation would they be entitled ? Let us look at
what happened in the case of the Irish clergy. We have the
actual net annual value of the livings of 1,382 clergy, 'including
archbishops, bishops, and incumbents (including holders of
cathedral preferments)' who commuted, given as £493,261.
The average of their incomes was therefore £356, a sum not
very much larger than the average income of the beneficed
clergy in England and Wales. This income was commuted for
a total sum of £5,815,223, which gives an average of £4,200, or
about twelve years' purchase of the income. But in regard to
the Church of England I am not writing of commutation. To
obtain a parallel in the Irish case, we must consider what the
clergy would have received upon compounding, and must take
this at two-thirds of the commutation money, in accordance
with the resolution of the Church Body. If, then, the 1,382
clergy in Ireland had compounded, they would have been
entitled to claim a total sum amounting to £3,876,816, which is
rather less than eight years' purchase of the net annual value of
their livings. In compensating members of the Civil Service
upon compulsory retirement, the Government does not in any
case, so far as I can learn, pay a less rate. I can find no precedent for a lower scale in the case of men of the age which it
would be reasonable to assume would be the average age of the
clergy. And if the clergy were to be dealt with upon the basis
of the 'Practical Suggestions' I cannot see how their claim to
this rate of compensation could be denied. They would have
no claim to special consideration, because there would be a
demand for their labour on the part of the disestablished

Church. But assuming that the calculation is to be made upon the ground that their dispossession is an absolute dismissal from the service, then there would seem to be no just cause for giving them less in the aggregate than eight years' purchase of the net annual value of the benefices. And if we take the aggregate annual value at £4,261,033, the amount of compensation payable to 13,300 incumbents would be £34,088,264.

As to the curates and 'other clergy,' I cannot concur in the 'Practical Suggestions' so far as they exclude the claim of any of these 'ecclesiastical persons' to consideration. Curates have enlisted in the service of the Established Church with a fair view to obtain its advantages, and it will never happen, when Disestablishment is brought by a Government before Parliament, that the party in power will be careless of making virulent enemies to their policy of the 10,000 unbeneficed clergy by denying them any claim to compensation. Their claim should not be large. A great number of them are attached to district churches built long since 1818, the year of the first of the Church Building Acts. In those cases the endowment would not be claimed by the State. Curates may not appeal to their prospects. In dealing with the Irish Church, Mr. Gladstone said : 'In all cases of the abolition of establishments, be they civil or ecclesiastical, the expectation of promotion is a matter into which, however legitimate it may be, it is impossible for us to enter.' They would, however, on the simple question of claim have the precedent of the Irish Church to which to appeal ; and if Disestablishment were effected peacefully, without revolutionary violence, the permanent curates would certainly make a good claim to compensation, and the unattached curates and clergy would find many friends to advocate their case. I should suppose that any estimate of the cost of Disestablishment would be erroneous which drew a hard and fast line in the matter of compensation between the beneficed and the stipendiary clergy. In Ireland there were 900 curates whose incomes amounted in the aggregate to £96,403. This income was commuted into a

sum of £1,730,781, and if all had compounded at the two-thirds
rate, about £1,282 would have been the average of compensation. This appears a large sum, and indeed it amounts to
more than twelve years' purchase of the average income of each
curate. In Ireland, the Church being overmanned, especially
when compared with that of England, it may be said that extra
liberality was due to this class of clergy. In England the
supply is less than the demand, and probably it would not be
wise to found an estimate for the compensation of curates upon
a higher scale than that adopted for the beneficed clergy. In
1831 the average stipend of curates in England was £83. I will
take £100 a year as the present average, and as I shall take that
rate for all the unattached clergy, very many of whom are
engaged in scholastic and other work apart from the Church,
the rate cannot be considered too low. Adopting Canon
Ashwell's figures, there are 5,765 curates, and of 'other clergy'
5,501—a total of 11,266 to be placed in this category, and the
compensation, calculated at £800 for each, would amount to
£9,012,800.

There are next the lay compensations, including the parish
clerks and sextons, the officers of cathedrals and of chapters,
the functionaries of the Ecclesiastical Courts and of the Ecclesiastical Commission. It would certainly not be prudent to set
these at less than £6,000,000, that is ten times the estimate in the
case of the Irish Church. And with this matter of lay compensation is closely connected the purchase of advowsons and rights
of presentation. It must be distinctly understood that the owner
of an advowson has no valid claim to compensation upon the
scale allowed to an incumbent. The income of the living is not
his, but only the right of presentation, and that right cannot be
regarded by the State as saleable property. Upon this point it
is well to bear in mind a recent expression of opinion, upon the
motion of Mr. Leatham, by the Home Secretary. Mr. Cross
said :—

' So long as a man held an advowson and the estate to which it was attached, he had no right to sell the next presentation. That was a sacred trust which ought no more to be sold than a vote for a member of Parliament. As to the direction which legislation ought to take upon this subject, he could not better indicate it than by quoting the conclusions arrived at by the Committee of Inquiry of the House of Lords. That Committee was of opinion that "all legislation affecting patronage should proceed upon the principle that such patronage partakes of the nature of a trust to be exercised for the spiritual benefit of the parishioners." That was a sound principle, and he hoped it would be unanimously adopted by the House of Commons. The Committee further declared that "the exercise of the rights of patronage without due regard to the interests of the parishioners, should, as far as possible, be restrained by law." ' [1]

The claim of the owners of advowsons to compensation upon the appropriation by the State of their property in those advowsons is therefore greatly restricted. It is not to be tested by the saleable value of an advowson, because advowsons are notoriously purchased in order that the buyer may traffic in presentations. In its legal aspect the property in an advowson is a barren trust, in the exercise of which the owner is, as Mr. Cross lays it down, bound to regard, not only in the first place, but solely, the interests of others. The Scotch Patronage Act of 1875 (37 and 38 Victoria, c. 82), which took away from private patrons their property in advowsons and their rights of presentation, is a very important witness in this matter. In fact and in law, the position of Scotch patrons before the passing of that Act was analogous to that of English patrons. Whatever rights of property English patrons have in advowsons, the same rights existed in Scotland. It is most instructive to observe how these rights were dealt with by the measure which the Duke of Richmond, on behalf of the present Government, carried through the House of Lords. . The Act provides that—

' In all cases in which the patronage of a parish is held either solely or jointly by a private patron, or any guardian or trustee on his behalf, it shall be lawful for him or for such guardian or trustee, at any time within six months after the passing of this Act, to present a petition to the sheriff of the county, praying him to determine the compensation to be paid to such patron.'

' *House of Commons Debates*, June 26, 1877.

But it was not obligatory on the patron to present such a petition, and his claim lapsed if he did not present a petition within six months.   In no case, however, could the sheriff award a sum more than 'equal to one year's stipend of the parish where the petitioner is sole patron.'   It may be said that public opinion permits the sale of livings in England, whereas in Scotland public opinion never held advowsons to be saleable property. But to this it may be confidently replied that Disestablishment is yet afar off, and that opinion in England is every day becoming more antagonistic to the traffic.   Lord Leconfield's dealing with the Irish Church will have some influence in this matter.   He had £20,000 awarded to him for loss of patronage by the provisions of the Irish Church Act.   Feeling that such patronage was a public trust, and in no sense private property, he has given the money to the parishes and to the diocesan funds.   In view of this and of the fact that, with regard to the Scotch Patronage Act, not one of the great Scottish landowners made claim for compensation, it is not difficult to assess the compensation which ought to be given upon the suppression of a trust of this nature. One year's value of the benefice, where any patron chooses to claim it, would seem to be quite sufficient.   To what would that amount ?   Referring to the figures compiled from the *Clergy List*, to which I have alluded as appearing in the *Financial Reform Almanack*, the number of benefices, the patronage of which is in private hands, is 8,222, and their value £2,594,105. If then to this amount I add nearly another half-million, and take £3,000,000 as the compensation payable to owners of advowsons, I shall probably have named a more than adequate sum.

If Disestablishment were effected upon the lines which have been indicated, the available surplus of Church property at the disposal of Parliament would be liable to be further reduced by the value of endowments made by private individuals living at the date of Disestablishment, and by the value of endowments created entirely or in part by voluntary subscriptions since the date of the first of the Church Building Acts (1818).

It is of course notorious that private benefactions made to
the Church within living memory have for the most part been
expended in church building. Not long since the *Times* estimated 'that a million a year for the last thirty-five years is not
in excess' of the sum which has been expended in the building
or restoration of nearly 9,000 churches, including, as to restoration, some cathedrals. That rate of expenditure is maintained,
if not now exceeded, by voluntary subscriptions. But church
building, repair, and restoration are totally different matters
from endowment. Taking into consideration the fact that of
this class of endowments many are, for obvious reasons, not
included in the estimate I have formed of the value of Church
property, it would seem probable that a sum of £5,000,000—
that is ten times the amount paid to the Irish Church Body as
a composition for private endowments which could be claimed
to the very remote date of 1660—would more than cover the
deduction to be made under this head.

The business of Disestablishment would cost at least £500,000
for official charges, and this completes the list of claims. It
would perhaps be unreasonable to suppose that the operation
could be perfected or the surplus realised in less than ten years,
and therefore it is not necessary to take into consideration the
deduction which, if the surplus were to be realised at once, must
be made for tenancies of glebe-houses and glebe-lands. Ten
years' purchase of existing life interests would be abundant
satisfaction. I may therefore proceed to recount the items of
compensation, which, in the order I have dealt with them, are
as follow :—

	Number.	Compensation.
Bishops and Dignitaries . . .	172	£3,440,000
Beneficed Clergy . . .	13,300	34,088,264
Curates and other Clergy . .	11,266	9,012,800
Church and Cathedral Officers . . ——		6,000,000
Purchase of Advowsons . . . ——		3,000,000
Private Endowments . . . ——		5,000,000
Official Expenses . . . ——		500,000
		£61,041,064

The estimate of the capital value of Church property was £158,503,050. The prospective surplus would therefore amount to £97,461,986.

With that statement my present task is practically ended. But certain considerations have arisen during the survey of this vast operation which it may be well to regard apart from the figures. And first of all it is unquestionably true that the country is not yet prepared to undertake this great matter. Briefly, it will not be prepared until a majority, and a considerable majority, of the electors are determined to vote for Disestablishment, and to maintain a large majority in the House of Commons pledged to accomplish that work. From this course many are now dissuaded by fear of the ecclesiastical vagaries of a disestablished clergy. We may presume perhaps that if it is not apparent that the clergy are manageable by the established order of things, this alarm will melt away. Many are dissuaded by fear that a Church Body would be established in such a manner as to defeat their hope of religious equality. The uncontrolled distribution of £46,000,000 among the clergy will be to many a terror dissolving all wish for Disestablishment, and inclining others, who desire to disconnect Church from State, to think it were better to institute a Church Body and commutation upon the plan adopted in Ireland. If anything like a clear conception of the business of Disestablishment should take the place of the crude, vague notions which are now floating in the minds of the people, it must check the demand for the moment, and give the subsequent appeal more steadiness and strength, if only because the magnitude of the operation and its vast consequences will be firmly grasped and comprehended.

There are other considerations. If those who promote Disestablishment are resolved that there shall be no simultaneous reconstruction by the State, as there was in Ireland, they defer the day of Disestablishment, though not without good reason. I believe that to this resolution they will adhere. But to the laity of the Church, to that body of Church people who have especially the ear of Parliament, this plan will probably not commend itself. The more they look upon it, the more earnestly they will oppose themselves to the policy of the Liberation Society. They will not find in it the most sure and certain hope of the resurrection of their Church after it has been cut off from the throne of State. But I do not therefore say that the general tendency of any exposition of this kind is to delay the action of Parliament. I believe that the more the whole matter is discussed, the more clearly does it appear that all classes would benefit by the operation. It is however certain that a further measure of Parliamentary reform will take precedence of the Church question.

Let there be no doubt, meantime, as to the value of the property held by the Church. There are compensations which I have omitted. But I have taken no account of the extravagant cost of the present management; I have made no calculation of prospective increase of value. It is stated as a consequence of the last dealing with Church property by Parliament, when some of it was transferred to the Ecclesiastical Commission, that there 'was a vast increase in the revenues, amounting in some cases to a trebling, and even a quadrupling, of the former sums received.' If Mr. Martin's researches have led him to this conclusion, there is good reason to believe that it is an experience which would be repeated in some departments. Nor need there be any doubt as to the plenitude and precedent of power in Parliament. The history of England, and notably the history of this century, records acts of authority by Parliament touching Church property. The bishops' estates have been made contributary, one to supply the deficiencies of the other, by Act of Parliament. By the same power the number of canonries has been reduced, the incomes of deans and canons regulated, and the surplus devoted to equalising the incomes of the parochial clergy. Looking further back, it is a noteworthy fact that the churches of London destroyed by the great fire

E

of 1666 were rebuilt by public rate levied by Act of Parliament
(19 Charles II. c. 3); that another Act of the same period
imposed a tax on coals for the same object; that coals were
again taxed and a public lottery established by Act of Parliament to provide endowment for clergy; and that later, by
the 58 George III. c. 45, more than £1,000,000 was granted
from public funds in aid of church building.   The origin of
Queen Anne's Bounty will not be forgotten, nor the Parliamentary grants of 1809-20 which augmented the Bounty fund
by the proceeds of taxation to the extent of £1,100,000.

Nor will the present composition of the Ecclesiastical Commission fail to convey a useful lesson to the laity of the Church.
Parliament always acts towards that laity with good intentions.
It set up the Commission in 1836 with a majority of lay
members, eight laymen and five ecclesiastical dignitaries.   The
laymen did not attend ; the clergy did ; and four years later the
dignitaries achieved a revolution which made the Commission
virtually an ecclesiastical body.   The Ecclesiastical Commission
is now to all intents and purposes the same body as the Upper
House of Convocation.   The secretary of that Commission,
which is the richest ecclesiastical corporation in the world,
once stated in evidence before a Parliamentary Committee, with
regard to the much-enduring laity of the Church of England,
that 'the flow of benefactions seems to be inexhaustible.'   That
generous flow would be immensely increased by Disestablishment, and the laity would be in fault if they did not make
better terms for themselves.   They have been pushed out by
the bishops from management of the funds of the Church, and
they will never regain adequate authority until those funds are
once more dealt with by Parliament.

II.

THE ABUSES OF A LANDED GENTRY.

I AM only in part responsible for the title of this paper. There was a discourse delivered in Edinburgh during the autumn of 1876 which had the same title with the exception of a single syllable. Mr. Froude held forth on 'the Uses of a Landed Gentry,' and called upon all men to accept and admire the laws and customs which have led to the present distribution of the British soil. It seems to me that the most mistaken and un-patriotic attitude which a public man can assume with reference to our land-system is one of easy contentment. I do not for a moment allege against Mr. Froude the conscious betrayal of the interests of his countrymen. Diligent in research, picturesque and powerful in literary display, he is probably short-sighted in the region of practice. He is profoundly distrustful of all popular movements. He is an apostle of the gospel of force. Mr. Froude has no confidence in the policy of extending the ownership of land, perhaps because of his declared conviction that the philosophy of progress is false in its principles.

I am constrained to suppose that Mr. Froude believes the actual distribution and apportionment of the soil of this country have the approval of Divine Power. In the fact that 523 noble-men hold in disability—for they are only life-tenants—one-fifth of the United Kingdom, I think he recognises high purposes of the Creator. I am sure I should respect Mr. Froude's creed if I comprehended it, but for my own part I have never been able to fathom that which appears to me the presumption of men who

profess to discern the decrees of an Almighty God.   Mr. Froude
has told us that 'the conditions under which human society
will cohere harmoniously are inherent in the nature of things ;
and human laws are wise or unwise, just or unjust, so far as
they are formed on accurate discernment of the purposes of the
Maker of the world.'[1]   He does not tell us who are the high-
priests of these oracles.   We are warned against neglecting the
important attributes of 'birth and station,' and against entrusting
the functions of government only to those who have given proof
of 'energy and ability.'[2]   We are assured that this power of
accurate discernment is not in the people.   He looks upon the
development of representative government as the growth of 'an
idol of spurious freedom.'[3]   He believes in heaven-born men who
scorn the *vox populi*.   As for 'the multitude, who are slaves to
their own ignorance, they will choose those to represent them who
flatter their vanity and pander to their interest.'[4]   But, I should
like to ask, was it not the heaven-born men—men of that past
which Mr. Froude loves so well—who held the multitude in
slavery to their own ignorance; and is the provision of universal
education—which is always a first demand of the multitude, and
is nowhere established until the multitude have been enfranchised
—is universal education an improper pandering to their interests ?

I wish some better man had stepped forward to rebuke this
audacious philosophy, which proclaims in the face of history,
glaring all the while with contradiction, that when the possession of power is the property of few, they will be less eager in
the pursuit of self-interest than the many—which, in violation of
the precepts of every writer on Political Economy, from Adam
Smith to Mill and Cairnes, ventures to assert that the distribution of land in this country is the result of 'economic laws as
absolute as the laws of gravity.'[5]

[1] *English in Ireland*, vol. iii., p. 1.
[2] *Ibid.*, p. 2.
[3] *Ibid.*, p. 3.
[4] *Ibid.*, p. 4.
[5] Mr. Froude, ' *On the Uses of a Landed Gentry.*'

But let us pass to consider what is the actual distribution of land in Great Britain, and in this matter we shall derive no small assistance from the returns recently made public in Blue Books which are commonly known as the 'New Domesday Books.' Pre-eminently these returns establish the fact that the soil of Great Britain is held by the landed gentry. The island is virtually in possession—I do not say of country gentlemen, because, through no fault of their own, they are not owners—in possession of the families which they represent. This cannot be regarded as an exaggerated statement of the facts when it is observed that 12,791 persons are returned as owners of four-fifths of the soil of this island, their aggregate property, outside the metropolitan boundaries, and exclusive of woods, other than saleable underwoods and waste lands, being 40,180,775 acres. This, I say, is the return; but, in fact, the number of owners upon that immense area is much less than 12,000, and if we could get at the truth it would not surprise me to learn that the number of so-called owners of four-fifths of the soil of Great Britain is nearer 5,000 than 10,000.

To begin with the nobles, of whom there are about 500. One —the Duke of Buccleuch—is counted as 14 landowners in the total, His Grace having estates in no fewer than 14 counties in this island. There are four peers who are returned as 44 land-owners, because these noblemen—the Dukes of Devonshire and Cleveland, the Earl Howe and Lord Overstone—are placed on the roll of 11 counties. Thus we have five persons returned in these New Domesday Books as 58 landowners; and if we include the Duke of Bedford, who has land in 10 counties, we may say six peers returned as 68 landowners. Let us see how any of them—say the Duke of Bedford—stands in the return. There can be nothing invidious in selecting one of the best landlords in the United Kingdom. In the lists for the counties of Bedford, Cambridge, and Devon, the Duke of Bedford appears as a great landowner. He is returned in each as the owner of more than 10,000 acres. In the counties of York,

Buckingham, Cornwall, Dorset, Huntingdon, and Northampton, he is returned as the possessor of more than 1,000 and less than 5,000 acres, while in the counties of Hertford and Lincoln he is returned as the owner of more than 1 acre and less than 100 acres. The effect of this is to make the superficial result of the New Domesday Books very misleading. Not only is the Duke of Buccleuch returned as 14 landowners and the Duke of Bedford as 10 landowners, but there is consequent error in any estimate of the various classes of landowners. In the category of great landowners the Duke of Bedford makes a threefold appearance ; then in the category which many assume is composed of squires, his Grace makes a sixfold entry ; and last and lowest of all, he is placed in the ranks of the small owners, who some would have us believe are peasant-proprietors or yeomen, and there he stands as two landowners. This is only an example, and undeniably a fair one, of the fallacious character of these returns.

But we should be on comparatively safe ground if we could assume that the Blue Books need investigation only in regard to the 12,791 persons who are returned as owners of four-fifths of Great Britain. It is published for our acceptance and belief that in this island there are not fewer than 269,299 persons among whom is distributed the ownership of 11,597,514 acres of land in parcels varying in size from 1 to 500 acres. I wish that these figures, which appear in the New Domesday Books, were true, or anything like true. I know they were compiled with care and assiduity under the supervision of an eminent public servant. But I fancy that if these big books had been issued by Liberal instead of Conservative authority, the grand totals would not have been promulgated without a large allowance for necessary deductions, to which I am about to refer. We who, from motives of national policy, desire to see a much wider diffusion of property in land, do not complain that in this category we have no indication of the number of persons contained in it who derive their subsistence from the cultivation

of their own land. It is, we know, in great part made up with
gentlemen-owners of two or three acres of lawn and shrubbery;
with tradesmen-owners of what is known as accommodation
land in the neighbourhood of towns in which their commercial
or other business is carried on. This confusion of classes was
inevitable. No one who has any positive acquaintance with the
facts would suppose that of the 130,000 persons returned as possessing more than 1 acre and less than 10 acres there is beyond
a mere handful of what may be called peasant-proprietors.

All this, however, applies to the figures when we have reduced
them to the actual number of persons owning land varying in
extent from 1 to 500 acres. But how is this to be accomplished? Officials sitting down to compile a New Domesday Book, with unlimited power of obtaining correct returns,
would not think of including the separate properties of corporations, in some cases giving the name of the corporation,
many times repeated, and in others the name of the occupier
or incumbent, as that of the landowner. Yet this is what has
happened throughout these returns. The North-Western Railway Company is counted as 28 landowners. 'Trustees of Poor'
stand as 40 landowners in the single county of Bucks. The
compilers have made an attempt to distinguish the lands of
corporations by italics, but in this respect there has been a
notable failure. I have selected for careful examination the
returns relating to the three counties—Bucks, Hertford, and
Lancaster. The choice was made for no other reason than
because the three principal members of the Government reside
in those shires. In the county of Bucks I find that the only
Church lands represented by italics are those of 1 perpetual
curate, 1 rector, and 3 vicars; in Hertford, there are only 2
rectors and 1 vicar; and in the county of Lancaster only 2
rectors and 5 vicars. But in the first county there are no fewer
than 235 landowners with the title of 'Reverend'; in the second
there are 159; and in the third there are 286 'Reverend' landowners. Of course, with very few exceptions, these clerical

landowners are in possession of glebe lands, and their names ought therefore to have been placed in italics. In the county of Bucks there are 273 ' owners ' or corporations in italics, and if we add that number to the total of the clerical ' owners ' of glebe lands, we have a deduction of 508, or about one-sixth, to make from the 3,288 reputed owners of more than 1 acre in that county. The areas of these public lands are generally small ; all, it may be said, are included in the category we are at present examining—that of the reputed owners of more than 1 acre and less than 500 acres, who are returned as numbering 269,299 in Great Britain.

We have learned from the case of the Duke of Bedford and others that a large reduction must be made in this category for the peers, baronets, and other great gentry who are also returned in the former division containing all owners of above 500 acres, and the allowance for these great gentry has to be added to the holders of public lands who are not rightly returned as land-owners. There are other errors; sometimes the name of a land-owner is repeated in respect of separate properties in the same county. But to reduce this category to its proper dimensions would produce no very interesting result. Take the actual number of owners in this category at about 150,000 ; that total would include a very large majority who are not agricultural landowners. They are, for the most part, residential suburban proprietors.

It is not unlikely that the true number of agricultural land-lords does not exceed the famous estimate of 30,000. The New Domesday Books were to establish the absurdity of that esti-mate. In this they are unsuccessful. But we are not on the whole dissatisfied with these ponderous volumes. They exhibit the one great characteristic fact of the English land-system— that the ownership of four-fifths of the soil, if properly recorded, would be inscribed above the names of a number of persons between 5,000 and 10,000.

It would be just as reasonable to say that the overflow of the

Thames was caused by the policy of the Government upon the Eastern Question, as to assert that this possession of four-fifths of the soil by a body of persons who could be put into Exeter Hall is the result of economic laws. It is the consequence of the feudal customs of this country, established, confirmed, and encouraged by the force and operation of law. We know how it is done. The law declares in every county, except I believe one, in this island, that if a landowner die intestate, the eldest son shall inherit the whole property, and that his brothers and sisters shall be dependent upon his bounty. In Kent a peculiar rule prevails, which is unnatural only as regards the daughters of the intestate landowner—the property being divided in gavel-kind among the sons, and the girls left destitute. The abolition of this law of primogeniture is sought because it produces injustice, especially in the class of small landowners ; primarily it is demanded because the English people will not consent to retain upon their statute book a law which is offensive to natural ideas of morality and justice. But this narrowed ownership is especially due to the custom of entail and strict settlement which has been allowed to fasten so banefully upon the soil of our country. This cannot be a free country while the freehold is reserved to an unborn generation. Of these 40,000,000 acres in Great Britain (I do not speak of Ireland) to which I have referred, it may be said that they are in bondage. By legal devices, which are not advantageous to the personal interests of the nominal proprietors nor to those of the people at large, these lands are, with insignificant exceptions, placed under permanent disabilities ; they are the preserves of entail, fenced with strict settlement ; they belong to no man, and to a certain extent they are doomed to infertility, because they are ever in waiting for the unborn hand of the next generation. We all know that this is opposed to the interests of the country ; we none of us doubt that it would be for the advantage of the landlords that the fullest energies of proprietorship should be brought to bear through each generation upon agriculture. The material interests of the country demand from us an effort to free the soil, and in this our labour will be sweetened by the knowledge that while we shall be conferring a pecuniary advantage upon those who are at present the nominal owners of this vast and valuable area, we may fairly claim a part of that increase of value for the revenue of the State. This law of primogeniture, with its allied customs, is not a natural growth of English soil. It was introduced by the Norman Conqueror, who, in deference to the power of the capital, provided in the charter he gave to London that the children of an intestate should continue to inherit equally. Yet it matters little to us what was the distribution of the soil 900 years ago ; our business and determination should be to provide in this our day such a distribution as, while it injures no man in his rights, shall be most beneficial to the nation.

It is now my task to show (1) the rights of the people in the land, (2) the abuses of the existing land-system, (3) the measures of reform to be proposed, and (4) the consequences which may be expected to ensue. It is easy to prove that absolute property in land has never been conceded. As Mr. Froude is an admirer of the English land-system, it may be well to refer to him upon this point. He is of opinion that 'private ownership in land is permitted because Government cannot be omnipresent, and personal interest is found, on the whole, an adequate security that land so held shall be administered to the general advantage. But, seeing that men are born into the world without their own wills, and, being in the world, they must live upon the earth's surface, or they cannot live at all, no individual or set of individuals can hold over land that personal and irresponsible right which is allowed to them in things of less universal necessity.'[1] I am glad to say that in every word of this statement I agree with Mr. Froude. As Mr. Lowe is understood to be opposed to the extension of the franchise in counties, he has also to some extent the confidence of those who are absolutists

[1] *English in Ireland*, vol. i., p. 131.

in regard to land-tenure. Mr. Lowe's opinion as to property in
land has lately been expressed with his customary candour.
'Land,' he says, 'is a kind of property in which the public must
from its very nature have a kind of dormant joint interest with
the proprietor.'[1] Let us adopt Mr. Lowe's words, and henceforth speak of the national property in the soil as our 'joint
interest' with the recognised proprietors. No intelligent person
will deny the existence of this joint interest, who considers that
the doctrine of absolute property in land might lead to a denial
of Mr. Froude's proposition that 'men must live upon the
earth's surface.'

Among the abuses of the present system perhaps the greatest
is that this 'joint interest' has, in its universal relation to the
soil, been not only 'dormant,' not merely neglected, but ignored
by Parliament. The people have been treated as if their
property in the land had no existence. Their interest demands
that the transfer of land should be simple, expeditious, and
inexpensive. It remains complicated, dilatory, and costly, the
percentage of expense being so uncertain and so onerous upon
small purchases as to favour the aggregation of land in few
hands and the annexation of small properties to large estates.
Their interest demands that the owner of land should be free to
sell, or exchange, or to improve for his own advantage; and in
the event of his becoming embarrassed, and therefore disabled
from exercising a beneficial ownership, the public interest demands that his creditors should be empowered to take and sell
his property for the discharge of their claims. The heir to one
of the most ancient peerages has stated that 'seventy per cent.
of the land in this country is held by men whose power over it
is limited by modern settlement.'[2] I think the figures I have
taken from the New Domesday Books will lead to the conclusion that even this is too low an estimate, and we may say that
nearly four-fifths of the soil of our country are placed in legal

[1] *Fortnightly Review*, January, 1877.
[2] Mr. II. R. Brand, in *Fortnightly Review*, 1874.

bondage.   Over by far the greater part of this island there are
no landowners.   It is a public grievance that our landed gentry
have but a limited interest in their inalienable properties, the
rents of which they are at liberty to farm for their lifetime.
Some of them from necessity, some from folly and extravagance,
have reduced their estates to the lowest level of impoverishment.   If these were freeholders, such land might be sold to
men who would treble its productive powers.   But it is 'settled,'
and the 'joint interest' of the people must suffer until death
passes it on to a new proprietor, who perhaps will be as much
embarrassed as his predecessor.

The interests of the people demand that the tenure of land
shall be such as will promote the best agriculture, and will therefore attract the largest amount of capital to be engaged in the cultivation of the soil.   But their countrymen, the nominal owners
of estates, have taken quite a different view, upon which they
have acted.   The land of England is now for the most part
farmed by occupiers upon a yearly tenancy, to whom, as well as
to leaseholders, landlords refuse a reasonable legislative security
for tenant-right. Mr. Mechi published in 1871 the statement of
a land agent that out of 1,500 farms he had let, fewer than 400
were on lease.   I am bound to say that several proprietors have
exhibited some consideration for the 'joint interest' of the
public.   In the article entitled 'Free Trade in Land,' I have
quoted at length the speech in which Lord Derby declared his
conviction that every acceptable tenant ought to have a lease:
There could be no condemnation of his fellow-landlords more
direct than this, or than that delivered by Lord Dufferin in the
House of Lords when he said: 'What is a yearly tenancy?
Why, it is an impossible tenure—a tenure which, if its terms
were literally interpreted, no Christian man would offer, and
none but a madman would accept.'[1]   But if we are rational, we
must admit that the landlord is free to take whatever view he
pleases of his own interest, and to act upon that view so far as

House of Lords Debates, January 14, 1870.

the law will permit; for my part I will never join in *ad miseri-cordiam* appeals to the owners of property. If they prefer the personal pleasures of ownership to regard for public interests, to the increase of production, and to a substantial improvement in the value of their property, I shall never dispute that they are free to choose, nor forget to extenuate their policy on the ground that the fault lies deeper in the laws and customs for which they are not personally responsible, which they and all together have inherited.

But regarding the 'joint interest' of the people, this is a very serious matter, and it is not difficult to form a just idea of the magnitude of that public loss which is the consequence. I will illustrate this part of the subject by a reference to the case of two of the best farmers who have lived in our day—one in the south, the other in the north of the island. The southerner was Mr. Prout, of Sawbridgeworth. Mr. Prout was too wise a man to expend his capital upon the conditions which are usually offered by the landlords of England. He farmed his own land, and in twelve years he raised the rental value from 27*s.* per acre to 42*s.* per acre. That this was due to his exertions and expenditure is shown by the fact that there was no such improvement in the value of the surrounding property. The produce of his land was double that of his neighbours, who had not his security of tenure. Now let us turn to the case of the northern farmer who fell into the power of his landlord—I mean the late Mr. George Hope, of Fenton-Barns, in Scotland. On the 30th of December, 1874, there appeared a letter on 'Tenant Right' in the *Times* from Mr. Hope, in which he said: 'For more than twenty years I have bought manures and feeding-cakes to the value of £2,000 annually. . . . I have known three adjoining farms on the same estate where the leases expired the same year, and two were re-let to the old tenants, one a little above, the other a little below, the old rents; *but the third was let to a new tenant at an increased rent of 50 per cent., and this large increase was mainly due to the expenditure of the former occupier,* *and to his keeping up its condition to the last.*' Upon the appearance of that letter, I wrote to ask Mr. Hope if the third farm was not Fenton-Barns, from which he had been evicted, and in reply he told me that it was, but that he did not wish to parade his personal grievance. He is dead now; he never recovered from that blow. Now I say this: if the individual who was Mr. Hope's landlord has, as a proprietor, a standard of duty which is not that of the public, and from the exercise of which the people at large are losers in regard to their 'joint interest' in his land, it is not the wisest policy to throw hard words at him for this transaction. The people are enfranchised, and it is their fault if they do not put it for ever out of a landowner's power to make a tenant regret that he lavished his life and fortune upon agriculture. We may learn by the letting value of these three farms that, had the cultivation been equal to Mr. Hope's, the produce of the two farms might have been doubled. The people lost that increase in the supply of food owing to insecurity of tenure. Lastly, the 'joint interest' of the people with the landlord demands the equitable taxation of land, so that this 'joint interest' should be, in every proper sense of the words, a beneficial interest.

Now what has Parliament done for the advantage of the people in regard to their 'dormant joint interest' in the land? Lord Chancellors, safely moored at the head of their profession, have bewailed the intricacies of transfer; and the failure of their feeble efforts has, I think, demonstrated the impossibility of obtaining adequate reform from the spontaneous action of Parliament. A late Liberal Chancellor, Lord Westbury, who had no scruples in regard to the abolition of the established doctrine of eternal punishment, was so fearful in touching this hoary abuse of our land-system, that the Act which bore his name, and which was devised to effect the registration of titles to land, made a progress in operation upon which I have calculated, in the paper (No. IV.) entitled 'The Transfer of Land,' that its work would not have been fulfilled before the year

2633, or about 760 years from the present time. As the evil to be dealt with is one which nobody denies, the Tory Chancellor, that eminent lawyer who now presides in the House of Lords, thought it his duty to prepare a Bill. In its passage through the House of Landlords, Lord Cairns' Bill was deprived of any promise it contained of being effectual, and its place among the statutes of England records only another and a contemptible failure. What has Parliament done to promote the best agriculture? It has passed some Public Drainage Acts, which were thinly disguised measures of relief for embarrassed landowners. In the preamble of one of those Acts, Parliament declared in plain words that £2,000,000 should be advanced from the public funds to mitigate the pressure of anticipated pauperism—*i.e.*, in reduction of poor-rates. 'Whereas . . . it is desirable to supply the demand for agricultural labour, especially at that season of the year when other sources are expended,' are the words of the preamble of 9 and 10 Vict., c. ci. Looking to the duty of Parliament, we turn in a case of this sort to see what regard was had in the expenditure of this £2,000,000 and other sums, to the 'dormant joint interest' of the people. What did the public obtain as their share? The answer is, Nothing. What, then, did the landed gentry do with it? Mr. Caird, a witness of the highest authority and a friend to the present system, wrote concerning Yorkshire: 'The Government Loan is repayable in twenty-two annual instalments of 6½ per cent., which repays both principal and interest. A few landlords charge their tenants 5 per cent. of this annual sum, and themselves pay 1½ per cent. Most frequently, the tenant is bound to pay the whole, and in addition to cart the tiles free of charge. And we are sorry to say that more than one instance exists in Yorkshire where the landlord charges his tenant 7½ per cent., thus putting into his pocket 1 per cent., besides securing a permanently higher value for his land by an outlay to which he does not contribute a single farthing.' I have no doubt that similar practice might have been observed in other counties. In Scotland, 'the custom was to charge the tenant a yearly percentage of about 1 or 1½ per cent. in excess of the Government rate.'[1]

But all this was honest and dignified compared with the policy of Parliament in regard to the Agricultural Holdings Bill. How sadly true is the proverb that 'corporations have no souls'! I don't believe there is one among the excellent and honourable men who form the great majority in both Houses of Parliament who, if the matter had been left to himself, would have conceded legality to a moral claim, and then have enacted that any one who pleased to put himself outside this legal sanction should be at liberty to do so. Such an act of legislation ought to close the long-drawn history which records the selfish, undutiful dealings of Parliament with the tenure of land. Recognising the fact that of the 1,100 or 1,200 members of both Houses not fewer than 800 are included in the landed gentry— a fact which those who run may read in the legislation of this island—the people must take this great matter into their own hands, resolved that from henceforth Parliament shall look after this 'dormant joint interest' under their close and continuous direction. There is no difficulty in the matter of tenant-right. Mr. Hope, in the same letter from which I have quoted, referred to the excellent cultivation he had seen in Lincolnshire, where there is an equitable custom in this matter. He wrote : ' These Lincolnshire tenants had no leases, but farmed under agreements to quit on six months' notice, being paid, however, on removal, for draining, marling, and manuring, either by the use of feeding-stuffs or otherwise. Now it is this Lincolnshire custom which I and Scotch farmers generally want to see added to leases for periods of nineteen or twenty-one years, being sure it would have the effect of adding one-third to the crops of the kingdom in a very few years.' Lord Derby and Lord Leicester think the produce of the country might be doubled by good farming ; Mr. Hope says that in a few years it might be increased by one-third if all landlords were obliged to do that

[1] *The Land Question.* By John Macdonnell. (Macmillan, 1873.)

which the force of custom compels in the county of Lincoln. We may therefore consider the fact established that if Parliament had not in this matter disregarded the public 'joint interest' in the land, the food-supply of the island might soon be at least one-third greater than it is at present, when landlords are free to appropriate the unexhausted expenditure of tenants.

If these things are done in the green tree of cultivation, what must we expect to find in the dry field of taxation ? While the prosperity of the country has been advancing by 'leaps and bounds,' what has become of the public 'joint interest' in the soil ? The income from real property has in fifty years increased at least 300 per cent. 'On the broadest historical survey there has been an increase of £8,000,000 in local burdens,'[1] which perhaps may be said to have doubled in that period. I have glanced at the history of the land-tax in the paper upon 'Free Trade in Land,' and will not now refer to that subject. But I must say a word with regard to the Succession duty. It is one of the abuses of our present land-system that the State—the representative owner of that 'dormant joint interest' in the soil which Mr. Lowe has asserted—has, under the guidance of Parliament, permitted the landlords to arrange this duty according to their own pleasure. The people have no 'dormant joint interest' in the money which any tradesman may bequeath to his children, yet a duty is imposed precisely proportioned to the amount, and I think justly, because the State needs a revenue, and because the State in the hour of a man's death renders service in the transmission of his wealth. But upon the land, in which the State has a joint interest with the proprietor, the charge is not made upon the body of the property, but upon the income. This is another indication of the method of Parliament, which in these days of free trade has been so specially protective of the interests of landlords that even if a bankrupt's estate is in process of liquidation, the

---

[1] Mr. Goschen's *Report on Local Taxation.* (Macmillan, 1871.)

F

landlord who is a creditor for rent can arrest the proceedings until his claim is discharged in full. Mr. Froude's indictment against the multitude is that they will choose those to represent them who pander to their interest. He has no words of censure for the class which, from the foundation of Parliament to the present day, has directed and controlled legislation touching the land for its own interest. I dislike class legislation, but no one will deny that the evil of it diminishes in proportion to the extent of the class which is seeking its own advantage. In regard to class legislation, I think no wrong so great can happen to this nation as that which has happened—that which has placed four-fifths of the soil of our country in the unreal, fettered ownership of five or ten thousand persons of whom the most important section have and hold places in Parliament.

I have endeavoured to point out in subsequent papers what I consider necessary for the liberation of the soil. The measures must substitute conveyance by registration of title for conveyance by deed, and proprietors must be brought to the registry by compulsion in case of sale, by attraction where they have held possession for a sufficient period. And in order that land may be saleable, and that the process of transfer by registration may be simple and speedy, the power of settling land for life estates, and of consigning the freehold to unborn persons, must be abolished. The 'joint interest' of the public in the land being admitted, the landlord cannot rightly claim to settle that which is not his. It would be obviously fair that he should be permitted to settle charges upon his land to such uses as those to which personalty may be secured. There must be abolition of customary and copyhold estates. We should need a Landed Estates Court, and trustworthy maps of all the lands of the country.

I have advocated reform upon Conservative grounds. I have pointed out that the position of the land*lords*—for the most part they are not land*owners*—in face of a Parliament continually more swayed by what Mr. Froude calls 'the multitude,' whom their laws have extruded from ownership of the soil, is a position fraught with peril to their own interests. I have appealed to low motives—to the same motives which directed the legislation to which I have referred—in asserting that land-lords would do well to strengthen their position by promoting the increase of their number through legislative processes, which there can be no doubt would add greatly to the pecuniary value of their interest in the soil. And it is only natural that proposals so moderate as to yield the strongest arguments in this direction should be distasteful to many earnest and energetic seekers after reform who demand larger measures. Indeed, that which is most needful is to convince the reforming party that the changes by which free trade in land may be established would result in a wide diffusion of landowner-ship.

The strongest crutches upon which our land-system still stands are two fallacies. One, that the aggregation of land in the hands of the rich is the result of that economic law which brings diamonds into their possession—namely, that com-modities of which there is a limited supply, and which are desired by all, will obtain so high a price as to be inaccessible to any but the wealthy. Mr. Froude, and those who think with him, firmly believe that were those obnoxious laws to which I have been referring, removed and abrogated, and were those other laws which I have suggested, in full operation, the large estates would still grow larger, and the number of agricultural landowners continue to dwindle. Now, I do not hesitate to say that if I shared their belief—if I thought that, after the esta-blishment of free trade in land, the dangerous and menacing contraction of landownership would tend to become yet more perilous to the fundamental interests of the country—I would from to-day cease to advocate the remedy I have proposed ; I would add to it a demand for something like the French law of compulsory division. But I do not agree in this with Mr. Froude. His theory of the inevitable tendency of landownership is, as I have said, based upon a fallacy which is generally formulated in words of this sort : ' Will men whose idea of life is to earn an industrial income of 10 per cent. from their capital, invest or retain an investment of a large part of that capital in the purchase of land for a return of 3 per cent. ? ' The supposition thus raised is regarded as preposterous. The addition of small properties to great estates which is taking place every day is referred to, and the matter is dismissed as affording no basis for argument. But I would ask, Why are the small properties added to the large, and why, when a large estate is for sale, is it not found advantageous to sell it in small lots, say of ten to fifty acres ? Mr. Froude would reply : ' Because the small capitalists are those who seek the highest rate of interest, and an investment in land produces the lowest or next to the lowest.' But this is a wild theory; it is not a fact. In every country in the world, the class of smallest investors is contented with the lowest interest. In Great Britain, being, for the reasons I have stated and will further explain, divorced from the soil, the class finds this in the Post Office Savings Banks, which return only 2½ per cent. But here, partly in consequence of their extrusion from landownership, the largest class is not a saving class. Outside this kingdom the savings of the multitude are invested in the land and in public funds. The debt of France is held by 4,000,000, that of England by 250,000, persons ; and a like proportion holds in regard to the land. The first demand of the small investor is never high interest; that form of folly belongs to the upper classes. His want is security, and the consequence is that at this moment an amount nearly equal to one year's revenue of the United Kingdom is held by savings banks, for a return less than the average received by the landowners of this country. The number of small proprietors is dwindling every year because there is no addition. And why is there no addition ? The answer is very simple. It is not, as we have seen, because of the smallness of the return from land; it is obviously because the small capitalist cannot afford, and will not consent, to encounter a certain delay in the business, and an uncertain risk in the cost, of purchase. The only man who goes free of care in this respect into the Auction Mart is the large buyer upon whose purchase the cost can amount only to a very small percentage. Say that a man, by years of self-denial and careful thrift, has saved £500, and the idea, so delightful to the minds of most men, of purchasing a small property upon which to spend his loving labour and the remainder of his life, presents itself to his imagination. In this country, and in this country only, the thought is chilled and checked because he has no assurance that the cost of purchase may not amount to a fourth or even a third of his store ; and if the purchase-money exceed his possessions, and he wishes to raise a further sum by way of mortgage, that process, to be repeated perhaps at the end of three years, may involve him in a lifelong charge for legal costs equal to the amount of the mortgagee's interest. He abandons, with a shudder, the coveted land to the men of ten and twenty thousand acres, and possibly his store of gold (for these small investors of the lower middle class may be thus imprudent) is transformed into the baseless fabric of a foreign bond, not because he loves the foreigner, and not because he hankers after a promise of 9 per cent., but because he is driven to the Stock Exchange by terror of the cost of law, and if he must buy a paper promise to pay he likes to have a high figure. Many of us know in our personal experience the truth of this. Many could mention cases in which this cost amounted to one-third of the purchase-money. I bought a small leasehold property lately. I thought the lawyer's account would not be more than £15 ; I had no assurance it would not be £150. It was £35. If that property had been in South Australia, the transaction would have occupied hours instead of weeks, would have cost me fewer shillings than it cost pounds sterling ; and the charge would have been one which I could have calculated exactly beforehand. Can any one fail to see what would be the consequence if a system like that which works so well in our colonies were established in this country? The purchaser, who always magnifies the uncertain cost of law, would then be prepared to add considerably to his bidding. There could be no objection to a part of that increase of value going to the landowner, but some of it should find its way to the purse of the State. Of course, to establish such a system of registration of title would be more difficult here than in any of our colonies, but no competent authority doubts that it could be done, or that in this island we should gain advantages as great as those which are being enjoyed by the people of the larger island of Australia. The benefits actually realized in South Australia are thus described by Sir Robert Torrens, the author of the measure :[1]

' 1. Titles being indefeasible, proprietors may invest capital in land secure against risk of deprivation and the no less harassing contingency of a Chancery suit; mortgagees, having also no further occasion to look to validity of title, may confine their attention to the adequacy of the security. 2. A saving amounting on the average to 90 per cent., or 18*s.* in the pound sterling, has been effected in the cost of transfers and other dealings, irrespective of the contingent liability to further expenses resulting from suits at law and in equity, the grounds of which are cut off by the alteration of tenure. 3. The procedure is so simple as to be readily comprehended, so that men of ordinary education may transact their own business. 4. Dealings in land are transacted as expeditiously as dealings in merchandise or cattle, *fifteen minutes* being the average time occupied in filling up the forms and completing a transaction.'

Compared with our restrictive system, this sounds like an announcement of the millennium. The English Law Reform Association declared twenty years ago that ' it has been estimated by persons of experience and authority in such matters that a cheap, simple, expeditious, and accurate system of transfers of land would add four or five years' purchase to the marketable value of land.'[2] From whence would this increase flow? Not from the pockets of the rich, for they are not hindered in

---

[1] *The South Australian System of Registration of Title.* By Robert R. Torrens. Adelaide, 1859.

[2] *On Registration of Transfers of Land.*

the acquisition of land by fear of the cost of conveyance by deed. It would come from the class of which Mr. Froude and the maintainers of the feudal system say that its members cannot afford to own land. The first fallacy is thus exposed. The highest price is never obtained where land is purchased as a luxury by the rich, but always where it is most suitably divided for industrial occupation. This is as true of Old Broad Street compared with Belgrave Square, as it is of the county of Bucks compared with Flanders, France, or Switzerland. There has been an approach to the system of free trade in land in the offer of the Church lands of Ireland to the tenants. And what has been the consequence? Four thousand sales have been effected at unusually high rates, and a small proprietary is being thus established on those lands. A man who can buy twenty acres of land, worth 30*s.* per acre in the hands of a great proprietor, and returning at that rent 3 per cent. upon the outlay, will commonly, by such diligent and unremitting labour as the magic of property can alone call forth, make that land worth 90*s.* an acre in a few years. His investment will then be paying 9 per cent. upon the purchase-money. Ownership produces on the part of the occupier labour which a leaseholder or yearly tenant would never give. It would be easy to point to many cases in which tenant-farmers, men of superior energy, would have been in a far better position had their capital been first employed in securing ownership. Take the case of Mr. Hope, of Fenton-Barns, as one of many. At any time he could have obtained two-thirds of the purchase-money of any breadth of land at 4 per cent. The 50 per cent. increase in the value of that farm, which was obtained by his landlord when he quitted it, would have been his own. There can be no doubt such men would be far richer at their death, could they be owners as well as farming occupiers of the soil, even though they were restricted to a third of the area over which their tenancy extends. The price of land in this country is low compared with what it would fetch if, by the establishment of what I have called 'Free Land,' the occupying farmer were brought in as a competitor. Land which would be worth £60 an acre in this island fetches £100 in the Channel Islands, and nearly £150 in Switzerland. 'In England, 30s. an acre would be thought a fair, and indeed rather a high, rent for middling land; it is only inferior land that in Jersey and Guernsey, where the average sizes of farms are respectively eleven and sixteen acres, will not let for at least £4, while in Switzerland the average rent is £6 an acre.'[1]

I think I have now demonstrated that the present distribution of land in England is not the result of economic laws. The distribution of land, where the unrestricted action of economic laws is permitted, will tend towards those who will give the highest price for it, and as a rule those are they in whose possession it can be made most productive. And the primary reason why, under a system of free trade in land, there would be a wholesome tendency to the restoration of that valuable but now almost extinct class, the small proprietors, is because in their hands an increase of produce, the possibility of which landlords like Lord Derby fully admit but cannot obtain, might most surely be accomplished. We shall see this more clearly in regarding the second fallacy, which may be thus expressed : 'That the agricultural production of England is larger than that of other countries because the farms are larger.' This fallacy is constantly in the mouths of those who uphold the English land-system. There is no lawyer of greater authority than the Lord Chancellor, and when he undertook in 1854 the defence of primogeniture, he believed he had reached firm ground in the argument that primogeniture is favourable to agriculture because it tends to large estates, and large estates tend to large farms. How is it that this belief, which I shall prove to be erroneous, has become rooted in the minds of British statesmen, even of some who I have no doubt endeavour to keep their intelligence open to the reception of truth upon this great question ? A too ready acceptance of statistics is in many

[1] *Peasant Proprietors.* By W. T. Thornton, C.B. (Macmillan.)

cases the cause of error. When the lesson of statistics runs in
the direction of national self-esteem, or the interest of a governing class, it is hard to throw over the favourable witness. And
official figures do undoubtedly show that the produce of wheat
per acre in England is much greater than that of any other
country. Herr Block, a Prussian official, compiled a table which
was promulgated by his Government after the great German war
of 1866, and which, through the action of our Foreign Office, has
been widely circulated in England.[1] No well-informed person
believes that it is strictly accurate, especially with regard to the
production of France ; but its general indication is no doubt
trustworthy. We may certainly accept as true the result that
the United Kingdom has the smallest proportion of the population engaged in agriculture, and the largest production of wheat
per acre. The following is Herr Block's table :

	Agricultural population to total population.	Average returns per hectare of corn.	Head of cattle per 1,000 inhabitants.	Head of cattle per 100 hectares.
	Per cent.	Hectolitres.	Number.	Number.
Russia in Europe .	85 to 90	16·0	693	86
Italy . . .	77	16·0	291	249
France . . .	51	14·6	494	346
Belgium . .	51	19·3	402	660
Prussia . . .	45	19·8·	540	369
Austria . . .	25	16·0	635	307
Spain . . .	25	16·0	.316	151
Holland . .	16	23·0	492	539
United Kingdom .	12	40·8	515	478

But how do these figures bear upon the question of small
farms ? They have been accepted by some politicians without
scrutiny. Mr. W. R. Greg flourished them over my head in
rejoinder to the answer I gave his terrific observations in the
character of Cassandra. Referring to the above figures, he
thought 'Mr. Arnold would be surprised to find that the average
annual produce of wheat in Belgium is 20 per cent. below that

[1] Part I. *Reports from H. M. Representatives respecting the Tenure of Land in
the several Countries of Europe.* 1869.

of England.'[1]   He seemed to think there was no appeal from
Herr Block's table. This is how the matter is put by politicians
such as Mr. Greg : 'Farms are large in England. Farms are
small in France and Belgium. The produce of wheat in England as compared with those countries is as 40 to 14 and 19
Therefore large farms are better than small, and therefore, whatever changes may be made in our land-laws, provided there is
free trade, there will be a constant tendency to increase the size
of farms. Q.E.D.'   Thus Mr. Froude and Mr. Greg, with perhaps three-fourths of Parliament in full agreement.

But let us try to put the matter more accurately. England
is a country of large farms; therefore the only proper comparison of English agriculture with that of any other country
would be where large farms prevail. By comparing large with
large, and small with small, we obtain a just comparison; we
see more clearly what are the essential differences of agriculture
in the several States.   Perhaps no possible error is greater than
to suppose that the system of one country can be adopted in
all its features in another country by a mere act of legislative
authority.   But, as a rule, the size of farms does follow the
tendency of legislation. The self-denial, the careful thrift, the
scrupulous frugality of the Flemish, the French, or the Swiss
peasant, could not be imparted to the English poor by any
statute of Parliament. These must grow from seed ; they
cannot be transplanted. But these domestic virtues, which
have become exotics by the maintenance of the feudal system
in this island, would surely spring up again when the law favoured the possession by the comparatively poor of that form
of investment in which alone their confidence in property can
take root and become established. The rude comparison made
upon the face of Herr Block's table conceals the real facts,
which I maintain are these: 1. That the soil of the United
Kingdom is well adapted for the varied forms of agriculture,
and has a greater natural fertility than the north and centre of

[1] 'Cassandra's Rejoinder.' *Contemporary Review,* November, 1874.

Europe. 2. That the large farms of England produce more than the large farms of the Continent ; but (3) that the greatest produce of grain of all sorts, as well as of meat, is gathered from small farms, from the land of peasant-proprietors ; and (4) that rent and saleable value are relatively highest upon peasant-properties. From which I shall argue that if we had free trade in land in England, even though we maintained the principle of non-interference with the distribution among living persons of a testator's land, we should find that the soil would, at least to a wholesome extent, return to the hands of yeomen and peasant-proprietors, in whose possession it would exhibit, as it does in those of the neighbouring peoples of the Channel Islands, of Normandy, and of Flanders, a higher level of agriculture, and a heavier produce, than can be shown by the general results of large farming in England.

The average produce of wheat in France would appear much greater, were it not for the inferior production of the large farms in the west and south ; and the same may be said of Belgium, the produce of the small farms in Flanders being very much greater than that of the large farms upon the French frontier. In fair comparison with English agriculture, which department is the garden of France? There can be no doubt—it is Normandy the most subdivided. 'The west and south,' says M. de Mornay, in an official report, 'have preserved more large estates than the north and east.' I do not wish to see the French law of com-pulsory subdivision established in England, but I do desire to see the peasant a successful competitor for land as he is in France and Belgium. It is quite a mistake to suppose that there are no considerable estates in France, and that subdivision proceeds only in obedience to the law. Together with five millions of small proprietors, there were before the loss of Alsace-Lorraine, according to the great authority of M. de Lavergne, 50,000 owners with estates averaging 500 acres. Division progresses from economic causes. The peasant is the highest bidder, and therefore, when estates are sold, the land is put up in small lots. M. de Lavergne has stated in a letter to Mr. Cliffe Leslie that 'the best cultivation in France is that of the peasant-proprietors, and the subdivision of the soil makes perpetual progress.'

If the average produce of France and Belgium is reduced by classing the inferior yield of the large farms with the superior yield of the small farms, then I have established the worthlessness of the comparison by which the advantage of the exclusively large farm system of England is sought to be maintained. And this is incontestably true. 'At the present day,' says M. Passy,[1] 'on the same area and under equal circumstances, the largest clear produce is yielded by small farming.' And with regard to Belgium, M. de Laveleye writes : 'The large farmers of Hainault and Namur do not buy manure, fancying they would ruin themselves by doing so. The Flemish small farmers invest from fifteen to twenty millions of francs in guano every year, and quite as much in other kinds of manure. Where does large farming make such advances?'[2] 'On the ten-acre farms of Flanders, the crops are heavier by a fourth than on the hundred-acre farms of La Hesbaie, and as heavy again as on the farms of two hundred and fifty acres in Le Coudroz.'[3] As to the objection that small farmers cannot obtain the best machinery, it is contradicted by the fact that the most costly machine in general use in England, the steam-threshing machine, 'is to be found everywhere in Flanders.'[4] So it is among the peasant farmers of Roumania. I have seen more steam-threshing machines of English make in a day's passage up the Danube than in any six hours of railway travelling in England.

We may, I think, consider the fact established that in France and Belgium it is the lands of the peasant-proprietors which are the most productive. But I have undertaken more than this. I

[1] *Mémoire de l'Académie des Sciences.*
[2] *Systems of Land Tenure.* (Macmillan, 1870.)
[3] *Peasant Proprietors.* By W. T. Thornton, C.B. (Macmillan.)
[4] *Systems of Land Tenure.* (Macmillan.)

have promised to show that large farming, which is seen to the greatest advantage in England, does not yield so much produce as small farming under less favourable conditions. I say less favourable, because of the superior soil of the United Kingdom. 'Not a blade of grass,' says M. de Laveleye, 'grows in Flanders without manure.'[1] He adds that soil of the United Kingdom 'might be bought to fertilise the soil of the Fleming.' But what do industry and thrift united to ownership accomplish? Mr. Caird gives 26½ bushels as the average produce per acre of English farming.[2] But in Flanders, in the district of small farms,— where, however wheat covers but a small area (to the disadvantage of Belgium in Herr Block's table),—the average yield is from 32 to 36 bushels.[3] 'Of barley, a more congenial cereal, the average is in Flanders 41 bushels, and in good ground 60 bushels ; while in England it is probably under 33, and would certainly be overstated at 36 bushels.'[4]

It will be admitted by all practical agriculturists that the surest test of production is the number of cattle, and in this matter Herr Block's table does exhibit our inferiority to Belgium and Holland. 'It would startle,' says Mr. Rham, 'the English farmer of 400 acres of arable land if he were told that he should constantly feed 100 head of cattle. Yet this would not be too large a proportion if the Flemish system were strictly followed . . . a beast for every three acres being a common Flemish proportion, and *on very small occupations*, where spade-husbandry is used, the proportion being still greater.' In 1873, on a farm of 32 acres, near Ypres, Mr. Thornton counted eight cows, six bullocks, a calf, and four pigs ; and was told by the farmer that over and above what his own cattle yielded, he purchased no less than £200 worth of manure annually. Again, take that part of Her Majesty's European dominions in which alone small farming may fairly be compared with the large farming of England—I

---

[1] *Systems of Land Tenure.* (Macmillan.)
[2] *English Agriculture.*
[3] *Outlines of Flemish Industry.* By Rev. W. Rham.
[4] *Peasant Proprietors.* By W. T. Thornton, C.B.

mean the Channel Islands. Certain lands in Guernsey yielded
of wheat an average, for the three years ending 1847, of 76, 80,
and 72 bushels per acre. In the Channel Islands, 'the agricultural population is more than four times as dense as in England,
there being in the latter country only one cultivator to seventeen
acres of cultivated land, while in Guernsey and Jersey there is
one to about four. Yet the agriculture of these islands maintains,
besides cultivators, non-agricultural populations respectively
twice and four times as dense as that of England. . . . There
are larger estates in England,' says Mr. Brock, a Bailiff of
Guernsey, 'than the whole of this island, but where will one be
found that produces the quantity of provisions sent to market
by our small farms?'[1]

Why should the Isle of Wight be less productive than
Guernsey or Jersey, and why should the latter be free from,
while the former is oppressed, in common with all England, by
pauperism? 'Certainly,' writes Mr. Thornton, 'there is not
a beggar within the limits of his [the Bailiff of Guernsey's]
jurisdiction, and an able-bodied person very rarely, if ever, seeks
admittance into either of the two hospitals or asylums for the
poor.' The pauperism of England is to a great extent the
consequence of our feudalised land-system.

I have endeavoured to set out the case fairly and honestly.
The abuses of a system which gives four-fifths of the soil to
fewer than 10,000 persons, and allows them but nominal
ownership, have now been exposed. Our race is deteriorating
by forced and unnatural confinement in the atmosphere of
streets. Owing to the size and character of estates, the rural
population does not increase, and pours no adequate infusion of
healthy blood into the towns. The primary cause of pauperism,
the great fault of the English poor, is want of thrift. Our land-
system denies to them the proper use of the best of all schools
for the acquisition of that virtue—the careful cultivation of small
freeholds. No people have ever exhibited frugality who were

[1] *Guernsey and Jersey Magazine.*

thus divorced from the soil. The production of our island is restricted because the occupier has not sufficient security of tenure. We are governed by landlords with a view to the main-tenance of the English system, because their estates give them power and place irrespective of personal claims. The value of land is kept down by terror of the cost of conveyancing, and we have to bear the heavy charge of a Socialist Poor Law in a country swarming with paupers. Mr. Wallace says [1] educated Russians wonder at 'our habitual callousness with regard to social danger,' and asserts that the Russians have, in their very widely diffused proprietorship, had in view the prevention of a pauper class. All these evils, we contend, would be in process of amendment and disappearance were free trade in land established. We should not see—we do not desire to behold— the extinction of large estates, nor the disappearance of large farms. But the man who could buy ten, or twenty, or thirty acres, would, in many places, compete successfully, and at far higher prices than are now obtained, with the man of broad possessions ; and from this increased value given to land, which would be augmented by the decline of pauperism, there would be an ample margin for the State to obtain by taxation on transfer or succession an income which might be employed in the reduction of the National Debt (to the further advantage of landowners) by at least £10,000,000 a year.

All this is no chimera ; it is not even an experiment. The requisite legislation has been highly successful in less favourable circumstances than we can offer. Without doing wrong to any man, with improvement to the property of all, this blessed change may be effected. If part of our dear fatherland were occupied by some hostile tribe, we should need no call to free the illustrious soil which has known no conquest for 800 years. Can we not see that our land in every part is now subject to a costly and enduring, though perhaps less humiliating, bondage ? The honour of liberating the soil of England by beneficent

[1] *Russia*, vol. i., p. 217. (Cassell, Petter, and Galpin, 1877.)

legislation will not be lost, now that the power in Parliament belongs, and will soon in the counties more fully belong, to the people.   It may be ours,—or we, neglectful of our duty and opportunity, may supinely pass it on to our successors.   Let this distinction be ours, and to the latest of English life men and women will recall the time in which we fought and won the glorious battle, as the day in which the grand old country, bating nothing of reverence and love for her traditions and history, became renewed with the bloom and vigour of youth, and, joining in the race with her competitors throughout the world, was able to preserve her lead, because she wisely determined to take off her feudal trappings, not to trample upon them nor to tear them in pieces, but to lay them aside as obsolete, antiquated, and outgrown.

III.

FREE TRADE IN LAND.

FOURTEEN years ago, in a vast mill-shed erected by the co-operative enterprise of working men, I listened to the last public speech of Richard Cobden. Never have I seen greater homage paid to living man. Some rough deal planks formed a sounding-board above his head ; the place was not well lighted ; his words could reach but little more than half the vast assembly. Five or six thousand people had congregated to listen to the 'unadorned eloquence' of that practical man, in a place most bare of ornament. He spoke with the measured tone of one who is sensible of great responsibility, as a man ought to speak whose words were carried to the magic needles ere the ink that recorded them was dry, and flashed away to all the centres of English intelligence, there to be reproduced a thousand, thousand times before the eyes of his countrymen. That night he offered to the competition of English statesmen a splendid prize,—the rich guerdon of a merit brighter than his own ; a reward nobler even than that respect betokened by the myriad of upturned faces, hanging, as it were, with unquestioning confidence upon his words. He expressed his belief that success would attend a properly conducted effort to establish free trade in land ; and he asserted that the man who should accomplish that work will have done more for the English poor than had been effected by the application of free trade to commerce.

And there it lies : the prize fell to the ground ; death sealed

the lips of the speaker; his words have assumed the solemnity
of a bequest; but nothing, positively nothing, has been done
towards the establishment of free trade in land. I really do
not believe that any one possessed of great authority in the
legislature questions the beneficial influence which a free exchange of land would exert. 'We Englishmen,' as Mr. Gladstone
said at one of the dinners of the Cobden Club, 'who have
received from Mr. Cobden a special commission and a special
charge,' have strangely neglected our calling. Believing in their
utterances, it can only be supposed that the conscientious men
who direct the powers of the State have been waiting long years
for a favourable breath of public opinion and for a clear channel.
The late head of the legal profession (Lord Hatherley) has said
that in 1815 he read Adam Smith, and that the study of the
works of that great economist was the cause of his taking up
the principles to which he has ever since adhered. In 1859
Lord Chancellor Hatherley—a man possessing, perhaps beyond
any of his predecessors, the respect and confidence of his
countrymen—spoke scornfully of the law, of which he was even
then a pillar, so far as it related to land. He said: 'Look how
the limitations of your law affect the transfer of your land. It
is only on account of these that you have difficulties as to title;
because, if it were not for the complexity of limitations, a
system of registration would long since have been established,
which so far as fraud and rapidity of transfer was concerned
would have freed us from any difficulty of title whatever. You
have now the combined effect of fraud and the complicated
investigation of title, which operate in the most serious manner
to prevent the free transfer of the land in our community.
What I wish, and have long wished for, is a free transfer of
land'—in other words, free trade in land. But it is not our
lawyers and statesmen only who have been content with the
expression of a personal opinion upon this great question. The
people have permitted the monopoly of land to become more and
more restricted, without interference. This surprised Mr. Cobden.

He said : ' It is astonishing that the people are so tacit in their submission to the perpetuation of the feudal system in this country as it affects property in land, so long after it has been shattered to pieces in every other country.' But he knew the reason why ; he declared the cause of this languid acquiescence to be that 'the great increase of our manufacturing system has given such an expansive field of employment to the population, that the want of land as a field for investment and employment for labour has been comparatively little felt.' 'So long,' he predicted, ' as this prosperity of our manufactures continues, there will be no great outcry against the landed monopoly.'

I say the time has come when this tacit submission exists no longer ; when the maintainers of the present land system must accept reform, or risk the rude chances of opposition. Slowly but surely the people are mastering this question. Every wind that blows brings to the shores of England testimony to her matchless wealth and to her unequalled poverty. Englishmen know, as a rule, very little of the land systems of other countries ; and the books which have been written are, for the most part, very superficial, or too ' dry' for popular reading. But not a few people are aware that our land system, so far as it is known abroad, excites the wonder rather than the admiration of the world. There is nothing like it. There are countries of peasant proprietors, such as France, Switzerland, and Belgium ; there are other countries with a class resembling our aristocracy ; but there is no other portion of the earth where the land is for the most part owned by one class, farmed by another, and tilled by a third. I anticipate the criticism of the opponents of reform, who at this point will exclaim triumphantly that such an exceptional position is the cause of that enduring stability which the institutions of this country have preserved, and that therefore the maintenance of the existing arrangement is desirable. It will surprise those only who are ignorant that free trade in land is both a truly Liberal proposition and also a thoroughly Conservative measure, that I should frankly admit this. I do believe that this singularity of our system has tended to preserve our institutions. How? Because it has rendered the voice of the rural districts subservient to the will of the urban population, and yet has presented a nearly equal power of resistance—aided by the peculiarity of our electoral system, which found grossest expression in the acknowledged and even lauded existence of 'rotten boroughs.' But this artificial equilibrium is passing away, and every day the rural party are losing power and influence in the State. To repair this balance free trade in land has become necessary.

My earliest recollections are some incidents of the free-trade struggle. I well remember the bitter words which, as a child, I heard spoken around me with reference to Cobden and Bright. As a boy of fourteen I sat on the stage of 'Old Drury'—never so crowded, even on Boxing Night, as it was then—with landlords who had travelled long distances to hear the turgid eloquence of Protectionist leaders. There was some fire in the movement, but it was borrowed—I will not say hired—light. A very untrained instinct might have detected unreality; they were defending a privilege, not a right; and of the agricultural class they had not the sympathy of the labourers. The peasantry of England could not be rallied to the cry of 'Dear bread and dear cotton stuffs!' But suppose it had been otherwise; assume that our land system had resembled that of France; grant that there had been 10,000,000 of people engaged in the cultivation of the soil, instead of 2,000,000; and that instead of these 2,000,000 inactively sympathizing with the demand for cheap bread, there had been 4,000,000 of peasant landowners and corn-sellers, with a far more weighty representation in Parliament than the landed interest possessed. Had this been the case in England, who will assert that our institutions would then have survived? It may be that civil war could not have been averted; for these peasants would hardly have condoned such a policy as that of Lord Derby and Mr. Disraeli—would never have displayed the intelligence and patriotism which induced the leaders of the English landed interest so readily to accept the victory of their opponents.

We must not be vain ; it is silly to suppose that we alone of all people in the world, are wise—that we only can construct durable institutions. We are of a busy, enterprising, conquering race, but we shall do well to remember that we are in possession of a country, the natural circumstances of which have moulded our institutions. Long before Adam delved or Eve span, rich store of metal, thousands of fathoms from the surface, was, as it were, distilled into fissures of the granite ; the trees of primeval forests were converted by decomposition and pressure into rich beds of coal; and then, fortunately, these and other treasures were so upheaved, that within the smallest area, probably, upon all the earth, were to be found, in this our island home, the greatest variety of natural wealth : stony districts, over which a thousand limpid and perennial streams ran ready to serve in cotton and woollen manufactures; coal-beds stretching in adjacent and parallel lines from Newcastle to Cardiff ; good soil for cultivation, and a climate assisting the husbandman—all these things tended to produce for England that balance of powers which, usefully acting upon each other, have yet tended to give to the concentrated, and therefore the more intellectual, population of the towns, the preponderance that in other countries has rested with the immobile and less educated class, the dominance of which has been productive of revolution and disorder. The shortlived triumph of the Communal idea in Paris, in 1871, was nothing but a revolt of citizens against government by ‘rurals.’ Had there been 10,000,000 of peasantry in this country, with a land system like that of France, we might have seen revolution followed by despotism, and have been subjects of the Emperor Benjamin Disraeli.

I propose to recommend the establishment of free trade in land as necessary for the interests of every class in the country ; but we must first glance at the land system as it now exists. The number of agricultural landowners is, I believe, decreasing ;

the causes which promote this decline are of increasing intensity. What are the chief of these causes? I should say, the increase of capital, and the cost, together with the uncertainty of the cost, of conveyance. The wealth acquired by manufacturing industry has tended to this result, for the overflow of these riches has narrowed the land market, because it has passed into the hands of men who are content to sacrifice a large portion of the ordinary profits of capital to purchase the social distinction which acres confer, and upon whose large purchases the cost of conveyance is not a heavy charge. Manufacture pays an enormous tribute to landlords in the shape of ground-rent, much of which is spent in the purchase of other land. As Assistant Commissioner of Public Works in Lancashire during the Cotton Famine, I became officially acquainted with some of the most striking instances of the conversion of land from agricultural to manufacturing uses. Estate maps were brought before me of a hundred years old, which showed the sites of towns now paying £20,000 or £30,000 a year in ground-rents to have been then nothing but obscure villages on a neglected moor, not worth £500 a year to the proprietor. I could give many instances where, by the competition of industrial capital, the rent of land has risen within a very few years from so many shillings to as many pounds per acre; and I cannot forget that I saw this vast industrial capital depreciated and jeopardized, charged with local burdens most grievous to be borne, and receiving but scant assistance from the landowners whom it had so enriched, and who, in full security, held the property of the leaseholders as a guarantee for their income.

Our manufacturing prosperity has done more than this to enrich the monopolists of land. Some of the princes of manufacture have become successful accumulators of the soil, and of many more the fair daughters have carried in their hands at marriage the gains of industry to expand the ring-fence of the landowner. The construction of railways was made subservient to the same end. There was once a feast—I could

name the day and the place—at which eight surveyors sat
round a tavern table in a home county, under the presidency of
a nobleman's steward. The *carte du jour* was unlimited, but
the favourite course was tasted first, and it went into the pockets
instead of the mouths of the company; there was a £50 note in
each man's dinner napkin. The incident is a trifle; but no
intelligent person who compares the cost of English railways
with that of those which the same hands have constructed in
other countries, will doubt that English landlords received
£100,000,000 over and above the actual value of their land,
from which sum there is only to be deducted the unnecessary
payments to lawyers, and for other professional services which
their opposition and vexatious processes demanded. This vast
sum was for the most part expended by landowners in the purchase of small freeholds; and besides these enabling forces,
they have had the advantage of the increasing value of land—
due not only to tenants' improvements, but also to the growing
wealth and number of the population—an increase which has
been at least as rapid as the increase of national expenditure.

The monopoly of land is directly fostered by the cost of
transfer. The landlord is willing to invest his money for a
return of $2\frac{1}{2}$ or 3 per cent., and the lawyer does all he can to
keep small capitalists from competition. Among industrious
nations of the Continent, the greater part of the cost of the
conveyance of land is a percentage on the purchase-money,
which passes to the coffers of the State, so that while the expense on a purchase of £100 would be, say, £5, that of the
conveyance of property worth £100,000 would be £5000. But
here the operation of the law imposes a system precisely the
reverse; it practically forbids the purchase of small properties
by imposing legal charges, the proportion of which invariably
declines with the increase of the purchase-money. A well-
known land agent asserts—and the experience of hundreds will
be similar—that he has often signed deeds for the purchase of
property of small value, when the legal expenses have equalled

one-third of the purchase-money. A member has stated in his place in Parliament that he has known the conveyance of half an acre of land to cost three times the purchase-money— the lawyer's bill having amounted to £150. Yet, perhaps, the uncertainty of the cost of conveyance exerts a more powerful influence in the limitation of the number of agricultural land-owners. The charge is unduly magnified to the prejudice of the small capitalist. An example of this occurred very recently within my own knowledge. Solicitors now permit them-selves to charge by a percentage for the cost of a mortgage, and an owner of land valued at £7000, anxious for certainty, agreed to pay 2 per cent., or £140, for all the business incident to effecting a mortgage for securing a loan of £5000 upon the property. The lawyer told me the title was so simple that he could not, if he had made out a bill, have charged more than £40; so that this unfortunate person needlessly paid £100, merely from fear of the uncertainty of the amount of law charges. It is not necessary to explain how much more strongly the same fear would press upon the man whose entire property consisted of land valued at two or three hundred pounds, nor can it be doubted that the soil of England, speaking of the country generally, is reduced in selling value to the extent of from two to four years' purchase by the incubus of this system of conveyancing.

The words which I have quoted as spoken by Lord Chancellor Hatherley, condemning the limitations of the law, place the axe of reform directly at the root of this system. Land-owners are now encouraged to fence their ownership, by their settlements, with limitations which swathe the soil of the country in parchments, and make of us, as Lord Westbury said, 'a lawyer-ridden people.' The soil of England is held under disabilities. When the House of Lords was crowded prior to the most memorable division on the Irish Land Bill, a friend who was with me, looking down upon the august assembly, whispered, 'And these men own one-fifth of the United King-

dom!' 'Would to God they did,' I answered. 'I doubt if
there are a dozen men there who have an acre of land that they
can call their own.' Their families, not they, are the owners of
that large part of the kingdom. Years ago, in their hot youth,
when they were neither statesmen nor practical agriculturists,
as many of them now are, they signed away to their sons, and
after the sons, to a long line of brothers and nephews—even
when they had not a thought of marriage—the freehold of their
inheritance. How then are the interests of the community
regarded in their limited ownership of the land? I speak of my
own practical experience and observation. On the majority of
great family estates the rent is far below what it might be if
the land were most advantageously prepared and divided for
cultivation; but the arrangement between the landlord and,
tenant is a mixture of a feudal and a business character. Each
thinks he sees his advantage in this. The tenant likes a low
rent; likes to remember that he and his father have had the
farm pretty much on the same terms; it is not difficult to get a
living, and ambition centres not so much in change of social
position as in the hunter which carries him to covert-side. He
has no lease, but his landlord is a kind and honourable gentleman; so long as the rent is duly paid, and he neither shoots
foxes nor, under some landlords, votes the wrong way, and does
not acquire a bad character in the neighbourhood, he will be
secure in his occupation. When he leaves the farm, he will be
paid, according to the custom of the country, for the unexhausted improvements he has made, which, of course, will not
approximate to those a thrifty man would have made if he had
been the owner and occupier, or the well-secured tenant, of the
soil. Says Adam Smith, 'It is against all reason and probability to suppose that yearly tenants will improve the soil;' and
is it much less contrary to reason and probability, to argue that
life tenants will to a necessary extent spend their incomes in the
improvement of estates of which they are but nominal owners?

I am amazed at the ignorance of people with regard to their

own country. Men talk of this as a free country; journalists wrote and politicians spoke of Mr. Goschen's Rating Bill as if it would impose upon landowners one-half of the local rates as they are now levied, and thus make them sharers with the occupier in the weight of extra burdens of such unhappy years as those of the Cotton Famine. But England is not a free country; in one most important aspect it is made up of life tenants and lessors, the former being the great power in the rural districts, just as the latter are rulers in the towns. We cannot liberate the soil by an Act of Parliament; all we can do is to legislate for the successors of the life tenants, as well as for those who may afterwards become leaseholders. The life tenants are, to a large extent, free from responsibility, or, surely, they could not bear to look upon the cottages which herd, rather than house, the people on many estates. I wish carefully to avoid invidious dealing with any class; the fault is in the system rather than in the men. Disgraceful and immoral overcrowding has been the result of the nominal owner's indisposition or inability to build new cottages, and hundreds of parishes will furnish such a scene as I will briefly describe from official records. In the thatch-covered roof of a single-roomed cottage—a loft ten feet square—three beds contained ten people; there were no curtains or divisions of any kind; one bed held the father, mother, and infant son; the centre bed was occupied by three daughters, of whom two were upwards of twenty years of age; and in the third bed lay four sons, aged respectively seventeen, fifteen, fourteen, and ten. Take 'S. G. O.'s' testimony as to cottage beds in a room thirteen feet square. 'On the first lay the mother, a widow, dying of consumption; on the second, two unmarried daughters, eighteen and twelve years of age; on the third, a young married couple, whom I myself had married two days before.' Looking on these things, can we wonder that the English peasantry is the most immoral in the world? The statistics on this point are shocking, yet they conceal the whole truth, because our population is so largely manufacturing, and

these marry and have generally excellent cottages. The following is the evidence of an English clergyman, who said: ' I
never recollect an instance of my having married a woman who
was not either pregnant at the time of her marriage, or had had
one or more children before her marriage.' I lay this frightful
immorality, which every country clergyman can confirm, to the
charge of the system of entails, which reduces the landowner to
the position of a life-tenant, and, not unfrequently, of a helpless
tenant.

And as with the peasantry, so it is with the farmers. In
many cases, the estate is mortgaged to the fullest possible
extent, and the nominal owner cannot obtain the means of
draining the land and improving the homesteads. Often have I
seen poor thrifty tenants imperfectly doing the work by filling
trenches with stones or bushes, or by dragging a mole-plough
through the cold, wet clay, so tenacious that the subterranean
mole-track made by the passage of the iron would ' perhaps
keep open for years. Though the nominal owner has under
various statutes a power of borrowing on the estate, why should
he in this way diminish his income—from which alone he can
provide something for his younger children—to improve the
property of his eldest son? Before the passing of Mr. Locke
King's Act, if he had saved a little money, this would have been
liable for the payment of the mortgage debt in the event of his
death, in spite of any testament by which he sought to bequeath
it to his otherwise penniless daughters. But, then, the farmer
may have money? Yes, he may; though more often he has not
a quarter of that sum which is needful for the most efficient cultivation of the soil. And if he execute works of improvement
he will want some consideration. He will demand a long lease
at the old rent, or he will ask a deduction from his rent to
repay, in so many years, the cost of the permanent improvements; and neither of these things is the nominal owner disposed to grant. If landowners could reasonably be compelled
to grant leases on equitable conditions, and for a sufficient term

of years, then the evils consequent upon the system of entails and settlements would be mitigated. But they dislike leases; and if they ever do contemplate such an instrument, it is often as full of vexatious limitations and restrictions as the deeds by which they hold nominal ownership of the land. The signal and peculiar misfortune of agricultural England is that for the most part it is 'no man's land'—that it is held in perpetual mortmain—the landlord is a life-tenant, and the farmer a dependent. There are exceptions to this feeling against granting leases; I record most notable words to the contrary with peculiar pleasure. Lord Derby said, in 1864: 'I think every good tenant, who is expected to stay permanently on the farm he holds, is entitled to ask for a lease from the proprietor. It is a very simple alternative: if a man is not fit to settle on an estate with a lease, he is not fit to settle without one; if he cannot be trusted with a lease, he cannot be trusted with the land. . . . I say this—and in what I am saying I am rather, in my own mind, addressing landlords than tenants—I say, if a tenant is to be expected to lay out capital on his farm, it implies no distrust of the landlord—it is simply an ordinary and proper business precaution that he should insist on having some lease. . . . I believe that these two things—one, the making the giving of a lease a general rule, and the other, having leases drawn more simply than as a rule they are at present—would go very far to settle that question of landownership of which we have heard something of late.' This is all very satisfactory, so far as it goes; but Lord Derby is scarcely an agricultural landlord. The broad acres of which he is the nominal owner attract bricks and mortar so fast that farmers let rushes grow—those infallible indications of the want of drainage. They would probably say, Where is the use of draining land which in a year may be wanted for a mill, or the level of which may be upset by coal-getting? 'Where do your rushes come from?' I asked once of a great candle-maker. 'Chiefly from Cheshire.' And when, some time afterwards, I

met a party of Cheshire landlords, and told them of the want
of drainage in their county, they assured me that the best
cheese came from the undrained farms, and that cows were
most fond of grass which grows about rushes. 'Are you convinced?' a worthy Cheshire baronet asked. 'Yes,' I said; 'I
am convinced that there is no evil in the world which will not
find defenders.' This question of land-drainage is one that
concerns the food of the people; and the operation of the
British system of entail and settlement is to retard its completion, and in other directions to keep from the land the
capital which would so greatly increase its produce.

It has been said by a practical man that the hostile passage of
100,000 foreign soldiers through our island, attended by all the
horrors of war, would not inflict so great an injury as this system
of land settlement works in a single year. The evidence of
farmers and land-agents proves that on heavy clay lands the
produce of the soil is trebled by proper drainage. But, as Smith
of Deanston said, 'Entail obstructs the substantial improvement
of the land.' Day after day, year by year, English capital is
flowing out of the country, to aid in every description of foreign
enterprise. Yet the agriculture of the kingdom in which this
ever-flowing wealth is made, is starved for want of more capital.
If Mr. Mechi finds that with £16 an acre he can make a better
return than with a smaller capital, we may presume that intelligent farmers generally would have the same experience. But
his land is thoroughly drained; the hedgerows are straightened
and cut down, so as not to obscure light nor shut out the passing
breeze; all is put in the best form for cultivation. I will not
venture to say that one-half the cultivated land of the United
Kingdom is properly drained; but if we assume that of the
46,177,370 acres which are now under cultivation, one-half requires drainage, and if we place the cost of this work at £8 an
acre, we know that a sum of £184,000,000 is required for this
subsoil labour. If we take the authority of experienced land-
agents, and assume that this would in time treble the produce

merely of the 11,755,053 acres under corn crops, the result would pay about 15 per cent. upon the outlay, and afford food, on the wheat lands alone, returned at 3,750,000 acres, for nearly two millions of people!

But this is only a part of the demand of the soil. I have said, quoting the experience of Mr. Mechi, that £16 an acre is not too large a capital for farming land to the best advantage. There are no statistics by which we can ascertain the amount of capital invested in farming; any estimate must be more or less a matter of guess-work. I am sure that to set the capital engaged in agriculture at half this amount—£8 an acre, is an excessive calculation. I have never met with an estimate which set the capital engaged in agriculture at more than £6 an acre. But assuming the higher sum, if then we take once more the 46,177,370 of cultivated acres in the United Kingdom, and compute the extra capital required to bring up the agriculture of the country to the high level which Mr. Mechi has maintained with such good results at Tiptree Hall, we find that in addition to the enormous sum required for drainage, the land of this country demands, and would well reward, a further investment exceeding £350,000,000. How is it possible for me to over-estimate the advantage to the people at large of the profitable expenditure of £500,000,000 upon the soil? Here at once we have the means for rectifying the position of the agricultural labourer. And why is the land thus starved? Why is its productive power thus abandoned? Because the landlords are but nominal owners of their property, and because the tenants have no sufficient security. We need free trade in respect to the land of the United Kingdom and the abolition of the system of imperfect proprietorship in which the main part of it is now held.

Then there are the 'waste' lands, which are slowly but surely passing out of the freedom of commonage into the fettered condition of most of the soil of this country. There are no trustworthy statistics as to the quantity of waste land; but I cannot say that the extent is over-estimated at 10,000,000 acres. The

total area of the United Kingdom exceeds 78,000,000 acres; that
of the cultivated land exceeds 46,000,000 acres. We have, therefore, 32,000,000 acres which are not cultivated; and allotting
22,000,000 to the towns, roads, rivers, etc., we have still 10,000,000
—or nearly three times the extent under wheat in England—of
waste or uncultivated land. There is sometimes clamour for the
cultivation of these lands, as though such a work would deliver
England from pauperism. No doubt there is much to be done upon
the waste lands; but the question in its relation to the wages
fund of the working classes is vastly inferior in comparison with
that of the general demand of agriculture for increased capital
and labour. I think Parliament should exercise great circum-
spection before sanctioning anywhere the enclosure of commons;
but this care is especially necessary when they are situate in the
neighbourhood of large towns; and though I am unable to
subscribe to what I understand to be the doctrine of some, that
in spite of law and custom, a property in rights of common
should be given to occupiers, I think that Parliament might, in
the cases where enclosure is sanctioned, demand a much more
liberal allotment for recreation and garden ground as well as
the preservation of all open spaces in towns, and of monuments
of peculiar or historic interest.

In order to establish free trade in land—of which in these
preliminary remarks I have endeavoured to establish the need—
I would suggest legislation directed to the following points:—

1. The devolution of real property in cases of intestacy in
the same manner which the law directs in regard to personal
property.

2. The abolition of copyhold and customary tenures.

3. The establishment of a Landed Estates Court, for the
disposal of encumbered settled property.

4. A completion of the Ordnance Survey of the United
Kingdom upon a sufficient scale.

5. A system of registration of title, which shall be compulsory upon the sale of property, the fees upon registration—

sufficient at least to defray all official expenses—being a percentage on the purchase-money; the same percentage for all sums. A certificate of title would be given free of all costs in respect of any freehold lands of which the reputed owner could prove undisturbed possession for twenty years. Any title could be registered in the Land Registry Office upon satisfactory evidence of title for twenty years; the fees being the same as in case of sale, when registration would be compulsory.

6. That, preserving intact the power of owners of land to bequeath it undivided or in shares, no gift, or bequest, or settlement of life estate in land, nor any trust establishing such an estate, should hereafter be lawful. Charges and mortgages upon land would be registered, and the position of trustees, as representing persons legally incompetent to hold land, would also be indicated upon the register. As to the tenure of land by corporations, I should be disposed, when the above-mentioned reforms were in operation, to recommend the compulsory sale of their lands.

The taxation of land is another, but a kindred subject. I would propose the charge of a percentage upon the value in fee of the estate, to be paid in the form of Stamp Duty, on transfer, whether by gift, sale, devise, or inheritance—the Succession Duty being remodelled to this end. The assessment might be so many years' purchase of the annual rateable value; and in the case of land and buildings, so many years' purchase of a proportion of the rateable value.

The question as to whether land can be the subject of absolute ownership is only debated by ignorant persons. Mr. Mill says: 'The claim of the landowners is altogether subordinate to the general policy of the State;' and this must be admitted. It is equally true of every other class of property, but specially of those which are limited, and which, being limited, are also indispensable to the existence of the people. If England were surrounded by hostile fleets, and famine was

over all the land, the farmers' crops and the bakers' loaves
would be limited, and 'the claim' of both farmers and bakers
would be 'subordinate to the general policy of the State.'
Again, with reference to the North-Western, or any other
Railway, of which we may assume that it possesses a monopoly
of the most direct line between two or more great centres
of population ; such advantages are limited, and the property of
the shareholders is equally 'subordinate to the general policy
of the State.' Of course it could not be allowed in the one case
that the landed gentry should exercise their admitted 'right' of
eviction, and condemn all the population except the members
of their own families to be crowded to death, in starvation
and plague, in such portions of the towns as do not belong
to their class—so small in number, so rich in land and luxury ;
nor, in the other, would it be permitted, if London were closely
invested, that the bakers should control exactly as they pleased
the distribution of bread. It appears to me that all rights of
property are 'subordinate to the general policy of the State,' it
being understood that the owner should receive compensation
if he is displaced. And with regard to the rent of land, this is
most truly defined as the result of competition for the possession of certain advantages of quality or position. The first
settlers do not pay rent ; they select the situations which in
time to come will command the highest rent if the channel of
communication—generally a stream—beside which they settle
continue to be the chief highway. The next comers are willing
to pay rent for this situation, and so the settlement spreads,
the increase of rent being mainly due to the competition of
capital. This causes the houses in cities to rise higher and
higher, from one storey to four or five, or in some cases ten
storeys high ; and land which was once unfenced, and where,
perhaps, any one might allow his beast to graze, becomes 'accommodation land,' worth £5 or £10 per acre per annum for
the horses and cows or the vegetables and fruit of the town
population. I have said this much upon ownership and rent,

because, finally, I have touched on the conditions upon which the taxation of land should be based. But my immediate object has been to show that free trade in land may be established by the means I have suggested.

In advocating the adoption of those suggestions, I would ask, and I hope to obtain, the co-operation of landowners. They are most largely interested in promoting reform. By the abolition of the law of primogeniture—by which I mean the gift by the State to the eldest son of all real property in cases of intestacy—when the State ceased to inculcate primogeniture, and forbade the practice of entail and settlement, parents might regain that proper authority which they do not now possess over the 'heir.' This scheme would leave intact their power to bestow their possessions in the customary manner, but in that important national as well as family work—the training of the masters of great property—the law would have put into the hands of parents a power for which those who are duly sensible of their responsibilities would surely be grateful. Insolvent landowners would be relieved of the millstone about their necks —restored to a natural position; not seeming rich and being unutterably poor. They would be real owners of their property. A large proportion of the families who mainly possess the agricultural land of the country could give, without trouble or expense, satisfactory evidence of acts of ownership for twenty years, and then, when registration was accomplished, they might burn those mouldy parchments, each reference to which at present costs £100, or they could preserve some of them as curiosities and as a part of the family history. The registration of their property would supply an indefeasible title in the place of these cumbrous and costly muniments, and would give an increased value to their land. When registration of title became general, as it would by this plan, being made compulsory upon sale, there would be an established preference for 'registered' land, and for such the price would be higher than for unregistered land, probably by two to four years' purchase upon all but the most extensive and costly properties.

Lastly, the agricultural landlords ought to accept free trade in land if they wish to avoid measures which will have less regard for their interests. Let them reflect on their position. See where they stand! They have and can have no indefeasible title for their privileges in Parliament. They are but a few thousands among 30,000,000; they have lost the rotten boroughs; they have lost the peculiar control they once possessed—which they usually exercised in a negative manner— over national education; they have lost, too, by the agency of a secret system of voting, their power of intimidation at elections. Stubborn resistance to reasonable reform will assuredly produce greater changes, and the first act of successful antagonism might impose heavy taxation upon the land, and decree compulsory distribution at death, proportioned by law. It is certain as sunrise that our land system will not be permitted to continue in its present form. Unwise opposition would foster the installation of the plan for 'nationalization,' the hobby of so many of the working classes, by which the State would purchase the interest of the landlords, and grant leases of the lands as part of the public domain. Property owners, friends of order, must condemn our land system, because it tends to deprive our country of the best resource against revolution. Our land system is very dangerously contracted in regard to ownership. There is in fact no real power in the rural districts to gainsay the will of the masses in towns. When a Socialistic Commune was erected in Paris, and demanded the exclusion of the city from the general law of the country, there were 5,000,000 landowners in France ready to say 'No,' and to enforce their views of property upon revolutionary Paris. Here there is no such force. The great landed families of the United Kingdom could not stand a moment against the breath of revolution; and, as for the peasantry, there are not (if they were the friends of the landed interest, which is not the case) more of them in England than a single branch of manufacture collects in the vicinity of Manchester. The Reform Act of 1867, the work of a Ministry of landowners, carried by the country party—Lord Beaconsfield having 'educated' them to the task—constitutionally placed the supreme power in the hands of the population of the towns, and the Ballot has confirmed their authority. The evident and irrevocable tendency is towards the equalization of electoral areas; one after another the smallest boroughs are disfranchised, and a stimulus in the same direction will be given when that defeated provision of the Ballot Bill, charging the necessary expenses of elections upon the ratepayers, is finally adopted; for these charges will fall heavy upon the 'pocket' boroughs, and will be unfelt by the populous constituencies.

I am no alarmist; I sincerely believe it would be dangerous for the landed interest to set its face against reform. To what could they trust in such a policy? The forbearance of the now legally, though not yet practically, all-powerful people? Why should these exercise forbearance? Does history read such a lesson to the people? Has the landed interest ever shown regard for their advantage when in supposed or actual conflict with landlord interest? About two hundred years ago the position in which the landowners and the people find themselves to-day was reversed; the former were mightiest in the land. And what did they do? They found a large taxation levied on the soil, of which it is not untrue to say that it was the purchase-money of their estates; they threw off those feudal dues, and substituted an Act which declared that 'the people of England should pay a tax of 1s. 3d. per barrel on all their beer and ale,' with a proportionate sum on all other liquors sold throughout the kingdom. And it was enacted that a moiety of this tax 'shall be settled on the King's Majesty, his heirs and successors, in full recompense and satisfaction for all tenures in *capite* and by knight service, and of the courts of wards and liveries, and all emoluments thereby accruing, and in full satisfaction for all purveyance.' This Act was carried in a House of 300 members by a majority of two. Then, again, when a land-tax of 4*s.* in the pound had been imposed, the landowners contrived, in 1697, so to frame the tax (9 Wm. III. c. 10) that it should not increase with the value of the land, as was at first intended, but should be a fixed annuity without rise in value. I do not bring forward these things as charges against the landed interest—they are now merely historical; nor do I refer to them as incentives to reprisals on the part of those whose ancestors paid so dearly for the legislation of the Caroline period. I hope the people will use their power wisely and fairly; but I have yet to see a party which, being in undisputed possession of authority, has been uninfluenced by motives of interest. I refer to these things as a warning to the landowners, suggesting their acceptance of such moderate, such wholly advantageous reforms as those I have sketched, in the friendly spirit in which they are framed. When Cobden said, in 1845, ' I warn the aristocracy not to force the people to look into the subject of taxation; not to force them to see how they have been robbed, plundered, and bamboozled for ages by them,' he spoke in days very far removed in reference to political affairs from our own. Were he with us now, he would be the first to admit this; but I am very sure that he would demand free trade in land, and, if it were withheld, he would not fail to arouse the people to a sense of their rights in this great matter.

The people! Who are they? 'The people at large'—of whom Cobden wondered that they were ' so tacit in their submission.' Why are they not agitating for these reforms—for free trade in land? I believe they will be tacit no longer; yet I must express my suspicion that the political education of the people is as yet so imperfect, that they do not quite comprehend the subject. Many think that *they* have no land, and *can* have no land, and that therefore it does not concern *them.* On the side of the people, I regard as important—though as standing by itself, utterly ineffective—that question of primogeniture, which would have been for ever decided if Mr. Gladstone's 'Real Estates Intestacy Bill' had become law. This measure —which since the overthrow of the Gladstone Administration has been introduced by Mr. Potter—would not affect the actual power of the landowner over his property, but it would reform the teaching of the State. The example of the State is a matter of supreme importance to the poor; for if the State, in making a will for an intestate person, follow the rule of primogeniture, which such men as Mr. John Walter, the chief proprietor of the *Times*, call a 'flagrant injustice,' then there is a process of 'dry-rot' going on within the body politic, which is ruinous to the interests of the poor. If the State regard not justice, it is the poor who will chiefly suffer. The leaders of society are corrupted when the teaching of the State may be directed by expediency. What is more sad than to have seen a man such as Lord Russell defending primogeniture, and saying that 'the law should adopt the general practice as the rule in cases of intestacy'? Surely Lord Russell then forgot that it is not the law but justice which is represented as blind, even to 'general practice.'

IV.

THE TRANSFER OF LAND.

IN these days of extraordinary projects, it is perhaps surprising that we have had no proposal for filling up St. George's Channel, so that a railway could be made direct from Bristol to Cork and from Belfast to Liverpool. But it may be doubted if we should not by that means lose any further development of those eminent services which Ireland has rendered to England as a trial ground and a motive power for great reforms. Had there been but one island, we may hesitate to believe that Mr. Gladstone's burning sense of justice would have enabled him to accomplish the destruction of a supremacy almost as unjustifiable and anomalous as would be the establishment of the Roman Catholic Church in England as the religion of the State. And as to the Land Laws of Ireland, who will assert that embarrassed landowners would so long since have been led or forced into an Encumbered Estates Court, and that with regard to real property, a system of transfer, which is virtually one of registration, would have been established in Ireland, had the waters of St. George's Channel been abolished ?

The very general embarrassment of Irish landlords led to the foundation of the Encumbered Estates Court, in which upon the petition, either of the owners or of the creditors of encumbered settled estates, these could be sold, and the land, together with its incumbent, set free. Matters were so arranged that the Court should inquire into and record the title with despatch and

economy, and should give to the purchaser a simple and indisputable claim. What has been the result ? The operation of
the tribunal was found so beneficial in regard to the transfer of
land, that the Encumbered Estates Court soon became the
Landed Estates Court, in the archives of which the titles of any
estates might be recorded after proper notice and investigation, and a sale of all or part conducted with economy and
credit.

This legislation may not have been designed to promote the
transfer of land, but such has undoubtedly been its effect. A
considerable step towards the establishment of free trade in land
in Ireland was taken to some extent unconsciously, and therefore
with much error, but the natural operation of self-interest is
making of the Landed Estates Court a register for the more ready
and economic transfer of land.   The Encumbered Estates Court
was established in 1849, and in less than five-and-twenty years
nearly one-sixth of the soil of Ireland had passed, with regard to
title, through the hands of the examiners. It is not asserted that
the whole of that area has been sold, though it is beyond question that the object of such examination has always had reference
to sale.   Any one who takes up an Irish newspaper may learn
much of the operation of the Court.   He will find that though
the laws and customs in regard to primogeniture, entails, and
settlement, obtain in Ireland as in England and Scotland, yet
that the sales of land are in proportion vastly more numerous ;
and especially he will notice the extreme rarity of a sale conducted otherwise than under the authority of the Court, and the
. still more rare occurrence of a sale of land without a title
stamped with the authority of that tribunal.   In fact, the landowners of Ireland have already learned something of the marketable value of a simple, indefeasible, registered title, and
accordingly there are many notices in Irish journals of application for registration, even when a sale is not immediately
contemplated.   Of course, the economic value of such an operation consists mainly in the fact that such transfers imply the

surrender of the great natural agent in production—the land—from ill-managing, unimproving, because embarrassed hands to those which also hold the means to make it bring forth in great abundance.

Nothing is more astonishing in this particular matter than the apparently wilful blindness of some political writers who pretend to authority. There are very influential journals which actually parade a statement of sales of real property in England having amounted in a single year to £10,000,000, as proof that the transfer of land is all that it should be in this country. How much more true to their proper function of rightly directing the public opinion would it be, if instead of taking this £10,000,000 as a text for glorification over the land system of the kingdom, they regarded its singular inadequacy to the circumstances of England! How much more true, for example, would it be to say: 'Here is a country of surprising wealth, a country in which capital has increased and is increasing at a rate which transcends even the imagination of the recent past, which is so rich that the world is to a great extent under mortgage to its people. Its realm is so secure that it is the savings bank of the universe; its soil is guarded not only by the sea, but by a dense and unconquerable people. And yet, such is the baneful operation of its antiquated laws and customs with regard to the tenure of land,—so clumsy and dilatory and costly is its method of transfer, that in 1873—the year of its greatest wealth and of its highest and most unexampled prosperity, the transfer of real property did not exceed the value of about ten millions sterling, an amount which in the shape of a six per cent. loan to the United States or to France, London would subscribe in ten minutes.' Is any one hardy enough to say that this would not be a more accurate way of putting the fact? Let me then, for his conviction, make one of the very few references I shall on this occasion permit myself to the land systems of the Continent. In France, the transfer of land is rendered onerous to the parties concerned by the imposition of a considerable tax on the

transaction, amounting, in fact, to more than six per cent.
But notwithstanding this, we find, from one of the greatest
authorities, that in France 'the value of immoveable (real)
property annually sold may be estimated at £80,000,000; that
which changes hands by succession at £60,000,000.' Thus in
France—which that great economist, Mr. J. R. M'Culloch, predicted fifty years ago would to-day be a 'pauper-warren' as a
consequence of its land-system—the ordinary annual transfer
of land by sale is eight times as great as in England, a country
overflowing with capital, of which millions are sunk, and much of
it squandered, in delusive foreign enterprises.

But we need not go outside the United Kingdom to show
the absurdity of this shallow jubilation. We may again refer
to the operation of the Landed Estates Court in Ireland, and
from that we may form some idea of what would be the result
of a more free transfer of land among this supremely wealthy
and home-loving English people. Through that Court nearly a
sixth of all the lands in Ireland passed, either for sale, or with
a view to sale or mortgage, in the space of twenty-three years.
Now let us suppose the real property of England to have been
dealt with in the same manner. The estimated rental of the
real property in England and Wales has been taken by Sir
John Lubbock and others at £150,000,000, representing (I am
taking Sir John Lubbock's figures), at thirty years' purchase, a
total sum of £4,500,000,000. It is not reasonable to suppose
that if even that small advance towards free trade in land which
has been made in Ireland had existed in England, the proportion both in extent and value of property transferred would
not be vastly greater than in Ireland. There the differences of
religion, which as a rule separate the owners and occupiers of
land; the terror of assassination, which was widespread in the
years to which we are referring; together with the comparative
poverty of all,—contrast forcibly with the teeming wealth of
England, and the pleasure, the security, the unmenaced influence which attach to the ownership of land in England. But

even if we make the unreasonable supposition that the transfer would be no greater than in Ireland—what do we find? Suppose that in twenty-three years, property to the value of one-sixth part of Sir John Lubbock's estimate had been dealt with; that would be £750,000,000, or more than £32,500,000 a year!

Is it not wonderful that we, in regard to the transfer of land, retain practices less civilised than those of the Plantagenets! But even that is perhaps less remarkable than that we should so utterly disregard the arguments of the greatest lawyers of our time, and of both parties in the State. In the preceding paper on 'Free Trade in Land,' I have quoted some memorable words of Lord Hatherley with respect to the transfer of land. From the opposite party in Parliament let us take, also before he arrived at the woolsack, a lawyer so powerful and eminent as Lord Cairns. What does he say? Lord Cairns has illustrated the evil in the following felicitous terms:[1] 'You buy an estate at an auction, or you enter into a contract for the purchase of an estate. You are very anxious to get possession of the property you have bought, and the vendor is very anxious to get his money. But do you get possession of the property? On the contrary, you cannot get the estate, nor can the vendor get his money until after a lapse—sometimes no inconsiderable portion of a man's lifetime—spent in the preparation of abstracts, in the comparison of deeds, in searches for encumbrances, in objections made to the title, in answers to those objections, in disputes which arise upon the answers, in endeavours to cure the defects. Not only months, but years, frequently pass in a history of that kind; and I should say that it is an uncommon thing in this country for a purchase of any magnitude to be completed—completed by possession and payment of the price—in a period under, at all events, twelve months. The consequences of this were stated in the Report of the Commission [on the Land Transfer Act]. The Commissioners state in their Report: "When a contract is duly entered into, the investi-

---

[1] Speech on Introduction of Registration of Titles Bill, 1859.

gation of the title often causes, not only expense, but delay
and disappointment, sickening both to the seller and the buyer.
The seller does not receive his money, nor the buyer his land,
until the advantage or pleasure of the bargain is lost or has
passed away." Unquestionably that is one and a very great
evil under which we labour. But that is not the greatest evil.
I can well imagine that the purchaser of an estate would be
content to submit to delay, and even to considerable expense,
if he were assured that when the delay and expense were over,
upon that occasion, at all events, he would have a title as to the
dealings with which for the future there would be no difficulty;
but unfortunately that is not the case. Suppose I buy an
estate to-day. I spend a year, or two or three years, in ascertaining whether the title is a good one. I am at last satisfied.
I pay the expense, the considerable expense, which is incurred
—in addition to the price which I have paid for my estate,
and I obtain a conveyance of my estate. About a year afterwards, I desire to raise money upon mortgage of this estate ; I
find some one willing to lend me money, provided I have a good
title to the land. The man says: "It is very true that you
bought this estate and that you investigated the title, but I
cannot be bound by your investigation of the title, nor can I be
satisfied by it." Perhaps he is a trustee who is lending money
which he holds upon trust. He says: "My solicitor must
examine the title, and my counsel must advise upon it." And
then, as between me, the owner of the estate, and the lender
of the money, there is a repetition of the same process which
took place upon my purchase of the estate, and consequently
the same expense is incurred as when I bought it; and for
the whole of that, I, the owner of the estate and the borrower of
the money, must pay. Well, that is not all. Months or years
after all this is completed, from circumstances I find I must
sell my estate altogether. I find a person willing to become a
purchaser. The intending purchaser says: "No doubt you
thought this was a good title when you bought this estate,

and no doubt this lender of money thought he had a very good
security when he lent his money; but you are now asking me
to pay my money. I must be satisfied that the title is a good
one; my solicitor must look into it, and my counsel must advise
upon it!" Then again commence abstracts, examinations, objections, difficulties, correspondence, and delay. I am the owner
of the estate, and I must pay substantially for the whole of
that, because, although the expense is paid in the first instance
by the purchaser, of course, in the same proportion as that
expense is borne by him, in the same proportion will he abate
the price which he will give for the estate.'

That is the English system of transfer described by the Lord
High Chancellor, and since that speech was delivered, Lord
Cairns has made attempts in the direction of reform. His
Bills were wrecked on the rocks of entail and settlement, the
removal of which will not be sanctioned by the landed gentry.
Lord Westbury was a great lawyer; he tried his hand at reform,
and of course failed. The establishment which Lord Chancellor
Westbury set up by way of improvement was merely a waste of
public money. The desolate Land Registry Office which his
Act established provided for three or four sinecurists, and that
was all. There was a registrar at £2,500 per annum; there was
an assistant registrar at £1,500 per annum; there were examiners
of title; there were solicitors; there was a chief clerk, with a
staff of subordinates. Four years ago I endeavoured to make
such inquiry as was possible into the business of this Land
Registry Office, and I found that the officials had literally
nothing to do. In ten years the office had registered titles of
land to the value of about £5,000,000, and in extent about
50,000 acres. I calculated that at such a rate of progress
(which there was no prospect of maintaining; for the most part
the business had been done while the Act was very new) it
would take about 760 years to accomplish the registration of
all the land in the country.

Of course there has been a Royal Commission. No one who

knows anything of England would doubt for a moment that a Royal Commission had considered the subject of the transfer of land. In Part II. of the Report which contains the views of Commissioners on the working of Lord Westbury's Act and the causes of its failure, we find them frankly stating that, 'As the number of applications for registration during the six years that the Act has been in force did not average more than eighty per annum, and are falling off, it is clear that the amount of business done is insignificant, and its progress affords no hope of increase.' The Commissioners thought that obstruction was caused by the requirement in the fifth section of Lord Westbury's Act, that the person who sought registration should make out not merely what is called 'a good holding title,' but a title such as the Court of Chancery would compel an unwilling purchaser to accept. The third cause of failure, described as 'the disclosure of trusts' upon the register, is that ever-present denial of reform which Lord Hatherley refers to in the speech that has been mentioned. There is something very pitiful in these attempts by men who know the evil and dare not deal with the cause. They fail one after another, because they submit to have the boundaries of reform marked out for them, somewhat after the fashion of a skating-ring upon the ornamental water in St. James's Park before the bottom was cleansed and made solid. One great area—the professional area—where clients tumble over head and ears in costs, is marked 'dangerous'; then the great area which belongs to entail and settlement is understood to be 'very dangerous'; and so on, until the poor law-maker, who is more to be pitied than some are ready to suppose, warned on one side of the peers and squires, on another of the lawyers, and urged above all not to be 'sensational' by colleagues who are themselves for the most part men imbued with the prejudices and the ideas common to the landed gentry, produces another of those legislative abortions of which the miserable skeletons are strewn upon the track of Parliament. There is probably not a lawyer of eminence who does not think that conveyancing by registration of title is superior to conveyancing by deed. I should be very unwilling to suppose that there is one who at any time thought it necessary that the title of every plot of land in the country should have its history written in crabbed letters, and written again and re-written for the immense space of sixty years. Why, it is little more than sixty years since the battle of Waterloo! I lose patience when I regard the construction of many of the laws under which we live—laws which seem retained only to add to the cost of existence and to the unprofitable expenditure of time and money and intellect, all of which might be employed in the service of more just and simple statutes ;—I say just, because those laws are obviously unjust which, by compelling needless expense, press so much more hardly on the poor than on the rich.

It is refreshing to turn from this 'lawyer-ridden country,' and to see what Greater Britain can do and has accomplished in regard to the transfer of land. The operation of Sir Robert Torrens' Act in Australia appears to be a complete success. Sir Robert has stated that the measure was suggested to him in the course of official duties connected with the transfer of shipping. He observed that 'at the Custom House, you may see an ordinary, uncouth clerk, without any difficulty, and with perfect security, conducting transfers and mortgages of property in shipping, and the time thus occupied in thus dealing with a vast property, such as that of the *Great Eastern,* would not exceed half an hour.' He saw that 'immobility and divisibility of the land, so far from preventing, do greatly facilitate the dealing with land by registration of title, especially as regards the complication of the record, through the frequency of joint ownership arising out of the indivisibility of shipping property.' His Bill became the law of South Australia in 1857. In 1872, he stated that no fewer than 18,000 or 19,000 'distinct titles (a considerable portion of them complicated or blistered) have been placed upon the record without practical injury or injustice to any one.' Under the system there in force, the requisitions

which the applicant for registration is required to satisfy are:
'(1) That he is in undisputed possession ; (2) That in equity and
justice he appears to be rightly entitled ; (3) That he produces
such evidence, as tends to the conclusion that no person is in a
position to succeed in an action of ejectment against him ;
(4) That the description of the parcels is clear and accurate.
These requisitions being satisfied, advertisement and the service
of notices, calling upon all claimants to show cause against the
applicant's title within reasonable time, are found to be sufficient
safeguard against risks arising out of technical defects, and (in
accordance with an ancient practice under English law) in the
event of non-claims within the prescribed period, indefeasible
title is issued to the applicant.' Under the Torrens system, all
that relates to a plot of land is to be found in one book, 'in
which a distinct folium is opened for each parcel, which folium
contains a map, and the record of every estate and interest which
it can concern a purchaser or mortgagee to be acquainted with.'
'The owner of each recorded estate or interest receives an instrument evidencing his title, which is in fact a counterpart or
duplicate of that portion of the register which relates to the
same ; and this contains a printed form of agreement for transfer,
discharge, or surrender, as the case may be, to be signed by the
parties, wherever they may be, in presence of notaries or commissioners for taking affidavits, and transmitted by the post for
registration.'

That our system as re-established by Lord Cairns' Act is a
failure, and that this Australian method is a complete success,
can surely excite no wonder. Our system, it is true, dangles
before the eyes of the applicant the bait of indefeasible title, but
on the other hand there are good reasons to keep him from the
office. In the first place he might be possessed of 'a perfect
marketable title,' and in that case he would be every way a
loser. A conspicuous merit of Sir Robert Torrens' method is
that it gives security to the possessor of 'a fair holding title.'
Then again, personal attendance is required in all the systems

which have been attempted in England; in Australia, the parties may transact their business in the localities in which they reside, and provide for the execution of the instruments 'in an easy and at the same time safe way.' The plain fact is obvious that our system is not registration of title, but rather certification of deeds; the very essence of a system of registration of title for the transfer of land is that the land shall be passed by the act of transfer upon the register. As the 31st section of Sir Robert Torrens' Australian Act puts it: 'No deed or instrument shall have effect to pass or charge any interest or estate in land; but so soon as the recorder of titles shall have entered in the record the particulars of any transfer, charge, or dealing, the estate or interest shall thereupon pass or become charged.'

Concerning two important points—the registration of trusts and of mortgages—the Australian system provides, with regard to the former, that mere trusts shall be excluded from the register; and in reference to mortgages, the transfer of the legal estate—an excuse for costs—plays no part. The Act plainly states that 'mortgage and encumbrance shall have effect as security, but shall not operate as a transfer of the land thereby charged; and in case default be made in the payment of the principal sum, interest, annuity, or rent-charge thereby secured, or in the observance of any covenant, and such default be continued for the space of one calendar month, or for such other period of time as may therein for that purpose be expressly limited, the mortgagee or encumbrancee may give to the mortgagor or encumbrancer notice in writing to pay the money then due or owing on such mortgage or encumbrance, or to observe the covenants therein expressed, and that sale will be effected unless such default be remedied.' Lastly, as to this admirable system, what do British mortgagors suppose is the cost of the operation? Ten shillings is the average cost of transactions— half being for transfer, and half for release. But more than this; the mortgage, being transferable by endorsement, may pass freely from hand to hand like a bank-note. As a specimen

I

of the transfer powers of the Torrens' Act, one gentleman writes, with reference to a very large transaction : 'Only two days before the packet sailed, I had an offer for my estate. The intending purchaser went with me to the Lands Title Office, and in less than an hour the business was transacted. I got a cheque for the purchase-money, and he got an indefeasible title to the land ; and as we did the business ourselves, the cost was only three or four pounds.' As to mortgage, another correspondent writes : 'Recently I purchased a sheep-station for my son, and being £5000 short of the purchase-money, I mortgaged some land for the amount. The transaction was completed in less than half an hour ; and as I did the business myself, the whole expense was only fifteen shillings.'

It appears to me that in legislating for the transfer of land in England, we could hardly do better than copy the Australian system in much of its detail. But we must not make the error of supposing that the registration of title is quite as simple a matter in the old country as in the new. Yet the greater error of assuming that all titles to land in the Colonies are very simple is more common. If the period for investigation were reduced to twenty years, it may be said with probable truth that titles in the Colonies would appear more complicated than in this country. Land changes hands in the Colonies with a rapidity unknown in England. I have heard Sir Robert Torrens say that the business of transfer in the Australian city of Adelaide is more than occurs in the whole of Ireland. Nor should we carelessly accept objections founded upon the immensity of the business which the number of transactions would involve. Sir Robert Torrens has alluded to the more complicated dealings with shipping ; and any one may see with what small trouble, and numbers and extent of offices, the transfer of the National Debt is conducted and the dividends paid, which latter is of course an operation altogether outside the work of registration. Mr. Thomson Hankey, in his valuable work on 'Banking,' says that 'to carry out the National Debt it is estimated that about 200 persons are constantly employed, with an additional staff of about 50 when the dividends are paid. Ten rooms are devoted to the purpose, and upwards of 1700 books are in constant use. The remuneration made to the Bank for this service is at the rate of £300 per million for the first £600,000,000 and £150 per million for the remainder of the capital stock, and amounts at the present time to about £200,000 per annum. The number of transfers is about 136,000 in the course of the year, and this operation necessitates 272,000 alterations of accounts, because for every transfer made the amount must be taken from one account and added to another.' Mr. Hankey gives the following 'number of transfers and of accounts in the Government Funds in the years 1839, 1849, 1859, 1865, and 1872':—

Years.	Transfers.	Accounts.
1839	201,190	279,584
1849	190,912	277,506
1859	171,881	269,304
1865	162,187	245,973
1872	136,000	214,000

In these figures may be seen that tendency to diminution in the number of holders which is also the most striking feature in the record of owners of British land.

In the foregoing paper, entitled 'Free Trade in Land,' I have put forward six propositions which it is unnecessary to repeat. I venture to think that those propositions would tend to facilitate the transfer of land. (1) The first would make the law equal, and easily intelligible in its operation in the case of intestates; whereas at present, if an owner of land in gavel-kind (so common in Kent) die without having executed a will, his land is distributed among his surviving sons; while we may say all over England, outside of Kent, the law of primogeniture prevails. (2) Copyhold tenure has a certain similarity to tenure by record of title, but it is absolutely necessary to abolish copyhold and customary tenures if we are to establish a register, because a universal registration of title, with transfer attendant upon the act of registration, is incompatible with the present system of the enrolment of copyholds. (3) The establishment of a Landed Estates Court would greatly facilitate the transfer of land. A large proportion of the soil of this country is in the hands of embarrassed holders, whose lands, on their own petition, or on that of their creditors, might be sold by order of the Judge of such a Court. The produce of the soil of England might perhaps be doubled by the application of £500,000,000 of capital in excess of that with which it is now so poorly provided; and it is probable that no inconsiderable part of that sum would be expended by landowners, if, by the operation of such a Court, their land could be taken from the hands of those who now are forced to starve it in order to keep themselves and their families from insolvency. (4) We cannot have an efficient registration of title without an effective means for the identification of each parcel of land, and to this end we must have a completion of the Ordnance Survey upon a sufficient scale. I have myself examined a considerable number of parish maps, and have found them generally so excellent and accurate that I have no hesitation in saying they might, in the great majority of parishes, be adopted at once for purposes of registration, being corrected when necessary by officers of the Government Survey. (5) With regard to the registration itself, we must not forget the holders of defective titles. It will not surprise any one who reflects upon the circumstances of the colony, to be told that these are in proportion probably more numerous in Australia than in England. But we need not go deeply at present into this matter, because it is now only proposed that registration should be compulsory upon the sale of property. On sale, by the act itself, every man may be held to declare his willingness to expose his title, and therefore there can be no hardship in making registration compulsory. A most important matter is to shorten the time for which evidence of title is requisite. I propose to reduce this requirement to twenty years (I believe that twelve years is the Australian limit), and the change would of course affect a vast number of titles which are now only 'maturing' in consequence of flaws beyond the twenty years of undisputed title. The presentation, free of all fees, of a certificate of title in respect of any freehold lands (the owner of which could satisfy some such queries as those which I have previously quoted from Sir Robert Torrens' method in respect of his title for twenty years), would, I anticipate, bring at once, and without difficulty, upon the register, the bulk of that vast portion of the soil which is held in settled or en-tailed estates. And this is needful, because, in order to make registration successful which cannot be, except on sale, com-pulsory, it is necessary to devise means for bringing owners of property to the position of applicants. The advantages of registration soon prove themselves when once their reputa-tion extends over a wide area. The superior selling value of registered land would attract the attention of all who might find themselves in the position of sellers or mortgagors. It is not needful in Ireland, and it would not of course be necessary in England, that an applicant for registration should be about to sell. Any title could be registered in the Land Registry Office upon evidence of title for twenty years; and as for the fees, the wisdom of Parliament would decide whether these should be of such weight as to contribute largely to the public revenue, as is the case in most continental States, or whether they should be sufficient only to defray all official expenses. (6) The final proposition I have put forward would have a powerful effect in promoting the transfer of land. It is stated on respectable authority that one-sixth of the soil of this country is held in mortmain by corporations; yet this considerable proportion is but small in comparison with the area which has no owner in fee simple, which is held by the nobility and gentry on a system of life tenure—of nominal ownership; a system under which the duties and responsibilities of parent and land-lord are so generally in conflict, and are often so inequitably regulated. I propose, however, to make no change in the status of the landed gentry; except in so far as these suggestions would tend to raise the status of the landowner by compelling him to be the real owner of his estate, with as much power to bequeath it undivided or in shares as he has over his money in the Funds.   Existing trusts would not of course be dealt with, except in the case of corporations which never die ; but I would strictly prohibit, with the exception I have named, the creation of new trusts, and this of course would greatly simplify the registration of titles.   The aim should be to have but one description of title to land—that of owner in fee simple.   Then the registry would be indeed a simple affair, dealing with owner- ship, with leaseholds, and with mortgages and other charges. In sight of so great a national advantage, I am disposed to think and hope that the real or supposed interest of any one class will not much longer be allowed to impede progress in that which would vastly enlarge the wealth and powers of the country.

V.

FREE LAND.[1]

DURING the Cotton Famine, when I was in Lancashire for
four years, administering in all its towns the business
of the Public Works Act, I often expressed, and I have many
times since repeated the opinion, that I knew no part of
England which seemed so free from stupid people. From that
time, I have felt an attachment to the people of this manufacturing district; and I have felt, too, that when any great
social question has to be placed before the public for solution,
there is no part of the country in which it is more important
that the subject should be well expounded and well understood
than in Lancashire. I am convinced that if the people of
Lancashire will master this question of free land, and insist
upon the necessary legislation being adopted by Parliament,
the thing will be done. This is a matter which concerns the
food of the people. There is not a pound of meat in the
butchers' shops, there is not a bit of bacon at the grocers',
there is not a loaf of bread at the bakers', there is not an
article of food which is not indirectly taxed—of which the
price is not made higher than it would be if the soil of England
were free land; if that soil were not withheld from increased
production by positive and permissive laws which have but
one object and one defence—that they maintain a privileged
class in a position of supremacy in the legislature and upon

[1] An address delivered at the request of the Liberal Association, at Bolton,
March 6th, 1878.

the land, whose power with regard to the land has always been used, and is now employed, to defeat the legitimate demands of the people of this country.

In the first place, this matter of free land is a food question. But man does not live by bread alone, and perhaps the greater part of this matter is that which connects it with the habits and status of the people. Now, in regard to self-help and self-elevation, there is nothing like thrift ; no man is rich who is improvident ; no man is poor who has all his life been wisely careful. But as to a nation, we look in vain for carefulness when the greatest of all incentives and encouragements to thrift —the possession of land—is withheld, as in this country it is withheld, from the people. We English are known all over Europe for the reverse of carefulness ; even our fellow-subjects in Jersey say, if they have a pauper, that he must be English or Irish. I have often noted the absence of thrift among our own people as compared with the saving, frugal habits of people of other nations, and have asked myself to what are the comparatively wasteful habits of the English people to be ascribed ? No candid and competent person will doubt that the response to this question involves a heavy charge against our arrangements with reference to land. People become thrifty through the desire to acquire, to retain, and to extend their property ; and wherever and whenever they are debarred from acquiring property in land, the consequence is painfully marked in the habits of the people. Our land system, to use Mr. Cobden's phrase, divorces the people from the soil, and, therefore, I lay to its charge that for which the people of this country have an unenviable distinction among the populations of Europe.

In sight then of these gigantic evils—evils which affect every one of us, we say we want free land ; and we are quite prepared to explain how it is that the land of England is held in bondage, and what we mean by free land. The old English term, a freeholder, implies a good deal of what we mean, but agricultural freeholds occupy a very small part of England. We wish our opponents, among whom there are certainly stupid people, to strive to comprehend and digest the fact (for it is a fact) that more than 50,000,000 acres of this United Kingdom—that is, nearly four-fifths—know no freeholder. These 50,000,000 of acres are not free land ; they are in bondage. Let us try to understand this great matter fully and thoroughly. Let us take, by way of example, the case of one who is known, at least by name, to all in Lancashire, and who, I believe, is as widely respected—the case of Lord Derby. He is not, he never has been, he never can be, owner of the Knowsley estate ; and of course his interest and his responsibility in regard to that large property are infinitely inferior to what they would be if he were the freeholder. Take the five hundred members of the House of Lords, who receive the rents of nearly one-fifth of the United Kingdom. They are not owners ; they are only life tenants ; they have small inducement and small power to improve the land. Some of them are, for their position and in their fashion, poor men, who are trying, regardless of the interests of agriculture, to scrape what they can out of their estates, which must all go at their death to eldest sons, for the benefit of the younger children. Some of them are insolvent ; but because the land is not free, they drag it with them through all the years of their struggles and into their occasional bankruptcies, and of course the interests of production are upon all such estates terribly neglected. Let us take a case recently before the Bankruptcy Court, by way of illustration. A property of 16,000 acres, with a rental of as many pounds sterling, was settled upon Lord —— for life, with remainder to his son Lord —— as tenant in tail. Upon the coming of age of Lord —— the estate was re-settled. Within a year after the re-settlement, the son, having run into debt, was made bankrupt ; the whole of his reversionary interest was then assigned to the creditors ; and—as Mr. Shaw-Lefevre has written in allusion to this case—'the result is that during the lives of father and son, and perhaps for many years after, this great estate will be in the position of being in the ostensible possession of men absolutely without means, and without any motive or probable power to sell.'

As I travelled towards Manchester to-day, I was thinking of this sad case—of the restricted production and the miserable future of that and of many other settled estates, while by a curious coincidence, a fellow-passenger, a Manchester man, whose name I do not know, was speaking of part of an impoverished estate of about 200 acres which he had purchased six years ago in the county of Chester. Fortunately for the interests of agriculture, the male line in the entail had failed, and a female inheritor had exercised powers of sale. When the land was conveyed to him from the possession of the long-embarrassed family, he said there was barely feed for thirty sheep, and that there was not a load of hay; indeed his own expression was, 'You could cart all the hay in a wheelbarrow.' In six years, by the due application of capital upon this land, so happily made free from settlement, he had raised the produce to fifty loads of hay; and he said he had at that moment six hundred sheep upon the land, which as 'settled' land barely afforded food for thirty. We want free land, because it would greatly increase the food supply by attracting capital to investment in the soil, thus adding to the wealth and strength of the country in the surest manner; because it would tend to increase the number of agricultural owners—a policy of the most wisely Conservative character, affording security such as none other can give for the rights of property, and the permanence of the most valuable institutions of the nation. Objections have been raised to my employment of the words 'free land.' I have given those objections full consideration. But though I have used 'free trade in land' as well as 'free land,' I am bound to say that I regard the latter as the closer and more correct designation of the reforms to which I am about to refer, and which it is certainly my fixed intention to advocate. It is not necessary, nor is it possible, that the general title of a programme of reform should convey detailed instructions to the legal mind. The tribunal, in an appeal of this sort, is the people; and the title will not be accepted by them unless it is intelligible and indicative of the direction in which it is desired that their movement should be made. I think 'free land' best satisfies this requirement. When I have confined my observations mainly to the work of facilitating and cheapening the processes of transfer, I have thought 'free trade in land' an adequate, though necessarily very imperfect, expression of the object. But in viewing the whole subject, of which the larger part is the emancipation of the soil from the bondage of settlement, and the establishment of freehold tenure, 'free land' is clearly more correct. It is not a valid objection that a title given to a programme of reform may, by uninquiring minds, be held to imply something foreign to the purpose of the reformers. 'Free trade' was the title of the great Manchester reform initiated at the time when I was but a child. You did not give up that title because it might have been held to imply free exchange of commodities without payment of carriage, or the abolition of the duties upon spirits, malt, and tobacco. When a Free Church was constituted in Scotland, when the same term is resounding throughout Europe, and is heard in every community, men were not and will not be persuaded to throw it aside because some pedant might suggest that it meant a Church in which every one was free to promulgate diverse and personal opinion. We ask for Disestablishment as a measure of justice to the whole people, and of real advantage to the Church; shall we abandon the word because, taken apart from the circumstances of the Church of England, the expression is vague, and might be held by ignorant minds to imply the abolition of that great and beneficial organisation? No; and I maintain that 'free land' has a claim as good as any one of these to acceptance, and that no other designation with which I am acquainted indicates so correctly that which is our most pressing need—the liberation of the soil from the influence of laws and customs which are of feudal descent and of most pernicious operation.

With very few exceptions, the estates of the landed gentry are settled for fifty or a hundred years, and are by that means practically withdrawn from all possibility of sale. Now I want to ask this question : Can it be for the advantage of the country that four-fifths of the soil should be without owners—should be settled by fetters immovable in many cases for a century? I assert that in order to have free land, we must insist that the tenure shall be freehold, and to that end it must be forbidden to create life estates in land. There must be no settlements of land. There can be no objection to settlements, for a reasonable period, of personalty, or of money charges upon land. But when we advance this preliminary demand in relation to free land, it will be asked, Why should not land be settled as well as money? Because, as Mr. Lowe has said, ' Land is a kind of property in which the public must, from its very nature, have a kind of dormant joint interest with the proprietor,' and because the public will not submit to be deprived—for a century it may be—of the beneficial advantage of that interest.

I must say a few words upon the nature of property in land. The ownership of land is and must always be a monopoly, and it is a monopoly of something necessary to the existence of every member of the community. Therefore absolute property in land cannot exist. No well-informed person has ever claimed that it does exist in England. In the standard book upon the Law of Real Property, we find it stated that ' no man is in law the absolute owner of lands.' This is true even of a freeholder, of whom we speak as one who holds an estate in fee-simple. I am a great stickler for the rights of property ; I never join in the cry that landlords ought to give leases or ought not to raise rents. We have moral obligations connecting us with all men ; but we are speaking now of legal obligations. Let every man do as he sees fit with his own ; but in regard to land, the definition of that which is his own must be determined by the State.

I say that the State must withdraw the power of settling life estates in land, because it is opposed to public interests, and that whatever is opposed to public interest in regard to the tenure of land should be made the subject of legislation. But to what extent should this be carried, and who shall judge what is for the public interest? I will mention what is my rule in the matter. It is this. Be sure that the legislation which is proposed will raise the pecuniary value of the interest of the landowners. This is, I think, the truest way in which legislators can inform themselves whether the change will be really for the public advantage. I say that it can never be for the public interest to lessen the value of the landlord's interest through any modification of the admitted rights of property. I have never met any one who had a doubt that if the power of settling land were abolished, and its transfer by registration made simple and inexpensive—as it is in the Channel Islands, or by a much better system in Australia—the result would be a large increase in the value of the proprietary right. And in completion of this point I would add that wherever it is clear that the proprietary interest runs with the public interest, then to legislate is an imperative duty, and to withhold legislation is to betray the interest of the public to the prejudices of a class. This is what is now happening in our country. Though every step in the beneficial progress of reform must augment the value of their possessions,—though no man who sought to violate their rights of property to the extent of a rood of ground would obtain a hearing from the British people, yet it is not to be expected that the vast majority of landowners will abandon their traditional policy of resistance. One reason why an unreasoning opposition to reform may be looked for, is because the most intelligent of the landlords are the least concerned with the management of their estates. Were they owners, it might be different; but as life tenants, with fettered powers of improvement, they prefer the paths of pleasure or of statesmanship. As for the majority, they will oppose, because, as Lord Beaconsfield has written of them in 'Lothair,' 'They live

in the open air, and they never read;' and because, as Mr. Mill
has said of them, 'Great landlords have rarely studied anything.'

But if the British people do not now proceed to free the
soil of their country from bondage in feudal forms of law
and custom, the fault is entirely their own. It is absurd to
speak harshly of the seven or eight thousand life tenants of
these 50,000,000 acres, as though they alone were responsible.
They are without question responsible for their own opposition
to reform, and for the self-interested legislation of their time.
It is undeniable that they have been guilty of class legislation.
But this selfish disposition cannot surprise those who have
taken even a cursory observation of the main stream of history.
Land tenure is the simplest of all its chapters; the proceeding
is, in outline, uniform in character. First the king claimed all,
and finding that he alone could not hold all against other kings,
he called in great nobles that he might have their swords at
need; then the nobles, finding that they could not keep their
great neighbours out of their castles with their own weapons,
admitted knights and esquires to landownership, who, as long
as the reign of force endured, secured the stout arms of meaner
men in the same way. There was at that time much subdivision of the land. But when law became supreme in place
of force, then the great people grew less liberal, and costly
processes of law which favoured the re-attainment of the soil
by the wealthy, were set up, and are still in operation. Thus
it happens that we now confront the greatest anomaly in the
world; and the danger which would menace this country—if it
were not quite certain that Parliament can and will deliver
us—is, that together with representation of an increasingly
popular character, we are maintaining a mediæval land system.
When millions rule, the ownership of four-fifths of the land
may not wisely or safely be left to a few thousands. If the
claim to constitute the best Second Chamber that could be
devised must for ever continue to involve the placing in mort-

main—for that is what it comes to—of 50,000,000 acres, or
four-fifths of our country, then, I say, unhesitatingly, that the
continuance of the House of Lords is not worth the cost, which
I believe to be a cost sufficient to discharge the national debt.
But there is nothing in the programme of free land which
demands the distribution of the large properties of the peerage,
and of course their titles of honour have no connection with
the matter. No one, however, who is wise will defend the
law of primogeniture, and the customs of entail and settlement,
upon the ground that these things are necessary and their
endurance justifiable for the maintenance of the House of Lords.
The nobility may count securely upon the goodwill of the great
body of the people, although I do not think that this tenderness
is, as has been said, peculiar to the English people. The fact
that a lord has an undoubted advantage over another man, is
due to that preference which is world-wide for those who are
in any honourable way distinguished ; to the traditions of power
and wealth with which that particular distinction is associated ;
and, last, but not least, to the undoubted excellence of members
of the British nobility. But I would warn its friends not to put
nobility upon a false basis. Those who are its natural guardians
must in this age be careful to keep its savour sweet before the
enfranchised people, and they must be careful not to identify
the uses of a landed gentry with those abuses of law and custom
which have placed 50,000,000 acres of the United Kingdom in a
condition of ownerless and settled disability.

Lately I read a debate in the House of Commons upon the
county franchise. In the speeches of honourable members I
observed a great many good reasons why the voting qualification should be made equal in counties and boroughs. But
the best reason of all found no place in the debate. I am sure
it could not have been so utterly absent from the minds of
honourable members. I suppose it was suppressed in deference
to that supremacy which the landed interest has always held
and still holds in Parliament. If I were asked what I thought

would be the best and most valuable result of the extension
of the franchise in the rural districts—if I were asked for what
purpose I think that extension is most needed—I should say
it was to make England free in regard to the system of land
tenure, to abolish the law of primogeniture, to release four-fifths
of the soil from the disabilities of strict settlement, and to
make the transfer of land simple and secure.   England is
embarrassed in her competition with other nations for want of
these reforms ; food is much dearer than it need be ; capital is
wasted in foreign enterprises which, if we had free land, would
be put to the most productive uses at home ; the population
in rural and most healthy districts does not increase ;—in other
words, the poor are forced into the already overcrowded towns.
All this is written most plainly upon the surface of English
life.   But we shall not get reform without a large extension of
the suffrage.   And it will need something more than that.   We
must educate the voters as to what must be demanded from
their representatives ; and then, when the whole country is
instructed and resolved, we shall have free land.

The evil is not denied.   There is not a great lawyer in the
kingdom who is not ready to abuse that crying evil, the English
law of transfer.   It is a needless and expensive protection to
the landed gentry ; a terror to the middle class ; an unknown
and unintelligible mystery to the mass of the people.   It is
bad in every point.   To this abominable system of conveyance
our country is condemned, partly because it suits that not
less injurious system of settlement.   In their utter aversion
from its intricacies, its costs, its delays, its uncertainties, its
responsibilities, the people of England have turned altogether
away from the land ; and the consequence is that millions
which might be spent with immense benefit to the interests
of labour and production at home, go abroad to provide such
despotisms as Turkey and such republics as Peru with those
most costly toys of sovereignty, iron-clad shipping.   The people
of England have been driven out from the possession of the soil

by the policy of Parliaments of landowners; I want them to be brought back to that possession by the policy of Parliaments of their own choosing; and a main part of the work of freeing the land is the substitution of transfer by registration of title for transfer by deed of conveyance.

I see that some lawyer has been imposing upon the good Bishop of Manchester by telling him that registration only adds to the cost of transfer. That is, though the Bishop does not seem to be aware of it, a crafty allusion to those costly shams which have been set up in this country—those wretched attempts of our legislature to make a system of registration square with the feudalism of English land tenure. We have been taxed to support such a legislative mockery as the Land Registry Office of Lord Westbury, which, at its rate of operation in 1873, would have completed the registration of English land in 760 years. That is not what we mean by registration of title. That is rather how not to do it. Assuming registration to be compulsory, and that the validity of a transaction could only be established by the fact of registration, then we may say there are two systems of transfer—one by registration of deeds, and the other by registration of title. Both are in operation within Her Majesty's dominions; both in that operation confer upon happier communities of fellow-subjects, the blessings of secure, expeditious, and cheap transfer; and either could be established in this country. If we want an example of transfer by registration of deeds, we have it in a part of the empire where titles are quite as ancient as in England—in the Channel Islands, which from the time of the Norman conquest have been annexed to the English Crown; while as for the far superior system of transfer by registration of title, there can be no doubt that the best example in the world is that which was established twenty years ago by Sir Robert Torrens in South Australia. Land is transferred in the Channel Islands in an hour, and at a cost of a few shillings; the title is secure, and there is no trouble about the custody of deeds. The system which Her

K

Majesty's Government has long ago approved for South Australia, and which is highly successful in operation, is still better, and that is a system which its founder, Sir Robert Torrens, has demonstrated could be adopted in this country. The cost of a mortgage under that system is 10s., and it need be no more in England ; the time occupied is fifteen minutes. The cost of transfer or release is 5s. ; the time occupied is five minutes ; and the validity of each step is guaranteed by an assurance fund supplemented by the security of the general revenues of the colony. When the title is registered it is indefeasible. Mr. Gladstone said in Dublin that he attached ' no value to our land laws in respect to entails and settlements,' and that in regard to these points he was ' in favour of bold and important, if not sweeping change.' Well, if we had much less complexity of limitations, there would be no insuperable difficulty in the establishment of compulsory registration, and we might then have transfer upon the Australian method. It is a common mistake to suppose that titles are of necessity simple in a newly-settled country. Land changes hands in a prosperous colony with rapidity quite unknown in England, where nearly four-fifths of the soil is settled for generations in the same families. Sir Robert Torrens has put the matter very clearly. He says : ' The first essential, therefore, in every measure for the reform of the law of real property must be to cut off the retrospective character of titles, thus removing existing complexities. The next essential is the substitution of a method of conveyancing, under which future dealings will not induce fresh complications. Both requirements are secured in South Australia by substituting "title by registration " for "title by deed," applying to the transfer of property in land the same principles under which, for more than a century, our dealings with property in shipping and in the Funds have been conducted with safety and satisfaction.'

But this is by no means the full measure of advantage to the landowner. With such a system of registration, the price of land of course rises, and the rate of interest on mortgages becomes substantially lower. An estate held by indefeasible title is as sound a security as can be offered—quite as good as Consols; and if we were rid of that 'tortuous and ungodly jumble,' as Cromwell called our law of real property, there is no reason why borrowers upon land should pay more than 3¼ per cent. for loans. Nor need their borrowings be less secret than at present, under the provisions of this best system of registration. We have parish maps quite sufficiently good for purposes of registration until the Ordnance Survey is completed ; and if we made registration compulsory upon sale or transfer, and the period for investigation were limited to twenty years, we should soon have the great bulk of land registered. We must give indefeasible title (with pecuniary compensation for error) where that could be given, and a good holding title in the comparatively few cases where the title would be maturing to indefeasibility. And if we got rid of entail and settlement, our registry would be even more simple than that of South Australia. We should then have free land, and what would be the consequence?

Let us look first at the altered circumstances of the landed gentry. If a landed proprietor died intestate, the abolition of primogeniture would give a share of his property to his wife and each of his children, instead of all going to the eldest son. But the landed gentry do not die intestate, and we may suppose that the majority would follow the rule of their fathers, and would give the landed estate by will to the eldest son ; the more so because titles of honour and nobility are so bestowed ; and those, of course, no alteration in the land laws would affect. It is in their marriage settlements that the landed gentry would be chiefly concerned by the changes we propose. They could not settle the land as they do now for the lives of their sons and their sons' sons, or their brothers and their brothers' sons—thus withdrawing it from risk of transfer, it may be, for a century. No such settlement would be valid. When a settlement was effected, it must be of personalty charged upon the land, leaving the soil free to the accidents of ownership. Trustees would be needed to hold lands for persons incapacitated by law, and their names upon the register, with 'No survivorship' attached, which is the Australian method of indicating trustees, would stop dealings with the estate until the expiry of their trust. The landed gentry, as they came under the operation of the new system, would be free to sell any of their lands, and we may presume that their interest in their property would be much more keen and intelligent than it is at present. Of course, the estates of the insolvent landlord would pass away from him, to his great relief, to the great advantage of his family and of the community.

But what of the people? The advocates of the present system say that if we make the land free in the way I have attempted to describe, the result will be the same so far as the exclusion of the people from landowning is concerned. I deny that, and I say that all the evidence leads to an opposite opinion. The proposition is true, however and where-ever it is tested, that industry always pays a higher price for land than luxury can or will afford. In Jersey, where the average size of farms is ten acres, the price of land is twice or three times as high as in England. The man who can afford to pay the highest price for land is he who intends to labour upon it for his own reward. People ask, Will he sink part of his capital in land at two or three per cent.? Yes, he certainly will, because that is the only way to security, and he will make it pay him 10 or 12 per cent. With free land, small farming would become a recognized business, as it has never been in our time; it would not be universal, any more than small shopkeeping is universal. But it would establish itself, and would tend to increase rather than to extinction.

Then, as to produce. I saw the other day that the Bishop of Manchester had been led astray by Mr. Caird's statement that with five times the extent of land under wheat in France, the

French produce little more than twice the quantity grown in England; and as farms are small in France, the Bishop rode away upon this as conclusive against the possible existence of small farms under a system of free trade in land. The worth of this statement, as an argument, is destroyed by the fact, familiar to every writer upon French agriculture, that the yield of wheat in France is most miserable upon the large farms; that of the small farms many produce as much and some much more than the English average. No useful comparison can, however, be made between the agriculture of two countries without taking account of the different amount of capital employed. Inadequate as that is in England, it is far larger than in any other country. Frenchmen have been known to take large farms with a capital of less than 10s. an acre. But the capital employed is not ruled by the size of farms. In Jersey, the average capital is greater than in England, and the result is that the average yield of wheat—a crop very widely grown, but for which the soil of the Channel Islands is not well suited—is much larger than in England. It is a delusion to suppose that capital and science must be the exclusive possession of large farmers. Agriculture is in this respect undergoing a great change. The farmer of 300 acres cannot afford to keep for his sole use such agricultural machinery as is coming into vogue; there is no article of that machinery of which the farmer of twenty acres need be deprived. The steam threshing-machine is far more commonly used in Jersey, where the farms average ten acres, than in the Isle of Wight. The progress of steam cultivation and steam carriage will be all to the advantage of the small farmer. The steam plough and the spade will be the implements of the future. The terribly expensive team of horses dragging a few sacks of wheat loiteringly along country roads will soon be a more rare sight. The traction engine or the light railway will take everybody's corn and potatoes at a fourth the price of horse labour, and bring back manure from the railroad stations for distribution at the farms by the roadside. We shall have fewer farmers standing about with their hands in their pockets, or riding their nags to the meet of hounds. A Jersey farmer who had just threshed a crop of wheat of his own growth, producing about fifty bushels to the acre, which is nearly double the English average upon large farms, said to me last autumn, 'How I should like to be an English farmer!' 'Why?' I asked. 'What I wish,' I added, 'is to see English farmers produce crops like yours.' 'Ah,' he replied, 'that's all very well, but what I should like would be to ride in a gig like an English farmer and take it easy.'

Now I must break off. I have touched upon many points, and there is not one which would not in detail furnish matter for an evening. If I have not succeeded in impressing upon your minds the economic importance of the consequences which would result from the liberation of the land, the fault is mine, for the case is plain and the arguments irresistible. I want to rouse the people of our country to fight this battle for free land. This is the first time in the history of England in which the people have had a prospect of being strong enough for the work —of power sufficient to ensure that no legal subtleties and no selfish interests shall defeat their demand for free land. I hope they will be worthy of the time and of their opportunities; and when they are asked, in reference to this great question, 'Shall England be free?' that their voices and their votes will demand reform and abolition of evils which affect not merely the character and the acts of the legislature, but all the circumstances of our daily life.

VI.

THE GOVERNMENT OF LONDON.[1]

IT would not be possible to address inhabitants of London upon any subject of greater importance than that of the government of the Metropolis, which, after ages of neglect, varied with partial and ineffectual legislation, stands before us discredited by every Administration, admired and approved by none,—except, perhaps, the typical Frenchman, who has a vague idea that the rule of Guildhall and of the Mansion House extends over all London, and that the loving-cup represents all the riches of contentment and satisfaction of all the citizens of the largest and richest city of the world. I shall assume, this evening, not only that you are better informed than he, as of course you must be, but also that you are acquainted with very much of the past and present condition of the government of London. I shall mention but two Acts of Parliament, those by which I trust the government of London will soon be remodelled. I shall suppose you do not approve of the undertaking of the local government of this capital of the British Empire by thirty-nine bodies, which bodies probably not a hundred out of London's four millions of people could enumerate. All of them, even to the least, deal with incomes derived from patient ratepayers—incomes amounting to tens of thousands of pounds; but whence they come, what they do, or whither the money goes, who is there can tell? As for our own ignorance of the matter—yours and mine—must we not

---

[1] An Address to the Members of the Social Science Association.

confess that we were fairly represented by the late Mr. Charles
Buxton when he said, in bringing to the attention of the House
of Commons those Bills, the outlines of which are in accordance
with the suggestions I shall offer: 'I have not the faintest idea
when I pay my rates, who those are by whom I am governed,
or how or why they have been chosen to govern me.'

Is there one person in this room who would not shrink with
horror, as I confess I should, from the task of explaining to any
inquiring foreigner our system of local government? Regarding
ourselves for the moment as inhabitants of this hall, is there any
one present so adventurous, so rash, as to assert that he could
off-hand say by whom we are here, in this particular spot,
governed for local purposes? He might bethink himself of one
board—the Metropolitan Board of Works; but the boards are
legion. Our paving and lighting are the work of the Vestry of
St. Martin's; our sewers are the province of the Metropolitan
Board, in regard to which body we, as ratepayers, are not
permitted the right of electors, that office being performed on
our behalf by the vestry, which has about it so much of the
clerical cloth from which it takes its name as to give colour to a
suspicion that London has thirty-nine governments for no better
reason than a blind concurrence with the number of articles of
the Church. If you commit an offence, that will at once bring
you in contact with another government—the police and the
police magistrate, of which the former dwells on neutral ground,
neither exactly local nor imperial, the latter being, in every respect, an officer of State. But nothing that you could do would,
so far as I am aware, bring to your notice, in its entirety, that
antique curiosity the Corporation of Westminster, in whose
dominions, however, you are assembled to-night. If you were
a candidate, in this city of Westminster, for election to Parliament, you might catch sight of a part of it in the person of
the High Bailiff; and another part of it, the Dean and Chapter,
may be seen occasionally at the Abbey; but I have never met
with more than one man who had beheld the entire collection of

antiquities. Again, you must not suppose, if, in quitting this
hall, puzzled with these mysteries, you should fall over the
Embankment and be drowned, it would be the duty of this
fossil Corporation, or of any body I have yet mentioned, to take
charge of your corpse. You would then be on the grounds of
the Conservators of the Thames, a body whose respectability
appears to be so nice, that while they have filled large Blue
Books with evidence about foreshores, they have shunned any
useful dealings with the filth which is poured into the river in that
part of its waters from which your drink is taken, and have been
inactive concerning the vast volume of sewage, which is thrown,
with waste of that which would make the bread of tens of
thousands, into the same river where its stream is open to the
traffic of the world.

The list is tedious, and my memory will certainly fail to
enumerate the many governments to which a dweller in this
house would be subject. But if we omitted the School Board,
the rate-collector of that beneficent organisation would not
forget us, nor would the company's officer who gathers the
water-rate, nor they who supply us with the artificial light so
much used in this murky city; and all three—Education,
Water, Gas—are the realms of separate and distinct authorities.
Lastly, if we succumbed to pauperism, we should fall to yet
another local government; and if we attempted, on any well-
drawn map of London, to identify the district which fared with
ourselves in each one or all of these matters, so that at least we
might know whom to call upon when we desired to unite in
protest, we should be involved in hopeless difficulty, for these
different governments have different districts, overlapping, inter-
lacing, intermixed—confusing to bewilderment. First, London is
seen seated on parts of four counties; then she is divided among
thirty-nine district governments, including the Corporation of
Gog and Magog and the Vestry of St. Pancras. But these divisions have no correspondence with the nineteen police districts
and fifteen police-court districts; nor these last with the thir-

teen county-court districts ; nor with the ten postal districts ; nor
with the thirty-seven districts into which the Registrar-General
divides London ; nor with the forty-four surveyors' districts; nor
with the fifteen militia districts ; nor with the ten parliamentary
and school board divisions; nor with the gas and water divisions : if we attempted to distinguish these divisions by colour,
our map would soon be blotted out of sight. I doubt if fifty
maps would be sufficient to show you intelligibly the anomalies
of London government.

You know, as ratepayers, and as practical people, what
all this means. Tens of thousands of your fellow-citizens
know also that it implies of necessity inefficiency, extravagance,
jobbery, and waste. But they are powerless, or, at least, they
feel powerless, because the area is so large, the grievance so
tremendous, the remedy so distant ; because the only organization in their own neighbourhood is so consciously interested in
maintaining the anarchy which I have vainly attempted to
describe. You know very well what are the best characteristics
of good government—efficiency, economy, publicity. We need
not speak ill of those who, in honorary and laborious service,
administer the government of London. They are a population
themselves. The House of Commons is sometimes regarded
as a numerous body. But the 654 members of that House do
not represent a tenth of the army which, for the most part
in various honorary official positions, administers the local affairs
of the Metropolis. There are more than 7,000 men, chiefly
fathers of families, engaged in it. Their number alone is sufficient to command respect ; but I need not tell you there are
very many of them to whom the community is under much
obligation. Yet it is obvious that, in order to secure efficiency
of government, our aim should be to attract the persons best
qualified for its due administration ; and no one will allege that
under our present system we succeed in this to the greatest
possible extent. In regard to the paid officers, efficiency is
clearly sacrificed by their mere multiplication. Agreeing, as we

all must, that this immense, this unparalleled complication of
governments is unnecessary, we must admit that in the maintenance of a separate staff by each division of local government
the efficiency of the officers is sacrificed. We see examples
everywhere. Why are there two sorts of pavement in the
Strand ? Because the Strand is under two governments. Why
have we seen some street lamps lighted with the expeditious
staff, while in other streets lamplighters were running about with
the old-fashioned ladder? For the same reason, of course.
And this condemnation on the ground of inefficiency, includes a
judgment also on the question of economy.

Who shall count the waste which ensues from this needless
subdivision of collecting and spending power ? I met a man not
long ago, a carter by trade, who told me that he let his horses
to the vestry of a West End parish, in order to give them a rest
now and then from the fatigues of their customary work. In
one parish we see a steam-roller at work, in the next our carriage wheels must plough through the raw macadam. I shall
endeavour presently to make an estimate of the saving which
might be effected by a reform of the government of London, and
no part of my task will be more easy than to prove that the
present system is most wasteful and extravagant. I have said
that another, the third characteristic—I ought, perhaps, in this
case to say the guarantee—for good government is publicity.
The opinion is somewhat cynical, but I accept it, and experience
leads me to endorse the view, that without publicity in matters
of administration there is always jobbery—unfair and improper
use of public funds. How can you make public—that is, how
can you interest the public in—the affairs of these thirty-nine
governments, especially when the governments are not composed (I will not be offensive) of first-rate citizens ? Some
years ago one of the many vestries did, indeed, obtain a passing
notoriety, but it was only upon charges which, if they were
proved, would make any government infamous. For the most
part, even the place of meeting of the minor governments of

London is unknown to the vast majority of the ratepayers whose money is there dealt with. In each centre there is a small *entourage* which is informed and is fattened upon parochial affairs, and beyond that all is darkness and blind payments.

It is clear, then, that to secure efficiency, economy, and publicity in the metropolitan administration, we must diminish the number of centres of control; and, inasmuch as all possible uniformity of area is productive of economy, and the divisions are otherwise very suitable, I see no reason why we should not substitute those parliamentary divisions which have been proposed in the Bills introduced by Lord Elcho, Mr. Mill, and Mr. Buxton, and which are now adopted in the elections to the London School Board. Originally it was designed that each of these boroughs should have a complete, separate, and distinct municipal organization, but that idea is, I am glad to observe, entirely abandoned. No doubt it would be better than the existing method, in which thirty-nine governments, more or less obscure, spend, unwatched and unchecked, the revenues of London. But I do not hesitate to object to the plan on another ground than that of perpetuating division and promoting injurious rivalry. I object to it, also, because the mayors of these boroughs must either be to the mayor of the City as a gig to the state-coach, or they must be useless, because subordinate to the potentate of Guildhall. It is with me a cardinal point in this great work to maintain, and not only maintain, but to enhance and to extend, the dignity and importance of the ancient mayoralty of the city of London. I have no sympathy with those who do not cherish the best traditions of the City; and I heartily approve of that part of the design of the late Mr. Buxton's Bills which places the Lord Mayor at the head of the government of the Metropolis. I cannot hear of any weighty argument to the contrary. Why should we sacrifice a tradition and a history of eight centuries of honour? To a fear of a Metropolitan Commune? I thought that bogey had at last been laid to rest. Our towns are not like those of France, outvoted by the country. In England the towns have always led ; and so far from there being a shadow of a shade upon their supremacy, the prospect is that, in any redistribution of electoral power, their influence must increase. I can understand narrow, old-world politicians being fearful that if the Lord Mayor were really what the French take him for—that is, Lord Mayor of London—his power would be a formidable rival to that of the Executive Government. But I cannot believe that this will be urged as an objection by any responsible person, now that the nation is fully represented in Parliament, and the supremacy of the House of Commons is so unquestionably evident. I am inclined to think that, apart from securing the efficiency of local government, we shall find, in strengthening municipal government everywhere, a useful counterpoise which it would be exaggeration to call a check, to the power of the House of Commons. In 1837, when Parliament enacted the scandal of reforming all municipal governments save that of London, it may be said, by way of excuse, that the nation was not then represented. Parliament had but just ceased to be the nomination club of an oligarchy, who might reasonably fear to touch a power possessing a title as good as their own. But now we have progressed to a more complete acceptance of the principle that taxation and representation shall go together, the government of London is an anomaly which cannot endure ; and no one has a right to contend that, because, for some silly reasons, he does not wish to see the ancient municipal government of London aggrandized, it is to remain in its present anarchical, wasteful, and inefficient state, divided against itself in all directions.

The division between Temple Bar and Aldgate, an area of about 650 acres, subject to the Lord Mayor and the unreformed Corporation, is now only the counting-house of the Metropolis : there has been no exodus comparable with that which has depopulated the City. In the ten years ending 1871, the number of inhabitants of the City declined from 41,076 to 25,360—a loss

of 38 per cent. ; and I doubt if there will be found 20,000 souls
in the City when the next census is taken.   But while this
drain has been going on from the home of the most prominent
and distinguished of the thirty-nine governments of London,
what has taken place in the dominions of the vestries and
the district boards ?   There the population, including all within
the districts of the City and Metropolitan Police, has reached
4,000,000 ; it was 3,883,092 (including the City) in 1871, and
had increased 20 per cent. in ten years.   The rateable value of
the property outside the City is £20,967,804, and those who pay
rates in respect of this vast property are closely interested in
the establishment of a government directly elected by themselves, and of sufficient importance, not only to attract the
co-operation of the most worthy citizens, but also to draw their
attention to the exercise of its powers in regard to the expenditure of their money.

It would seem desirable to extend municipal government to
the whole of the Metropolis, the mode of election of councillors
being the same as that which prevails in the boroughs of the
kingdom.   But while it is of the first importance to have
unity of government, not only for the dignity of local authority,
but in order to secure uniformity in design and execution of
works of improvement, it would at the same time be necessary
to decentralize sufficiently to ensure due attention to the wants
in detail of each neighbourhood.   And this, it appears to me,
might be accomplished by constituting the councillors to be
elected in each of the parliamentary divisions a Standing Committee for the government of that borough,—their chairman,
elected by themselves, to have the title and dignity of alderman,
unless it was thought better to choose the aldermen by separate
election, as at present.   The council might consist of three times
the number of the School Board, and I should certainly prefer
that the cumulative vote adopted in school board elections
should obtain also in those of the Corporation of London,
though this would be a feature new in municipal elections·

With a view to obtain men of great position to serve in the office of Lord Mayor, it might appear desirable to retain the separate election of aldermen, who should take the chair in rotation, as at present, subject to a veto by two-thirds of the council.

I had unusual opportunities for close observation of a similar form of local government in Manchester during my official residence there in the years of the Cotton Famine. The population of Manchester is perhaps about twenty times that of the city of London ; and, for the purposes of local government, the northern metropolis is divided into six townships, each having a town hall, with a staff of officers for the execution of public works. The elected councillors for each of the federated townships are appointed a committee for that township, and to this committee is practically left the carrying out of the powers applying to objects which are paid for out of township rates, the proceedings of all committees being submitted for approval at the meetings of the council. I have transacted business with the Corporation of Manchester in all its departments, both with the superior officers of the council in the negotiation of loans, and with the township officers in reference to the execution of public works ; and if my approval of the system be qualified, it is only because I observed that further improvement might be made in the direction in which I am informed the Corporation is now moving—that is, of stronger central control to ensure greater uniformity of excellence in public works of every description. In London, we should have a town hall in every borough, and an election of one-third of the members of the council every year. For the sake of economy it is most desirable that rates should not be made by separate levy in each borough, but obtained for each, as in the case of the townships of Manchester, by precept issued to the overseers. By adopting this method, avoiding the trouble and expense of levying and collecting separate rates, Sir Joseph Heron, the town clerk of Manchester, tells me that the Corporation has saved not less than £3,000 a year.

The government in any city or town should be one, or there can be no proper execution of public works, no uniform observance of sanitary and other regulations, no convenient construction of new or improved streets, and no satisfactory provision of water and gas. At present there are hardly two of our thirty-nine governments which perform any function in the same manner or at the same cost. Let us take an instance, and one in which you will agree with me there is least room for divergence of expenditure : I allude to the charge for watering the streets. From the reports issued by the vestries at the request of the Metropolitan Board of Works, we are able to compare the charges for watering. The cost per mile, including labour and cartage, in Marylebone, is £82 12s. 9d. ; in St. Pancras it is £52 a mile, where the authorities discover that a saving of £22 per mile is effected by the use of a meter. In Lambeth, the cost is reported at £70 per mile. Paddington spends £97 17s. per mile ; and while St. Martin's does the work for £90, Rotherhithe accomplishes it for about £30 per mile. On the whole, the cost varies from £30 to £115 per mile, and I ask you, as I fairly may, to judge from this example the inevitable waste attaching to such a system of minutely divided, complicated, and obscure government. I regard Mr. James Beal's calculation—and no man has given more time, thought, and practical ability to this question—that a saving of £150,000 a year would be effected by establishing a Corporation of London, in place of these thirty-nine governments, as extremely moderate ; but even that amount would pay your education rate. Yet this is certainly but a small part of the gain which might accrue to the people of London from the establishment of a duly elected municipal government. I say elected, to distinguish it from any government in existence. I have no word to utter in disparagement of the Metropolitan Board of Works. Though that board was brought into existence as a compromise, though it has but little of the dignity which would belong to a metropolitan corporation, and though the election of its members is a travesty of a real election by ratepayers, yet the board has done good work and service—such as I am quite sure will, in the reconstruction of London government, ensure a place for every one of its members and officers in the new and more stately fabric. I can fancy the day when, without regret, the members of the Metropolitan Board of Works will see their offices become those of the City of Westminster, and of the committee of the Corporation of London acting for the City of Westminster.

If we look forward to the time when a municipal government shall control the metropolitan supplies of gas and water, we may anticipate much larger reductions of expenditure. Some one may ask, Why should the provision of water and gas be the work of the municipality? As the matter is only part of the subject we are discussing this evening, I cannot go into it fully; but I will touch upon some of the reasons for, and the advantages accruing from, this course. To begin with, the quality of the water is sure to be better. Do you suppose that people would pay rates for water which contained cholera poison or diluted sewage, to the Corporation of London, as quietly as they have paid rates to companies whose water has been reported to be so affected? Do you suppose that the recent water-famine in Bermondsey would have been possible if the supply of the rest of London could have been thrown into the mains of that district? Of course that scarcity, which in its effects might have been so terrible, would thus have been entirely avoided; and that incident, from which we may learn something of the economy of distribution, will teach us also how wasteful in point of expenditure is the present system, by which we are dependent for a supply of far from first-rate quality, upon eight companies, —every person in the west of London being forced to drink Thames water taken at points above which the stream has received the sewage of thousands of people and the manurial washings of the farm-lands of the river basin. Water, unlike gas, is a necessary of universal consumption; it is therefore,

L

the interest of all the ratepayers to supply themselves with water, and at cost price. Even assuming the existing sources of supply to be the best attainable, and sufficient (which I do not concede), then by unity of management and supply at cost price, we could certainly reduce our water-rate by twopence in the pound, and thus again we should save an amount equal to the present payment for the education rate. In Manchester, water of excellent quality is supplied on these conditions : the works have cost more than £2,000,000, but the united charge for the public and domestic water-rate does not exceed tenpence in the pound. And that is not all; the Manchester people have the advantage of constant service, and of service at such pressure that from any of the street mains I believe water may, without a fire-engine, be thrown into the upper rooms of any house in the city. Such a system as this can, of course, only result from unity of management, under the control of a single municipal authority.

The supply of artificial light, which is almost as necessary as that of water, and is absolutely needful at night in all public streets, should be the work of the local authority. It is not only the profits of the supply that are lost by the ratepayers, but because the supply is a matter of private concern, they are forced to burn gas of various qualities and different prices. What benefits have the ratepayers of London received from the concession of this monopoly to nine companies? Can any one here point to a shilling's worth of advantage, except the example of shareholders pocketing easy dividends of 10 per cent.?—an example which, I hope, will not be lost upon ratepayers. Why should not the profits of our gas supply free our bridges and repair our roads? Profits there must be, for we must not supply gas as we should supply water, at cost price, because the gas-works, being the property of the ratepayers, they would be entitled—those who consumed no gas equally with those who burned the most—to share in profits, and therefore the supply of gas should be fixed at a fair, uniform market price. I think the Corporation of Manchester have acted wisely in strictly adhering to this method. No one will say that their supply of gas is not infinitely superior in general quality to that we have in London; and the price is less, which is partly due to the proximity of coal-pits. But, charging a fair market rate, what have they done for the ratepayers? We shall make the inquiry more interesting by looking to the gas supply of Liverpool, which, like that of London, is a private monopoly. Liverpool has quite equal facilities with Manchester for obtaining coal and cannel, yet at the present time the price in Liverpool is 3s. 9d. per 1,000 cubic feet, while in Manchester it is only 3s. 4d. But this is not all. The Corporation of Manchester have received profits from the supply of gas already amounting to upwards of £1,500,000; and this sum has been expended in the execution of works of public utility and permanent improvement within the city. I feel sure there is no exaggeration whatever in the estimate that an annual sum of £300,000 might be saved if the supply to the metropolis of gas and water were in the hands of such a Corporation of London as has been suggested. There is yet another great work which, not less than those I have mentioned, demands that the metropolitan area should be under one local authority. That which would afford a splendid revenue is now poured out in monstrous waste and defilement at Barking and Plumstead. The main sewers of a city should of course be under one management. To a general ignorance of this fact I have seen tens of thousands of pounds sacrificed by petty Local Boards whose territory adjoined, and which for drainage purposes should have formed one district; and to this fact the Metropolitan Board of Works owes its existence. But only a Corporation of London will be sufficiently powerful to deal aright with the utilization of the sewage of the metropolis.

It would be in accordance with my ideas that this Metropolitan Council, or Corporation of London, as I prefer to call it, should perform all the functions of government which are not within the domain of the State. I should advocate this course

in order more fully to promote the advantages which I anticipate from the institution of the new corporation—efficiency,
economy, and publicity. The body would gain in dignity by
this absorption of authority ; the advantage to the ratepayers in
point of economy is very considerable by the concentration of
establishments ; and the proceedings of a public body attract
attention in exact proportion to their importance. If the change
were not simultaneous with an election to the School Board, it
would of course be desirable to accord seats in the council to
the members of that board, who would then form the first
committee of the Corporation of London for education. The
administration of justice, and the control of the police, should,
I think, belong to the State. For if the control of the police
be not conceded to the general government, we must, of course,
expect to see the palace of the legislature and other property
of the State guarded by soldiers, and that would not be con-
sonant with English feeling. If time permitted, it would be
easy for me to speak of the long train of indirect advantages
which would follow the erection of such a local government
for London as I have described, and such as is substantially
defined in the Bills which have been submitted to Parliament.
The strongest opposition will come from those who think that
reform would bring back the funds they now control to the
service of the people.   And we must here avow, that while every
proper provision should be made for the enhanced dignity
of the Lord Mayor, the sheriffs, the aldermen, and common
councillors, and for maintaining the time-honoured reputation
of civic hospitality and splendour, it would be necessary that
every item of receipt and expenditure should be brought to
audit, and that the ratepayers should be able to look down and
to see clearly into the lowest recesses of the budget of London.
This, which would involve some surrender on the part of the
Corporation, would be incomparable when contrasted with the
enormous increase of authority and prestige which would be
thus established in the Guildhall, securely and for ever. At

present, when the Lord Mayor emerges westward from Temple
Bar, he is a foreign potentate whom the people regard with
feelings far less acceptable than those which would greet their
own chief magistrate.

I should like, if I had not already trespassed too long upon
your patience, to speak upon the educational, the ecclesiastical
and the industrial endowments of the City of London, which
could not fail to be affected by the change. Why should not
such endowments as those of Christ's Hospital be equitably
appropriated for the higher education of boys and girls, and why
should £500,000, which might promote this grand work and
help forward the best scholars of the elementary schools—why
should this vast capital be locked up in the site of that great
school, which could not have a more disadvantageous position?
As to the ecclesiastical property in the City of London, when
I think of it I am reminded of what Sir Charles Trevelyan
said in this room three years ago : that 'while, notwithstanding
the most strenuous efforts, only £389,000 of the million required
to relieve the spiritual destitution of the outer circles of the
metropolis has been raised, at least two millions are lying at
waste and abuse, to the scandal of the Church, in her ancient
stronghold of the inner circle of the City of London.'

Lastly, in speaking of the industrial endowments of London,
I am alluding to the funds of the Livery Companies, which
should, of course, be devoted to promote the welfare of the
respective trades—of the operatives as well as the employers ;
and I can imagine nothing more likely to aid us in overcoming
the difficulties that beset the co-operation of labour and capital
than the due employment of the historic influence and the
funds of these trade guilds for this object. I might speak of
funds for the provision of 'comfits,' which have developed into
boxes of rich Parisian *bonbons*, or of the trust for providing a
postprandial draught which, I am informed, bears the name of
' Lady Cowper,' because a lady of that name once gave the
testator a glass of pale brandy when he had gorged himself

at an eighteenth-century dinner.   It cannot be regarded as
satisfactory that the Drapers' Company should expend £70,000
in building a dining hall, or that the Goldsmiths' Company
should relieve the indigence of decayed members by giving
to one man as much as would serve to keep hundreds from
the workhouse.   All these, and a thousand other ills, would be
righted—I would almost say, would right themselves—if we
had a duly elected Corporation of London.   And in giving our
energies to the accomplishment of that great end, let us not
fear to be proud of much that is written in the annals of the
Corporation of the City.   Eight hundred years of honourable
history constitutes a treasure which no wealth could purchase, and
which nothing but folly could destroy.   But even these splendid
traditions would be too dearly bought by a continuance of the
misgovernment of London.   To the citizens and ratepayers
there is every inducement to press forward in this matter of
reform, which is to them a subject of sanitary, moral, and
pecuniary interest.

VII.

'THE CITY.'[1]

THOSE who denounce the Corporation of the City of London are not always wise in their mode of attack. They do not distinguish and discriminate; they confound and confuse the evil with the good. Abuses, the growth of centuries, and due rather to inertness of prosperity than to activity of corruption, have fastened upon a historic corporation, honourable through all its long career and for ever illustrious in the annals of local government. The absence of reform and the overwhelming growth of riches through the increase in the value of property, have fostered the existence of drones and gluttons, lovers of pay without labour, wanton consumers of charitable funds, sycophants and social hypocrites. Yet, in spite of all this, the Corporation is sound and vigorous still in its public life, and its existence is in no danger. The history of the Corporation of the City of London forms no mean part of that of England, and to strike with the axe at the stem of a stately tree, in order to destroy parasites which infest its branches, would not be more impolitic and reprehensible than is the action of some of these municipal reformers.

If the Corporation of London were a corrupt body, as venal and infamous as that which till lately ruled the city of New York, it would deserve the language with which it is assailed. This language misses its mark because it is not justifiable; because the Corporation of the City of London is not a corrupt

[1] *The City: an Inquiry.* By William Gilbert. Daldy and Isbister, 1877.

body. The fruits of a thoroughly corrupt corporation are not such works as the Holborn Viaduct, the new Smithfield Market, the popular victory in Epping Forest, and the construction of Queen Victoria Street. The officers of a corrupt corporation are not men of distinction such as the late Recorders, Mr. Russell Gurney, and Mr. Stuart Wortley. A corrupt corporation is as a rule popular only with those who are in its pay : the Corporation of London has admirers in every town and village in the United Kingdom. Of all this we find no word in such a book as that lately written by Mr. Gilbert. He believes that the government of no capital in the world enjoys a reputation so far above its merits as that of the ancient city of London,' and that the majority of its admirers 'are directly or indirectly interested in the continuance of its abuses.' That is a statement which upon careful examination could not be sustained.

What then is really the matter with the London Corporation ? Simply this : it is suffering from disease which has assailed many corporations, and from which others were relieved in 1834. The symptoms in the capital have become aggravated, as we might expect, by delay. To confound the splendid hospitality of the Mansion House or of the Guildhall with the sordid gluttony of committees in back rooms of the well-known City taverns, or with the squandering of charitable funds by City companies, is a blunder which reformers would do well to avoid. In no part of this great capital is order better maintained in the streets, and nowhere is improvement in paving, lighting, archi-tecture, and in the lines of communication, more noticeable than in the City. In all this the Corporation of the City of London justifies the hopes of those who are its most judicious critics, and who are most anxious for its reform. The disease, by this diagnosis, is seen to be not organic. In fact there is no difficulty in determining what is wrong with the London Corporation. There is not another corporation in the kingdom which would not exhibit the same symptoms under the same conditions. Where the wholesome light of publicity shines upon the work of

the City Corporation there is little to complain of : your leading
article, read by a hundred thousand people, is a great purifier.
The notebook of the reporter is as needful in the affairs of
corporations as the bull's-eye of the constable in the dark alleys
of the City. The conscript fathers of the Guildhall are by no
means the only persons who cannot be trusted to deal with the
public funds and endowments uncontrolled by the public eye.
Deans and chapters were found unworthy of such blind confidence. Time was, and that not long ago, when bishops rolled
untold thousands into their private treasuries. It is not fifteen
years since the present writer saw a prelate preside at a meeting
for the relief of 'spiritual destitution' in London, whose demise
in that chair would have benefited the inferior clergy to the
extent of about £10,000 a year. He was then the only unreformed bishop. We are all the better for the greater publicity
of the present time. This then is what is needed in the City.
Who has not witnessed the good results of candlelight on
various occasions ? It happened lately to the writer to enter
upon a six days' occupation of a cabin in a Russian vessel during
the dark hours of morning. On striking a light he saw that the
sides, and floor, and roof, were covered with greedy creatures,
and that the only condition upon which that cabin could be
occupied was that of keeping a light burning. It is just so
with the London Corporation. Light and air ; public control ;
popular election ; public audit ; the training and transfer of
endowments from obsolete to beneficial uses ; the kindly
operation of public intelligence upon public affairs ;—that is
the cure for all that is wrong in the City.

Attacks upon the Corporation imputing 'foul injustice' as to
dealings with the houses of the poor have not much of our
sympathy. That the poor will continually demand and continually obtain improvement in their dwellings is our earnest
hope. But the destruction of the wretched lanes and courts,
the fever-nests of the City, is matter for congratulation. Nor
do we agree with those who appear to desire that the con-

struction of workmen's houses—and of workmen's houses exclusively—should be the business of local or imperial government. Let designs be multiplied and perfected; afford all possible facilities for obtaining land; but to bemoan the fact that the smoky heart of this vast city holds fewer inhabitants at night than it did twenty years ago, is a regret in which we cannot join. The doctrine that the provision of superior dwellings for any independent class of the community is a proper function of imperial or local government, is one to which we cannot subscribe. The demand for land in order to erect workmen's dwellings in places where land would not be thus devoted without the intervention of authority, is to us vain and unsound. Those houses of the poor, the demolition of which is thus deplored by reformers of the City, were condemned by the possession of every vice of unfitness and insalubrity. The general, we may say the universal, construction of the homes of the poor in London five-and-twenty years ago was far worse than that of any other capital in Europe. It is nearly as many years since the present writer met one morning in Paris a gentleman who is now a highly distinguished medical officer in one of the largest of English towns. 'Where do the poor live in this city?' was his puzzled, anxious inquiry. 'I cannot find them,' he said; a confession which pointed directly to the superior condition of the poor of Paris. The sanitary inquirer in the French capital could not find the miserable, narrow courts and streets, bordered with shabby little houses constructed for the wants of a single family, but tenanted by half a dozen families, with which he was so sadly familiar in London. He was directed to find the poor of Paris in the entresols and the garrets of houses inhabited, as to their best apartments, by persons of somewhat superior quality. The houses from which the poor of central London have been 'ejected' were of the worst description. How could a girl learn to be a tidy good housekeeper who was one of a family which had its 'home' in a bedroom, or perhaps in two small rooms of a mean little house, with no sink, no dustbin, no sanitary appliance whatever? There would be a sink and scullery in the basement or on the ground floor, but that would be occupied exclusively by another family. On the Continent it has been otherwise. Bad as the homes of the poor were and still are in Paris, they have been for the most part constructed for separate homes. This is the reason why the Model Lodging Houses and Industrial Dwellings are so valuable and successful in London. By all means let the imperial and local governments insist upon the observance of sanitary regulations in dwelling-houses, raising the standard higher and higher as the knowledge of the true economy of life descends and widens in the social scale ; but let us beware lest we sap the virtue of independence in the name of philanthropy.

The evils which we shall now have to disclose and to descant upon in connection with City government have nearly all one origin, that of misdirected, misapplied 'charity,' and the least pardonable error which reformers can make is to imitate the evils of which they complain, to foster the breed of parasites which they should utterly sweep away, and to cheer on the poor to assault this citadel, so full of treasure, with the promise that they shall be, by possession, at least partially secured against the need of thrift, of frugality, of temperance ; that in fact they shall be endowed with houses, or elementary education, without labour and without price. We shall see as we proceed that much at least of the funds is directed to the encouragement of sloth, hypocrisy, intemperance, and hereditary pauperism of the most expensive kind. But it were better that the endowments were turned into money, and the gold sunk in the deepest furrows of the Atlantic, than that it should be employed in relieving the poor from those obligations which must be sustained in order to win and to wear the blessings of civilisation.

It was a glaring evil—one not yet wholly removed—that legislation should encourage the extrusion of the poor from parishes in order that the owners of property might gain by ceasing to be responsible for their support in case of distress or incapacity for labour. It is not long since the parish of St. Michael's, Cornhill, paid a poor-rate of only one penny in the pound, while another in Farringdon Street paid five shillings. Mr. Gilbert tells us that ' the parish of St. Christopher-le-Stock, containing the Bank of England, paid one-tenth of a farthing in the pound, on an assessment of half its value, while the parish of St. Ann's, Blackfriars, containing the space between Ludgate Hill and the river side, paid eight shillings ; and the greater part of this amount was levied on persons scarcely above poverty themselves.' So that while the proprietors of the Bank of England were paying a tenth of a farthing in the pound, the proprietors of the *Times* office paid eight shillings in the pound. Yet in that iniquity of fiscal injustice a limit had been fixed, and it was this. A parish which had no pauperism was obliged to pretend to have some, for if a parish had no poor of its own it was liable to be joined to some poverty-stricken parish in the neighbourhood. It is needless to say that this condition of utter freedom from pauperism was carefully avoided. There was, however, a parish which was at one time separated from this dangerous prosperity by a single life. St. Bartholomew-the-Great, containing the Royal Exchange and the Stock Exchange, had, some forty years ago, but one pauper, a sort of pet old man, whose valuable life stood between the parish and a poor-rate. He was boarded and lodged in the country. He was visited and inspected by guardians, who had a pleasant jaunt and a heavy dinner now and then, all for the sake of this cherished old pauper. But this pet pauper, dear to St. Bartholomew-the-Great, died at last. The guardians looked anxiously round, hoping to find a poor parishioner. They were ready to stretch a point, there can be no doubt of that. But they found no one who, with any decent pretence, could assume the requisite condition of poverty. They were driven, Mr. Gilbert says, ' to the painful necessity of advertising for a pauper, though for some time without success.'

It is observed that the ejectment of the poor from the City within the last fifteen or twenty years has, for the most part, been caused by the construction of railroads, which are, in fact the means whereby the industrial classes are carried to and from their labour. It was probable—indeed it was inevitable, during the construction of these railroads—that there should be shocking and numerous cases of overcrowding in the neighbourhood of the works. We observe that Mr. Gilbert, who is very full upon this subject, and very severe upon the 'ruthless' conduct of the civic authorities, quotes occurrences in 1861,—and, in fact, that all the saddest tales of overcrowding are of that comparatively ancient date. It is our impression that there has been from that time a steady and continuous improvement in the homes of the poor ; that they live in better atmospheres than formerly ;—that they are, on the whole, less crowded ; that the death-rate among them has diminished ; that epidemics are more rare ; that their food is of better quality, especially as regards freshness ;—and we believe that for all these things they are indebted to those improved means of communication, to make room for which so many of them were ejected from less wholesome places of abode. Can it be seriously contended that the construction of the Blackwall Railway, or of the Metropolitan Railway, or the South-Eastern and Chatham and Dover Railway extensions into the City, have not benefited the artisan more than any other class ? There can be no question of the benefit. The advantage of the railways and tram-cars has been greatest of all to the labouring classes. To write about the necessary clearances of the ground in a tone almost suitable for a description of atrocities in Turkey appears to us to be a pitiful misdirection of force. The Farringdon Road works caused the demolition of houses which covered, perhaps, fifty thousand people. To quote the *Building News* of 1860, or the Medical Officer of Health for Blackfriars in the year 1861, as to the consequent suffering of that large population, may be useful as teaching us in future how to avoid the temporary hardships

of such dislodgment; but to bring such evidence forward as
proving that the works have been a curse instead of a blessing,
is sheer folly.　For the terminus of the Cannon Street railway
more than twelve hundred persons were dislodged.　'In the
formation of the Moorgate Street station, three thousand
householders and lodgers, the latter principally shop assistants
and lodgers, were ejected.'　Mr. Gilbert seems to regard this
and similar operations as among the great sins of great cities.
Let any one go and look upon the narrow piece of land occupied
by the Moorgate Street station, and ask himself whether every
philanthropic heart should not rejoice that there are no longer
'three thousand householders and lodgers' upon that small
area.　If this demolition had been carried out merely to
beautify the City with open spaces, it would, after temporary
suffering by overcrowding, have benefited those whom we call
the poor by an improvement in their sanitary condition, and
the same may be said if the object had been to make new
streets, long and airy, from which the contamination of the
atmosphere due to animal life would be quickly removed by
the passing wind.　But these dislodgments were owing to
constructions more beneficial to the working classes.　The
wealthy classes have, in fact, invested their savings, some at
4 per cent., and to a great extent for no interest at all, in
providing those railway carriages by which the labouring
people can be swiftly and cheaply carried to and from any
part of the metropolis.　They have been made 'carriage-
folks;' the power of their legs has been multiplied; while the
shareholders of the Chatham and Dover, and of the Metropolitan District Railways, have never seen a penny of interest
upon their outlay of millions sterling.　Mr. Gilbert's attack
is almost ludicrously misdirected at this point.　The *employe*
of one City tradesman lives, say, at Notting Hill, and in the
same day does one piece of work in St. John's Wood, and
another piece of work at Mile End.　Is he the loser because he
has been expelled from his wretched tenement in Farringdon

Street to make way for the railroad which enables him to do all this without fatigue?

Mr. Gilbert's attack is, as we have said, misdirected. His statements of fact are of great value, the evident result of careful and long-continued inquiry. He marks the evils in the City, and adds them up with rising indignation, but does not carry forward the proper inference. For example, in this matter of dislodgment, he sums up the atrocities of City government in the following sentence: 'They have been driven so far from the City that they have lost not only their identity as citizens of London, but also their right in the thousand and one charitable endowments and educational institutions of enormous wealth which it contains, as well as their constitutional privileges as voters in the City elections, parliamentary and municipal, to which, had they remained, vast numbers of them would have been entitled.' Properly valued, all that would appear a loss incommensurate with the gain they have achieved. But we should have been better pleased with the argument had it proceeded to show that these advantages ought to follow the removal of the people, and that just as they have passed out from the narrow limits of the old wall-bound London of the City, so should these influences, and powers, and properties be made, as far as these are good, advantageous to the whole of that Greater London in which the people are dispersed; that Metropolis, which is now divided into thirty-nine territories, governed by persons who are, for the most part, unknown to the ratepayers; who have not obtained, and do not claim to possess, the confidence of those with whose affairs they are concerned; who, so far as they are elected by vote, are chosen by a vicious and contracted suffrage, and whose operations, subdivided into a merely parochial significance, are, because of their subdivision, conducted in obscurity. It is wiser, we know, to look for figs from thistles, than for the fruits of honest and wise government where the proceedings are not enlightened by a commensurate publicity. We shall see as we go on that what is wrong in the City is that the area of administration and of the application of benevolent endowments has not grown with the growth of London, and that misdirection is principally due to the exigencies of reconciling the natural increase in the value of property and the altered conditions of life, with the selfish interests of men who have retained for themselves advantages which should have been distributed, and have done this with such unreflecting perseverance and persistent greed, that they have been blind to the increasing absurdity of their position.

The expenditure of many of the parochial charities of the City has long been scandalous, and a reformed application of the funds is much overdue. Take the case of the parish cited by Mr. Gilbert, which has a fund of £300 a year—originally perhaps not a tenth or twentieth part of that sum—for the support and repair of the parish church. Unable to get rid of the money in any preferable way, the rector and churchwardens have been wont to invite their friends to an entertainment at Richmond, and there to spend about £40 a year, a churchwarden having recorded his opinion that it is 'very advantageous for the interests of the parish and the promotion of good feeling amongst the parishioners, that an opportunity should occasionally be afforded them to meet together in a sociable and friendly manner.' Another 'charity' is charged twenty guineas for an 'audit dinner at the Crystal Palace,' the total income from the property being less than £500 a year. In one case, eighteen trustees have made a triennial visitation to inspect a property worth about £300 a year, and have charged fifty guineas for the day's outing. These eighteen persons were, both in their cups and in committee, unanimously of opinion that it was 'very desirable that the whole of the trustees should be intimately acquainted with the nature of the property.' But for a case of 'devouring widows' houses,' none perhaps equals that quoted by Sir Charles Trevelyan, who refers to a 'charity' for poor widows, freemen, etc., with an income of

£60 a year, the whole of which is derived from dividends. In 1868 the charge for management was:

	£	s.	d.
To the seven trustees for dinner, etc. . .	8	0	0
Secretary and solicitor	11	4	6
	£19	4	6

Not a few of the City parochial charities are distributed in doles given on condition of attendance at church. Founded, we may say, for the encouragement of hypocrisy and religious mendicity, it is not, perhaps, to be wondered at that these 'charities' are plundered by their appointed guardians. Take the case, for example, of a 'charity' founded in 1461, when it seemed doubtful whether, after payment for masses for the repose of the soul of the testator, it would yield 40s. a year. The money is now invested in a farm yielding £275 a year, 'which is applied to doles and church purposes.' Although this farm is let on lease for twenty-one years, the trustees seem to charge about £15 15s. annually 'for supervision.'

To call these things 'charity' is gross misuse of a word which suggests an association with virtue, benevolence, and misfortune. The confiscation of these 'charities' is a duty which the State cannot long neglect. Directly their administration is exposed, it is seen at once how hurtful to public morality is their present distribution. We have employed the word 'confiscation' advisedly, and here we may introduce the argument of Mr. Freeman touching that word which is precisely in point. Mr. Freeman says,[1] 'We use the word "confiscated" in its proper sense, not in the sense in which it has often been used by Mr. Disraeli and others when they wished to put a measure in a bad light by giving it what they thought an ugly name. In vulgar use the word has got a wrong meaning. "Confiscation" is vulgarly used to mean "robbery." But the word has a meaning of its own, a meaning which is wanted in this discussion. Confiscation is an act of the State, and of the State

[1] *Disestablishment and Disendowment.* By E. A. Freeman. (Macmillan.)

M

only. It is the taking of property by the State. It is a perfectly colourless word, which does not rule whether such taking
be just or unjust. When a magistrate inflicts a fine, he does an
act of confiscation. So when a man's land is taken from him by
Act of Parliament because it is wanted for a railway, his land is
confiscated. To be sure, he gets compensation ; but the land
may be taken from him quite against his will, and the compensation may be one which he thinks quite inadequate. . . .
The one sound principle is that the State may, when it sees
good reason for doing so, take or confiscate any property of
any kind. From this rule property given to ecclesiastical
purposes can claim no exemption. It is liable, on just and
sufficient cause, to be taken and applied to some other purpose,
and of such just and sufficient cause the State itself is the only
judge.' But I presume that no one would question the power
of the State to confiscate these miscalled 'charities.' The real
question is this : Are we convinced that their organisation is
so bad, that their application is so baneful, that any plea for
their continuance in their present form must be disregarded ?
The condemnation which we pronounce against them is no new
thing. They have been condemned already. For years they
have been waiting execution. Mr. Gladstone is a good Church-
man, and fourteen years ago was, perhaps, more convinced of
the benefits of Establishment and Endowment than he is at
present. Speaking of these City parochial charities in 1863, he
said, as Chancellor of the Exchequer,[1] 'It might be alleged, and
with some truth, that a multitude of these charities are positively
bad, injurious, demoralising, poisoning and sapping the principles
and independence of the poor, not one jot better, in many cases,
than the old poor-law doles, which at an epoch of courage and of
wisdom, the House of Commons swept away in 1834, under the
guidance of Lord Grey's Government.'

Mr. Gilbert sees no small part of the evil in the fact that 'the
poor who have been driven from the City are deprived of all the

---

[1] Debate on Customs and Inland Revenue Bill, May 4, 1863.

benefits which were solely intended for their use and comfort.'
That is one way of looking at the matter; but to us it seems
that the exodus of the poor from the City is not to be regretted,
and that as for the benefits of the 'charities,' those must follow
them into Greater London.

Now let us turn to the Livery companies, and here again we
must say that the attack is not wisely directed. These companies have large incomes; some are enormously wealthy.
The misuse of these funds is unquestionable, is glaring; with
paltry exceptions these funds have been diverted from their
original design. But there is this important difference to be
marked in comparing the Livery companies with the parochial
charities. The design of the City companies was sound, and is
not, nor is it likely to become, obsolete. These companies were
formed and established for the advantage and dignity of labour
of the higher sort, and of the commerce of the City; and to
those uses, if we are not much mistaken, they will some day
return. What is the future of labour in this and other countries?
To us it seems brightening into a time, and that not very far
distant, when skilled handicraft, and when excellence in every
branch of production, will meet with adequate reward and social
acknowledgment. Those who remember the artificers of fifty
years ago must be filled with hope of this sort on comparing the
best work of that time with the productions of to-day. Less
and less, as time goes on, will the middleman be able to over-
shadow and to hide the artist-workman; and the tendency in
all trades, but especially in those which are concerned with art-
workmanship of any sort, will be to elevate the importance of
the skilled operator. Probably the time will come again when,
if we speak of a goldsmith, we shall mean a goldsmith, and not
a capitalist who buys and sells gold ornaments. At all events,
as skill increases, and a longer and more intelligent pupillage is
requisite in every trade, the body will become more closely knit
together, there will be a new growth and increase of corporate
feeling. With that prospect we do not think it will be possible

or desirable to destroy the ancient guilds of the City of London. But their present form is monstrous. We should very much like to read an argument by Lord Selborne, the Prime Warden of the Mercers' Company, justifying his acceptance of that position. One of the Prime Warden's particular duties, it appears, is to satisfy himself that the wine taken from the company's cellars at each feast is replaced by other wine of equal value; an office which leads to buying hock at 104*s*., and other wines at 120*s*. to 150*s*. a dozen. That clearly cannot be a suitable or satisfactory occupation for the dignified and erudite ex-Chancellor. Lord Selborne cannot be ignorant that the original charter of the Mercers' Company, granted in the reign of Richard and confirmed by Elizabeth, denotes the composition and objects of the guild. By its charter, the company was founded 'for the perpetual sustentation of the poor belonging to the mystery of mercery in the City of London.' In 1701, Sir William Gore, mercer, and Lord Mayor of London, commended in pointed terms the exclusive admission to the company of men belonging to his trade. These were the original circumstances of the Mercers' Company. A vast change has taken place in the value of the company's property, but none in its charter and statutes. This company, members of which have been lately described as boasting that they drink wine at enormous prices, was in recent times again the subject of notice from a Lord Mayor. Mr. Cotton, than whom no one is more convinced that whatever is, is best in the City, gave a special entertainment to the masters and wardens of the companies, avowedly with the benevolent intention of keeping up their spirits in depressing days of reform. And the Prime Warden of the Mercers' Company, having newly cast off the robe of the highest judicial office in the realm, stood up to speak for the City guilds. When we are told that one of these companies lately built a dining hall at a cost of £74,000, and that another spent £30,000—Mr. W. H. James, said in the House of Commons that 'when one of the members of the Goldsmiths'

Company was charged with this fact, he indignantly repudiated it, and said that not £7,000 was the amount '—in the feasting of a single year; that not one company can claim to represent the trade the name of which it bears ; that, for instance, in the Mercers' Company there is said to be not a mercer,—it does seem strangely bold on the part of so modest and moderate a man as Lord Selborne, that he should, with all his legal honours thick upon him, declare that no other trusts had existed so long and remained so unaltered and unimpaired as those appertaining to the City guilds; that their funds were well, honestly, charitably, and conscientiously administered.

Lord Selborne could probably find no more favourable example than that of the Joiners' Company; yet it seems difficult to suppose that he could repeat his laudation after perusal had been given to the following account of the expenditure of the Joiners' Company :—

EXPENDITURE OF THE JOINERS' COMPANY FOR 1875.

Court and Livery Fees	£300
Pensions and Donations	130
Salaries	130
Investments	560
Dinners and Entertainments	760
Sundries	200
Balance	170
	£2250

What will his Lordship say to the average expenditure for ten years, from 1860 to 1870, of the Innholders' Company—also quoted by Mr. James in the House of Commons,—which shows, he said, the following particulars : ' Provisions £229, wine £97, court £214, casual expenses £118, salaries £150,—making a total of £808 ; that is, £808 a year is paid in fees, salaries, and feasting for the management of a total of £852 a year, the Court concluding the decade by pocketing and swallowing down the balance previously carried over from year to year.' The malpractices are not confined to gluttonous feasting. Take as a sample of other evils the charge posed by Mr. James against 'a man of the highest honour and integrity,' who it appears has several leases from his company at £10 per annum, which he underleases to some one else for several hundreds. How is it possible to maintain that these trusts are conscientiously administered?

We may surely take as evidence that all has not been right, the new line of action assumed by the Goldsmiths' Company. This guild, probably the richest, is said to possess property worth more than £100,000 a year. The Goldsmiths' Company has offered prizes of £50 and £25 and a scholarship of £100 a year for the encouragement of skill in gold-working. This is the company which is reported as having expended £30,000 in the dinners of one year. This is the company which occasionally endows 'decayed' liverymen, not necessarily goldsmiths, with £300 a year. This is the company whose clerk has emoluments estimated at the annual value of £4,000. This is the company which has built *alms*-houses worth £60 or £70 a year each, for house-rent alone. And these prizes are its grand deliverance in the line—the acknowledged line of its duty! It comes to this, that whenever and wherever a City company is found doing something meritorious and praiseworthy, it is simply prudent to believe that the dutiful outlay is but a trifle in comparison with that which is expended in a way not so well suited for the public eye.

We are not of those who object to reasonable hospitality, or even to a certain amount of magnificence in the halls of these ancient guilds. But at present neither hall nor hospitality has any meaning beyond what is for the most part a sordid gluttony. We shall pass on presently to speak of the Corporation and of the Mansion House, and shall not deprecate the Lord Mayor's hospitality. But there is no 'hospitality' in the proper sense of the word at the dinners of the City companies. Most of the men who assemble there are unknown outside their own parish; they are self-trained athletes in the labours of gastronomy.

There is no performance of a due and useful function. For the
most part it is eating and drinking with splendid accessories,
and nothing more. The stately hospitality of the Mansion
House has a meaning; the position of the Lord Mayor is so
dignified that honour can be shown in this way even to distinguished guests. It is one thing to dine at the Mansion
House, and quite another to dine with a livery company, or
with a committee of the Corporation. The livery companies'
dinners are dull and solemn for those who do not care for the
luxuries of a costly banquet. But to see a City dinner in its
grossest form, one must, perhaps, undergo the gastronomic
labours of a guest of a committee. The especial vice of civic
expenditure in feasting is in committees; it is there that one
encounters the typical turtle-eater, with no redeeming accessories
of good-fellowship. The committees of the Corporation are, it
has been stated, allowed £4,000 a year for refreshment!

We now come to the lands held by these City companies, the
extent of which is estimated at more than three hundred thousand acres. For our own part, we should like to see an end to
the holding of land in mortmain. Free trade in land will never
be complete while colleges and companies are permitted to hold,
century after century, lands such as those in the possession of
these guilds. Moreover, a great loss to the revenue is involved
in this ownership by undying corporations. The succession
duty on land is far from what it ought to be. But nothing of
the sort is levied upon the lands of corporations. Mr. Gladstone said in that very eloquent speech upon the taxation of
charities to which we have already referred: 'I maintain that
exemption is a grant.' It is undeniable that to these corporate
holders of lands, the State does make a grant to the extent of
their exemption from succession duty.

When Mr. Gladstone used in 1863 the words we have just
quoted, he was referring to the case of the great endowed schools
and medical charities of the City in connection with the exemption of their funds from income-tax. Of these schools, Christ's

Hospital is by much the most wealthy and important. We do not say that the best expenditure of its vast resources, amounting to nearly £100,000 a year, would be the provision of elementary schools in the metropolis. That would simply be a reduction of the education rate. But we do say that such a direction of the funds would be much more in harmony with the original foundation of the school than the present expenditure. In the first place, Christ's Hospital was established for the poor. Secondly, it was established without distinction of sex, and girls have just as much claim as boys to its benefits. Thirdly, there is no justice in any restriction of its advantages to the walls or to the government of the City; these belong to the metropolis. Stow's *London* is a book of great authority, mentioned with all respect by Mr. Samuel Pepys, himself perhaps the best-known man in the long line of Presidents of Christ's Hospital. Stow, in 1556, said of Christ's Hospital that 'it was established to take the chylde out of the strete, which was the sede and increase of beggary, by reason of ydle bringing up. And to nouryshe the said chylde in some goode learninge and exercise profitable to the commonweale.' In another place, he says that in one month from the opening of the school, November 21, 1552, 'chyldren had been taken from the stretes to the numbre of fower hundred.' No closer analogy to the Board School of the present day could be obtained. There was originally no limitation to boys. Machyn, in his Diary, referring to attendance at the Spital sermon and to Christ's Hospital, wrote: 'And alle the chyldren of the hospital, boyth men chyldren and women chyldren, that be kepte with certayn landes and the cherete of the nobul citie of London.' Restrictions appear to have begun in the time of Charles I., when it was declared that no child of illegitimate birth could be admitted. But even to that there was a proviso, 'except in cases of extremity where losse of life and perishing would presently follow;' and the proviso is important, because it shows the character of the school as devoted to the most necessitous

children. Mr. Gladstone complained in 1863 that Christ's
Hospital was in fact receiving a grant from the State of £6,000
a year in the form of exemption from income-tax. And when
he was told that if this exemption were no longer accorded
at the cost of the general body of taxpayers, the educational
advantages of the Hospital must be curtailed, he put the very
pertinent question, to which, of course, there was no response,
'Why then do you spend £220 in a feast?' Mr. Hare, one of
the Charity Commissioners, reported in 1864 that the Hospital
possessed property worth about £85,000 a year, devoted to the
education of twelve hundred boys and *twenty-seven girls.* The
appropriation of this great 'charity,' as one belonging in its
government exclusively to the City, is unjustifiable, and the
system of nomination to the benefits of Christ's Hospital is open
to grave objections. There is a pretence that, in accordance
with the rules of Charles II., dated February 9, 1676, 'None be
admitted but suche as are without probable means of being
provided for in other ways'! But it is flagrantly untrue that
such are the circumstances of the pupils. It seems an act of
great munificence for a person to contribute £500 to this institution, and those who give this sum are, as a rule—which has we
believe no exception—elected governors. But in truth, if they
wish to enjoy for themselves or others the educational advantages of the 'charity,' the money is excellently well invested,
and, in fact, a bonus of nearly double the amount is added to it
from funds which most clearly belong to the poor and miserable,
who have no claim but indigence and the danger of neglect.
The nominations are sometimes of so gross a character that
the committee has been known to remonstrate; but there is
abundant evidence that they are not over-scrupulous; while as
regards the education of girls, a grave misappropriation is continued without reproach and under the highest patronage.

We have alluded to Christ's Hospital as fairly typical of the
endowed schools of the City. To a certain extent they are all
well managed. No one says that the education obtained at

St. Paul's School, which belongs to the Mercers' Company, is not good, but no fair inquirer will deny that it is limited by unsound restrictions, of which the fanciful arrangement of 153 pupils is a fair example. A clear insight into the general administration of City 'charities,' including parochial charities, endowed schools, and hospitals, may be gained by a glance at the affairs of St. Paul's School. St. Peter is supposed to have included in his net when he hauled in 'the miraculous draught of fishes,' a hundred and fifty-three of all kinds, and when St. Paul's School was founded in 1509, the number of pupils was designed for perpetual commemoration of the miracle; just as the Escurial was built in the form of a gridiron to commemorate the martyrdom of San Lorenzo. There was another provision in ·the original rules, concerning 'the littel dinner, the cost whereof was not to exceed foure nobles, and which was to be held as near Candlemas as possible, the time not to exceed three days after or before.' The value of the noble never, we believe, exceeded ten shillings—the cost of the 'littel dinner' in money of our time was therefore 'not to exceed' two pounds. Attention has been drawn to the expenditure by the managers of St. Paul's School of £229 for the 'littel dinner' in a single year; and supposing that the value of their property and their consequent ability in regard to the business of the foundation had increased in the same ratio as the cost of their dinner, they ought now to be providing for the education of at least a hundred times 153 scholars,—for more than 15,000 children.

If we were in turn to visit the Charterhouse, or Merchant Taylors' School, or any other of the endowed schools of the City, we should find only a repetition of these things. We must pass on to consider the position of the three great medical charities which pertain to the City of London. The management of St. Bartholomew's, of Bethlehem, and of St. Thomas' Hospitals, belongs to the Lord Mayor, Aldermen, and Corporation, only as representing the government of London. Until their jurisdiction is extended over the metropolis, their claim to the exclusive control of these hospitals is not equitably good. These hospitals were founded at a time—St. Bartholomew's in 1143, and the other two about a century later—when they may be supposed to have been sufficient for all the necessities of the sick, the wounded, and the afflicted of London. To fulfil the same function as nearly as possible in the present time, the enormously increased funds should have been devoted to the erection of a number of small hospitals, where poor persons who are sick, or any who are suffering from accident, could be received without having to travel miles, which in case of accident may and sometimes does involve death. There is, as things are, no just or reasonable proportion between the increase of funds and the extension of benefits. St. Thomas' Hospital has been lodged in an imposing fabric, which suffers nothing even by the close proximity in which it stands to the Palace of Westminster; a great medical school has grown up, has become established, and only 600 patients are provided for. It is a modest statement to assert that ten times the number might have been cared for in several parts of the metropolis with the funds belonging to St. Thomas' Hospital. We may learn from the accounts of the Poplar Hospital, that for building, fitting, and furnishing, beds may be provided at £50 each. These charges, in the case of St. Thomas' Hospital, have amounted to little less than £850 for each bed!

We entirely agree with Mr. Gilbert that 'the original establishment of St. Bartholomew's Hospital was simply and purely that of a parish workhouse under the Local Government Board at the present day.' This is clear from the deed dated 27th December, 1546, which recites that 'Our Sovereign Lord the King is pleased and contented that the said Hospital of Saint Bartholomew shall from henceforth be a place and house for the relief and sustentation of poor people, and shall be called the "House of the Poore," in West Smithfield, in the suburbs of the City of London, of King Henry the Eighth's foundation.' There was also a power of taxation which was resorted to when necessary for the maintenance of the Hospital. St. Bartholomew's has had a splendid career, but its present distinction is rather as a great medical school. The population which up to twenty years ago surrounded St. Bartholomew's has gone, and the funds of this great institution would be ‑much more equitably bestowed in maintaining the workhouse hospitals of London. But there is and will be increasing need for branches of these great hospitals in various parts of London. Medical science must be encouraged and diffused, and it cannot be expected that masters of that science who now attend in these hospital schools could give their services in all quarters of London. These are considerations which must not be lost sight of. But it cannot be denied that the primary object of these hospitals is, and ought to be, the care of the sick and wounded. Yet this is not the first concern of the Governors. So recently as July, 1877, the Governors of St. Bartholomew's Hospital determined upon an expenditure of £50,000 in a resolution which contained no reference to the public; and the Charity Commissioners, replying to the Governors, stated that, 'having regard to the great development of the School of Surgery and Medicine, and the rapid augmentation of the number of students in recent years, which is apparently due to the position and other advantages possessed by the Hospital, the Commissioners think that their sanction may justly be given to the erection of the new theatres, library, museum, and other buildings devoted to instructional purposes.' We are disposed to maintain that this is a misdirection of the funds, and that these medical charities belong by right to the people and to the government of the metropolis, and not to the government of the City while that represents but a small portion of the people of London.

The Lord Mayor, the two Sheriffs, the 26 Aldermen, and the 206 Common Councillors, who govern the City, ought numerically to be sufficient for the metropolis. How their jurisdiction is to be reformed and extended has been shown in the Bill

which Sir Ughtred Kay-Shuttleworth, in succession to Lord Elcho,
Mr. Charles Buxton, and Mr. John Stuart Mill, has recommended
to Parliament.   When the municipal government of London is
reformed, a change will follow in regard to the property and endowments now controlled by the Corporation of the City.   Our
contention is that this property and those funds belong to London,
and not to the particular space between Ludgate and Aldgate.

Not willingly would the people of England see the illustrious
Corporation of the City of London pass away.   But its existence
can be secured only at the price of real and thorough reform.
The election of members must be made upon the same method
which is practised in other municipalities—there must be abolition of election by the Livery.   'Nothing,' said Mr. James, in
the speech already referred to, 'can be worse than the powers
of voting which these bodies possess.   I have a return moved
for a year since, bearing date August 15, 1876, according to
which it appears 1,932 liverymen within the City have on
various occasions bought their votes.   In one of the companies,
it was a well-known fact that not long ago the duties of the
master, assistant, and clerks were all consolidated in one person,
who had it in his power to increase the Livery entirely at his own
choice.   From the return of the Loriners' Company, it appears
that 273 persons purchased their vote; in the Coachmakers, 79;
the Curriers, 43; the Butchers, 69; the Founders, 75; and
many others in like amount.   I am not going to insinuate
against any of the large companies that they pack their
register by unfair or improper means, but as long as you have a
system of this kind there are always those who will avail themselves of any artifices or dodges which are within their means,
and which no just person by any sort of casuistry can defend.'
If the proposal of Lord Camperdown in the House of Lords
had been adopted, the Metropolitan Board of Works would have
been elected, as a School Board is elected, by ratepayers.   At
present the members of the Metropolitan Board are nominated
by the vestries and district boards.   Had the change been

effected, the Metropolitan Board of Works would have gained a
great increase of popular strength and approval. Much of this
would have been achieved at the cost of the Corporation, the
election of whose members is a sham, having no substantial relation to the present circumstances of the real constituency.

The prestige of the Corporation of the City is historical, and
is supported by its properties, and its powers of banqueting.
That all which is good in this may be retained and extended in
conformity with the altered conditions and with the growth of
London, that all the utility it possesses may be preserved, and
that the needs of the vast population of the metropolis may
obtain the benefits of the best local government, is the hope and
the object of the present writer.

VIII.

WATER SUPPLY OF LONDON AND ELSEWHERE.

I DO not think the alarming language which some have used in treating of this subject, is either called for by actual circumstances, or that it can be productive of good results. It is far more likely to lead to the adoption of crude and ill-advised schemes, requiring a large investment of capital in works which are not most advantageous in the present, and which will be obstacles to future improvement.

It is very true that the quantity of water which the soil of the country annually receives is limited. Fortunately there is but little variation in the amount, though a considerable difference in the intervals, of rainfall. But assuming an average annual fall of thirty inches in depth, it is at once seen that the quantity received may be regarded as practically unlimited, and that our care should be concentrated upon the most economic mode of obtaining the largest possible quantity which is demanded by the most liberal estimate of our wants.

The term 'water economy,' if not used, has certainly been interpreted, in the sense which would be applicable to coal economy. The difference between the supplies of coal and water is, that it is quite possible to imagine the day when the coal-fields of England will be exhausted, while it is quite impossible to suggest any operation which would reduce the rainfall by an inch. We know, for instance, that the Northumberland coal-field is not a thousand square miles in extent, that the greatest thickness of workable coal is not more than one hundred feet, while the mean thickness scarcely exceeds twelve feet ; and resulting from this, we can calculate with tolerable accuracy that a consumption of twenty millions of tons annually will exhaust this coal-field in about three hundred years.   But the rainfall remains undiminished.

It has, indeed, been suggested, that land drainage has reduced the rainfall by an appreciable degree : but it should be remembered that this interesting statement is made with respect to an island which, from east to west, nowhere measures more than three hundred miles.   Undoubtedly, the primary effect of land drainage is to reduce the amount of water evaporated from the soil ; I say, the primary effect, because the quantity of water of which the soil is relieved by these drains is not so important in its actual effect upon the producing qualities of the soil, as is the rise of temperature in the earth above the level of the drains, which is the result of reduced evaporation.   It is certainly true that less water is evaporated from a well-drained than from a marshy country, and that the soil of England gives out much less watery vapour than it did fifty years ago ; but when we remember that the division of the surface of the globe is three-fourths of water to one of land, and that a hundred and forty-five millions of square miles of sea are constantly supplying the heavens with rain,—and, moreover, that we in this small island are surrounded by seas of great extent, with an infallible and immense rain machinery close at hand in the junction of the heated Gulf Stream with the icy Arctic waters, —it should excite a smile rather than alarm when we are threatened with thirst because of agricultural land drainage.

Probably there is no equal area in the world upon which so many geological strata are exhibited at the surface as in England.   Speaking with reference to the general industry of the country rather than with scientific minuteness, it may be said that mountains and metal mines characterise the older and harder formations ; that coal mines and manufacturing industry abound upon those which are next in degree of solidarity; while to agriculture are devoted those beds of more recent and lighter composition. This division affects the supply of water, inasmuch as the first and second have generally an impermeable surface, and the water must either be utilised during its passage to the sea, or be stored upon the surface for use in times of drought; while in the third division the supply, running through the permeable beds until it falls upon some impermeable stratum, finds a natural storage beneath the surface; and, saturating to the level of its outfall those beds through which it has passed, it is lessened only by artificial depletion or by the slow process of capillary action moving upwards to the drier surface of the soil. Of all English reservoirs, whether natural, like Windermere, or artificial, such as those of the Manchester water-works, none above-ground are so capacious as the great bed of New Red sandstone, which, with an enormous thickness, underlies so large a part of mid and north-western England, or as the great bed of chalk, upon which rests so much of the wealth and population of the south and south-eastern portions of the kingdom. When it is considered that these are the thickest strata in our geological series, and that while sandstone will take up a sixth of its bulk in water, chalk will absorb double this quantity, or one-third of its bulk, it needs but little acquaintance with the extent of subterranean reservoirs to be certain that they are not filled by the rainfall of a single year.

It follows, then, from this brief description of the water resources of the country, that generally, those districts which are mountainous and manufacturing obtain their supply by means of storage reservoirs constructed at high levels, pouring forth their contents by gravitation; while those localities which are agricultural are mainly supplied from underground sources, the water being lifted by pumping and then carried away for consumption. Yet this distribution of rainfall by the geological strata is much more equable than appears upon the surface

N

For instance, the rainfall of Lancashire is about double that of Middlesex, while the fall of portions of the Lake country is twice that of Lancashire. But it cannot be doubted that a large portion of this excessive rainfall finds its way into the red sandstone stretching to the south, just as the increased rainfall upon the South Downs is distributed throughout the vast bed of chalk of which those hills form the most elevated portion.

There is no question that a plentiful supply of good water is one of the first requisites of public health, and with reference to any increase in the northern division of the country, nothing would seem easier than to advise utilisation of those natural reservoirs—the Lakes, and the construction of additional reservoirs. If water-closets should in time to come be generally used among the population in the North, a largely increased supply would be needed. But the difficulty of obtaining this increase in the immediate neighbourhood of existing water-works is complicated by vested rights of landowners and mill-owners in the neighbouring rivers and streams,—rights which offer a far stronger resistance to extension than any caused by the expense of works. These water rights form a subject of perpetual litigation, of endless intrigue, and continual anxiety to manufacturers. Yet such are the economic advantages of the storage of excessive rainfall, that by the construction of reservoirs constant flow can be given to a river or stream, for manufacturing purposes, exceeding its average flow, although a large portion of the drainage of the watershed is abstracted for household and urban consumption. But in a densely populated district the expense of contesting and satisfying these rights increases to an alarming extent the cost of extensions, and suggests a wider search for any large addition. The supply of the chief towns in Lancashire is generally of very excellent quality ; and indeed it may be said that no other city in England possesses a water supply equal to that of Manchester, whether as regards its purity or volume. The waterworks of that city belong to the Corporation, who have power to supply nearly thirty townships, including a population considerably exceeding half a million. The water thus distributed by gravitation, which is gathered from high lands, of the millstone grit formation, is very soft and pure, and at a distance of nearly twenty miles from the storage reservoirs, the Corporation are able to supply other local authorities at the price of threepence per thousand gallons, and at this rate to realise a considerable profit.

The difference between pure and impure water does not pass the public comprehension, yet it must not be hastily assumed that they can appreciate this distinction by sight or smell or taste with sufficient certainty to protect their health. But analysis will detect all impurities. That admixture of bi-carbonate of lime which constitutes the difference between ' hard ' and ' soft ' water, is not, when it exists to a moderate degree, deemed an impurity sufficient to cause a supply to be rejected for domestic purposes, though it affects the real value of the water for such uses. ' Hardness' is defined by Dr. Clark's test to imply, ' one grain of bi-carbonate, or sulphate of lime, in each gallon'; but commonly if water contain six grains per gallon, it is called ' hard '; if less than six, ' soft ' water. Among the physical advantages attending the consumption of soft water are said to be a comparative freedom from granular and calculous deposits in the bodily system, and a greater delicacy of complexion, to which circumstance some ascribe the reputation of the ' Lancashire witches' for personal beauty. But this is not all. The water supply of the Lancashire district as compared with that derived from the chalk formation in the South, requires but one-half the quantity of soap and one-third the quantity of tea to effect the same results in the washing-tub or the teapot, an advantage which is equivalent to an immense reduction in the price of those articles, to say nothing of the saving of labour and linen in the process of washing. The master of the Bolton workhouse, some years ago, crucially tested this difference, by making the 'old women's' tea with hard water. Their allowance was four ounces of tea, but he put six ounces to the usual quantity of water, substituting hard for soft. Nothing was said respecting the experiment, but after three days of the 'six ounce and hard water' tea, a deputation waited upon him to complain 'that the tea had not been so strong as it had been formerly; the person making it must have made a mistake, and forgot to put the usual quantity of tea to the same quantity of water.'

In course of time it may happen, through the increased demand for water in the manufacturing districts by the rapid growth of the towns, by the general use of water-closets, by a large addition of manufacturing power, by the diminution of surface supply owing to the construction of sewers and drains, by a demand on the part of owners of great industrial works for a supply free from all dangers of litigation and impurity, that it will be necessary to go farther in search of water, and to utilise, for the consumption of a very extensive area, the excessive rainfall of the Lake district, which about Seathwaite averages 140 inches per annum. It has been proposed to make use of the water of Thirlmere,—a proposal in regard to which the Corporation of Manchester have been met with inconsiderate opposition. The first and best utility of a fresh-water lake situated upon high ground within reach of a dense population must be for water supply ; no other supply can be equally pure or attainable with such certainty and economy. The rainfall must be greatest in that region, and thus the quantity and freshness of the water are secured, and the elevation natural to such a lake is in fact an important and advantageous circumstance in distribution. If the neighbourhood of the lake possesses great beauty of scenery, there is utility in that, which, though of a secondary order, is not likely to be forgotten. And it may be confidently asked,—which would more probably preserve the natural charm of the Lake district,—a policy which leaves all the land open to the erection of buildings, or one which would necessitate the preservation of the land in a state of nature ? In fifty or a hundred years, with all the changes in the tenure of land which that period may be expected to bring, I doubt if there will be an acre in the Lake district without a house upon it, unless, owing to the utilisation of the Lakes for the health and the largest benefit of the community in the storage of water, the increase of building is forbidden except under strict regulations which would allow very rare exception.

In seasons of drought, the Corporation of Liverpool have experienced great difficulty in ekeing out their store of water, and may yet have to resort to the plan suggested some years since by my friend Mr. Rawlinson, who proposed to bring the waters of the Bala Lake to the banks of the Mersey. A comprehensive scheme was about the same time brought forward by Mr. Dale, the manager of the Hull waterworks, who proposed, at the cost of eight and a half millions sterling, to utilise the waters of Ullswater and Haweswater, leading them by a line of not less than one hundred and fifty miles, to supply the following towns, daily, with an aggregate of 131,000,000 gallons, distributed in these proportions : Liverpool, 40,000,000 gallons ; Leeds, 15,000,000 ; Bradford, 10,000,000 ; Lancaster, 2,000,000 ; Preston, 8,000,000 ; Wigan, 4,000,000 ; Dewsbury, 3,000,000 ; Wakefield, 3,000,000 ; Bingley, 1,000,000 ; Kendal, 2,000,000 ; Bolton, 8,000,000 ; Blackburn, 6,000,000 ; Keighley, 2,000,000 ; Huddersfield, 4,000,000 ; Burnley, 4,000,000 ; Rochdale, 4,000,000 ; Halifax, 4,000,000 ; Colne, 1,000,000 ; Bury, 8,000,000 ; and St. Helens, 2,000,000. Whether this proposal will ever be carried into execution, I cannot venture to predict, but I am confident that the demands of manufacture alone will induce a much greater storage of the northern rainfall.

It is, however, in London, that the question is of the highest importance. The water supply of the metropolis is bad in quality, deficient in quantity, and faulty as to the sources from whence it is obtained. Nothing is more certain than that 'progress' involves a large increase in the individual demand for water. The quantity delivered in London rose from 44,383,332 gallons in 1856 to more than 108,000,000 gallons in the year 1866. One-half of this supply is filched from the river Thames; not economised from the storm waters of rainy seasons, but drained from the sluggish stream in the thirsty summer, more largely even than during the impetuous floods of winter. This water is fouled by the sewage of many considerable populations scattered throughout the Thames basin, which includes 1,000,000 inhabitants above the point at which the lowest supply is obtained; it is further polluted by the surface drainage of many thousand acres of highly manured land, and by the incidents of an extensive traffic, including the corpses of innumerable dogs and cats, which, after a frequently cruel death, are thus noxiously avenged. And the same objections may be urged against so much of the remainder of the supply as is derived from the Lea and the Ravensbourne, in the east and south of London.

The Thames can ill afford to lose this quantity of water, which amounts to one-sixth of the dry-weather flow at Hampton; and now, less than ever, when the diversion of the sewage has prevented the restoration of this water in the place where its outfall would much affect the flow of the river. But that the Thames should bear a further abstraction is not to be tolerated, nor are there adequate sources of supply in the neighbourhood of the metropolis sufficient to meet the increasing demand. It is quite possible that a more rigid inspection may prevent, to a great extent, the pollution of these and other rivers. We may yet see the Thames Embankment lined with anglers; but we must not expect that populous river basins will afford a supply of pure water, nor is it right, upon sanitary or economic principles, to take water for domestic consumption from the dry-weather stream of such rivers.

I have said that the water supply of London is not only unsatisfactory in quantity, but also in quality. I will not refer to the wells—many of which are directly fouled by poisonous contaminations, of which the Broad Street pump, of cholera notoriety, was a signally fatal example,—but to the quality of water furnished by the eight great companies which together pour in the daily drink of the metropolis. In point of organic impurity, as expressed in analytical tables, the London water does not appear much inferior to that of the northern cities, but the organic impurity of the first is, we should remember, of a very different character from that of the organic impurity of the latter. Organic impurity is hurtful in proportion to its power of putrefaction, and the humous peaty matter which forms so large a portion of the organic impurity contained in the waters from the northern moors upon the millstone grit and Silurian formations, is comparatively harmless when contrasted with the matter which pollutes the river supplies of London. Again, in reference to the important quality of hardness, the whole of the London supply appears distinctly inferior to the northern waters. The water of Lake Bala, to which I have referred as a possible source of supply for Liverpool, contain but 0·8° of hardness, while the London water contains from 12° to 16° by the same test. It may perhaps be safely assumed that the presence of this quantity of lime in the metropolitan supply of water involves the waste of not less than 3,000,000 lb. of tea and 3,000,000 lb. of soap every year ; nor is it a high estimate to set the money loss thus involved at £525,000, a sum which, capitalised at 4 per cent., represents £13,125,000. But this is only part of the waste occasioned by the hardness of London water. To this must be added the loss in coffee, in the preparation of chemicals for manufacturing purposes, the large item represented by wear and tear of clothes in washing, and other sums, which as positive loss would swell this total probably to £20,000,000 sterling. I will leave to the readers of this paper the task of computing the sum which should be added for the sanitary advantage of a soft water supply. Once, to be sure, there did appear an advocate of hard water, on the ground that lime was necessary to renew the osseous framework of the body, but he retired abashed upon the suggestion that 'bone' was rather a characteristic of the Scotch people, who are, in general, consumers of water containing but 1° or 2° of hardness.

Assuming, then, it is necessary that increased supply should be obtained for the metropolis, and that it is desirable the water should be as soft as can be procured, I will refer to the localities from whence this addition, or entirely new supply, could be obtained. It is the opinion of the best informed persons upon this matter, that a large addition to the existing supply might be obtained from the chalk which underlies the metropolitan district, and from the Bagshot sands of Surrey. The first would, of course, be very hard, though if the lime which it contains were precipitated, this evil would be to a great extent annihilated. The latter would be soft water. But neither would of itself furnish a supply sufficient for the total demand of London, which is the prime necessity of any scheme proposing the largest measure of reform. The eight companies to which I have previously referred have an invested capital of about £7,000,000 sterling, with a gross annual revenue of about £700,000; they compose an obstacle of very formidable dimensions; but not insuperable, if we may judge from the scheme promulgated about ten years since by Mr. J. F. Bateman, who proposed to supply London with 220,000,000 gallons a day from the sources of the Severn, comprising two drainage areas, each of about 66,000 acres in extent. One of these 'is situated a little to the east of the range of mountains of which Cader Idris and Aran Mowddy are the highest summits, respectively of 2,914 and 2,979 feet in height, and forms the drainage ground of the rivers Banw and Vyrnwy, which join the Severn about half-way betwixt Welshpool and Shrewsbury. The other district is situated immediately to the east of Plynlimmon, 2,500 feet in height, and forms the drainage-ground of the upper portion of the river Severn proper. The discharge pipes of the lowest reservoir in each of these districts would be placed at an elevation of about 450 feet above the level of Trinity high-water mark.'

The idea is not novel, but the details are original, and appear to have been well considered. The water would be of a far better quality (containing only 1·6° of hardness) than can be obtained from any nearer locality; indeed, the high mountain lands are, as I have said, 'the natural water-fields of a country. Mr. Bateman proposed in these districts to construct four reservoirs, containing an aggregate storage capacity of 4,991,000,000 cubic feet, the embankments in no case to exceed 80 feet in height. By aqueducts of 19 and 21½ miles in length respectively, the waters of the two districts would be united a little to the N.E. of Montgomery, and from thence by a common aqueduct of 152 miles in length, open or tunnelled, according to the level of the intervening country, be conducted to high land near Stanmore, from which point water could be supplied to the metropolis from service reservoirs, 'at high pressure, and under the constant-supply system.'

For the present the waters of those districts, estimated at 130,000,000 gallons per day, would be sufficient; and the necessary works, including the long aqueduct, of such dimensions as would conduct the full supply when it was needed, and the cost of connecting new pipes with the existing systems, Mr. Bateman estimated at £8,600,000 ; the total estimate for a supply of 220,000,000 gallons per day being £10,850,000. But then there are vested rights to be dealt with, and the engineer calculated 'the gross cost, after capitalising the present dividends and interest of the existing companies, if they are to be purchased, viz., £450,000 per annum, at twenty-five years' purchase, will be £19,850,000 for the first instalment of 130,000,000 gallons per day (exclusive of any of the New

River supplies, which may still be retained), or £165,416 per million; when the full quantity from North Wales is introduced, viz., 220,000,000 gallons per day, the total cost will be £22,100,000, or £100,454 per million gallons per day.'

I do not see anything in this scheme which should alarm our civic economists, although it will probably be some time before they rise to a full appreciation of the benefits to be derived from it. The cost would amount to about one year's rateable value of the property within the district receiving the supply, and that is a charge which in many northern towns has not been suffered to withstand the effort to obtain a good supply of water.

From a sanitary point of view the question of water supply eminently demands attention, in its relation to the small scattered towns and villages, hundreds of which have no regular supply whatever, and are dependent on ditch-water, or wellwater, which is in many cases very impure. I have heard of 117 people waiting around one pump; of poor women rising in the early morning, three hours before working time, and walking more than a mile in order to be first at the tiny stream upon which their village was dependent for water. There are many rural districts, too, where the poor are drinking dungdiscoloured water; many, where the supply is drawn from old wells, the mouths of which, trodden to a funnel shape, mingle the washings of the surface with their contents. In very many towns which have a supply, the poorer classes are obliged to fetch their water from standpipes—a mode of distribution not only wasteful to a very serious extent, but involving continuous and unnecessary labour on the part of working people, when, by a proper application of machinery, a quantity equal to the contents of 30,000 pails could be lifted to their housetops for a shilling.

At a meeting of the Society of Arts, a paper was read upon the subject of 'water supply, especially to small towns and villages in rural districts,' by Mr. Bailey Denton, in which he recommended the storage of agricultural drainage water in small reservoirs, and assuming the population of a village to be 400, requiring 10 gallons each per day, he estimated that it would be necessary to store 120 days' supply, or 480,000 gallons, the reservoir containing 720,000, to allow for evaporation and waste, and covering four-tenths of an acre with a depth of 7½ feet. The cost of this work was set by Mr. Denton at £415.

It is impossible not to feel grateful to him for having so assiduously called attention to the real suffering which a very large proportion of the population endure, owing to the want of a proper supply of water. But I cannot convince myself that the ills they suffer are much more grievous than would be the wholesale execution of a system of small works of this description. The fact is, that the reform must be made, each place for itself, in the manner and under conditions which the locality suggests. I have seen a small township construct very efficient waterworks for £450, which held a good supply during a very prolonged drought. But this is quite an exceptional case. The construction of a number of small, shallow, and exposed ponds throughout the rural districts, is an undertaking which cannot be recommended on sanitary or economical grounds. There are many cases where such reservoirs may be constructed with great advantage ; but the reform cannot be carried out upon a system which ignores the capacity or incapacity of separate districts. It might be thought desirable that the funds should be borrowed from one common source ; but there can be no common treatment in the design of the required works, which, both to secure greater purity of the water and economy of cost, should be made as large as possible, feeding the widest practicable area which could be supplied from one centre.

To the proposal to collect effluent water from land-drainage for domestic consumption, there are, however, obvious objections to be made. As a rule, this water would be considerably softer than that to be obtained by pumping from the under-lying strata. There are grounds for believing that the habitual use of water drawn from the chalk formation tends to impair the digestive organs, and predisposes to calculous disease. It is said, too, that the presence of carbonate of lime in water is a frequent cause of sore throat, and is invariably found where goitre is a common affliction. But this objection applies principally to the chalk beds, and there are many water-holding strata throughout the agricultural districts to which it is not applicable. Of the water which is carried off by land drains, it is true that sometimes none whatever comes directly from the surface of the soil. The drain may mark the level of saturation of the soil in which it rests ; but during the season in which these small reservoirs would become full, the soil below the drains would be saturated, and all water carried off by the pipes would come directly from the surface. This season is also concurrent with the time of manuring, and if it be possible for taint of manure to remain in water after per-colating to the drains, the outfall would certainly be impure.

On this point the General Board of Health took evidence, some years since, at the suggestion of the late Lord Carlisle. Among other witnesses, they examined Mr. Smith of Deanston, who, in reference to land-drainage, has the place which Adam Smith holds in political economy. Mr. Smith said : ' The water flowing from drains is generally very limpid and pure, although at times, when much manure has been put upon the land, it is impregnated to a considerable degree with soluble matter and sometimes colouring.' But unquestionably, the water issuing from drains four feet deep, especially from land under grass, is generally very soft, and of good quality ; and if the main drains were carefully led away, so as to avoid contact with any impure washings from the surface of cultivated lands, a valuable supply of water might thus be gained. Yet in place of con-structing one small reservoir for each village, in which it might be very difficult, if not impossible, to preserve the purity of the water, it would, when practicable, be far more economical and serviceable to construct the needful storage for each watershed. By such aggregation the quality of the water would be improved, and its cost lessened. If works could be constructed for a population of 400 persons, at a cost of £415, they would obtain a supply of 480,000 gallons for this sum. That was Mr. Denton's proposal. But the Manchester Corporation are enabled to sell this quantity at a considerable profit, and at a distance of twenty miles from their reservoirs, for an annual charge of £6; while if a pumping system is considered desirable, not less than 80,000 gallons may be lifted upwards of fifty feet at a cost of one shilling.

I have made these remarks in order to prove that in this, as in every other undertaking, there are great advantages in association. The provision of a pure and sufficient supply of water, especially in rural districts, has been very much neglected ; and if regard is to be had to the health of the people, this is a matter which presses for immediate attention. The want is felt keenly among populations too small to possess local authority capable of executing considerable works ; and in the endeavour to remedy a state of things which must be characterised as disgraceful, it may be found desirable to give to local authorities greater facilities of union for this object.

IX.

THE LIBERAL PARTY AND THE CATHOLICS.

WHEN Lord Melbourne was Prime Minister, in the first December of Her Majesty's reign, there was a question before the House of Commons touching Irish Election Petitions. A young man addressed the House for some twenty minutes, amid 'murmurs' and 'interruption,' until at last the 'shouts' of members overwhelmed half a sentence. 'The noble lord,' said the maiden speaker, 'might wave in one hand the Keys of St. Peter, and in the other ———.' Since that day Mr. Disraeli [in writing of Lord Beaconsfield's life in the House of Commons, it is still well to use his family and familiar name] has sketched for us, with the fine satirical pencil of his tongue, a long gallery of Parliamentary portraits ; they troop in the mind's eye, some with the supple step of his 'red Indian of debate,' others with the 'Batavian grace' of his honourable friend the member for the University of Cambridge,' but he was never permitted to finish his first Parliamentary painting ; and in place of Lord Melbourne's left hand he had to raise his own in deprecation and in prophecy that 'the time will come when you will hear me.' England had then effaced part of a great blot ; some years before she had conceded a tardy measure of justice to Roman Catholics, but even then there were few indeed of the Protestant majority who were sensible of the wrong, or in any way pained at the maintenance of religious disabilities of the most odious and insulting character.

The attention I propose to invite to the relations of the

Liberal party and the Catholics has been suggested by the paper entitled 'The Tory Party and the Catholics,' which Mr. Pope Hennessy contributed to the *Contemporary Review.* He himself appears in the paper in two parts,—conspicuously as a political Rip van Winkle, who, while the European world has been boiling in the caldron of controversy, has been slumbering among Labuans and West Africans, and as a Colonial Governor removed from the 'struggles of party,' who must not venture into the whirlwind of current politics. This, however, I should say, is a reserve to which Mr. Hennessy pretends ; he is quite unable to maintain the *rôle* which he thinks most fitting for a Colonial Governor who was once a busy member of Parliament. In his swallow-flight through more than 200 years of history, he dips, like the bird in stormy weather, again and again to earth, pecking now at Mr. Gladstone, now at Cardinal Cullen, and chirping always when he meets with Mr. Disraeli, in whose brilliant and bejewelled utterances Mr. Hennessy delights to mirror himself. His paper is a eulogy of the policy of Mr. Disraeli, from the hour in which we have seen that distinguished man first rise in the House of Commons ; and it is a censure of the Catholics for those wanderings from their 'natural alliance' with the Tory party of which they have been, as he alleges, especially under the leadership of Mr. Gladstone, so frequently and foolishly guilty.

I have followed his example in giving Mr. Disraeli a leading place in this reply, because Mr. Disraeli is the hero of Mr. Hennessy's paper—'the highest living authority on political parties' ; 'the most successful party organizer that the Conservatives of England have ever known' ; the consolation of a Tory Catholic in a State of which the vast majority is Protestant. And we shall understand Mr. Hennessy better if we recognize how gladly he would be Mr. Disraeli if he were not Mr. Hennessy. I had a special object in referring to Mr. Disraeli's maiden speech. His hat once covered a party in Parliament, and so did Mr. Pope Hennessy's. It is a matter of history—Mr. Hennessy says so—that 'the Tory Catholic party that was formed in 1859' had a 'solitary representative,' one who has for a little while returned from places far more outlandish than the home of Lord Macaulay's New Zealander, to contemplate the stability of the Church of Rome from a seat upon the ruins of his party. And now in what his political master would denote as his 'historical conscience,' Mr. Hennessy thinks that minute and single-voiced body 'attracted some attention, and may, perhaps, be said to mark a turning-point in the recent history of the Catholic party.' To those who object, Mr. Hennessy might well say, 'Why smile, why envy me, why not let me enjoy that reflection?'—as Mr. Disraeli pleaded when the House, on the evening to which I have referred, met with 'loud laughter' his assurance that he stood 'not formally, but in some degree virtually, as the representative of a great number of members of Parliament;' and for the present, until in due course we refer to the noble lord, the Tory Catholic and Home Ruler, upon whom Mr. Hennessy's mantle has, in these days, fallen, and who, with more sweetness and less light than his predecessor, does his best to preserve the solitary traditions of the party, we must leave Mr. Hennessy in sole possession of the Tory Catholic representation.

I do not propose to tarry long in the far-extending plains of historical record; but to touch Mr. Hennessy's ideas at their fount, we must pass up the stream of history to the time of Charles I., when that thing, so horrid alike to Mr. Disraeli and Mr. Hennessy—when 'Puritanism' had its origin. The Catholics then fought in company with the Church of England for the Crown. 'The faith that is associated with loyalty to the Crown and an aversion to Puritanical tenets compelled them to do so.' Mr. Hennessy, like Mr. Disraeli, is full of *finesse* of this sort. You may infer, if you please, that the Catholics of that period rather liked the Protestantism of the Church of England, and that the Puritanism of the coming

Lord Protector was the only thing that their souls abhorred. We shall probably do no wrong to Mr. Hennessy if we trace his indebtedness to Mr. Disraeli for this stroke, so clever in a country where Protestantism is powerful and Puritanism is but a dim idea and a vague recollection. In 1844, the present Prime Minister (Lord Beaconsfield) ascribed the then condition of Ireland—with, as he said, ' a starving population, an absentee aristocracy, an alien Church, and the weakest Executive in the world '—' not to Protestantism but to Puritanism.' That Puritanism, as a reaction from the unprincipled rule of Charles I., and afterwards as a protest against the licentious reign of Charles II., was marked with excesses, there can be no doubt ; but Puritanism was the warden, the depositary, the very essence and power of Protestantism. The two things were, in fact, synonymous. Mr. Hennessy himself shows this in his complaint that ' the Puritan Parliament was constantly quarrelling with the King (Charles II.) on account of his attempts to protect the Catholics.' ' Protect ' is a mild word to employ in this connection. There would have been little Protestantism remaining in the Church of England, had it not been for the Puritanism of the period. Mr. Hennessy is all for the Merry Monarch and against Puritanism. He says : ' No period of English history has been so misrepresented as the reign of Charles II. ; even Catholic writers have blindly copied the Whig calumnies against the King.' We do not wonder at this ; the alliance is natural; the Stuarts always, as Macaulay says of Charles, ' liked a Papist better than a Puritan. The Protestant Church of England would certainly have passed away, had it not been for the strength of Puritanism. Mr. Disraeli, in apology for the speech from which I have last quoted, has spoken of ' the heedless rhetoric, which is the appanage of all who sit below the gangway,' but his ' historical conscience ' recognizes the sentiment of that speech as ' right.' The same high court of appeal will, no doubt, reconcile his abuse of Puritanism in times when men like Laud, the greatest of Ritualists, ruled the Church of Eng-

o

land, with his ardent support in 1874 of a Bill to 'put down Ritualism' in the Church of England. What was that period, and who was that monarch of Mr. Hennessy's eulogy—that Stuart period when the alliance of Tory and Catholic was cemented in blood?   If wasted opportunity be the truest measure of failure, then Charles II. was the worst sovereign who ever occupied the English throne.   And I believe that he fully deserves this title.   His profligacy and prodigality have been painted in that famous death-bed scene in which his sultanas muttered 'Aves,' and gamblers counted their gold, while the French Ambassador helped to smuggle the priest Huddleston to his bedside in order that he might die a Catholic.   He violated the most sacred public law, in allowing more than three years to elapse between the dissolution and convocation of a Parliament ; he encouraged fraud in the public service, and as Macaulay says of his time—

'From the nobleman who held the white staff and the great seal down to the humblest tide-waiter and gauger, what would now be called gross corruption was practised without disguise and without reproach. Titles, places, commissions, pardons, were daily sold in market overt by the great dignitaries of the realm, and every clerk in every department imitated to the best of his power the evil example.'

I do not grudge the Tory party the fullest recollection of the period in which Mr. Hennessy dates the foundation of the Catholic alliance,—an alliance the true basis of which was confirmed by the late Lord Derby—'the Rupert of debate'— when that Cavalier politician said at Liverpool in 1859—

'I am happy to say that I have for some time past perceived a growing inclination [on the part of Roman Catholics] to alienate themselves from the advanced Liberal party, and to unite themselves with those who are *their natural allies*, the Conservatives of this country.'

As Mr. Pope Hennessy is a distinguished servant of the Crown, I will not, though he has given us to understand that there was but one Tory Catholic in Parliament at the time, inquire too closely whether he is the gentleman who decorates himself upon the birthday of 'King James III. ;' but, in follow-

ing the 'natural alliance,' it is instructive to notice that he and
Mr. Disraeli are at one in repudiating the settlement of the
Crown in 1688. The present Prime Minister [Lord Beacons-
field], in 1841, 'had not the slightest doubt that those [the
Liberals, who at that time had Lord Melbourne at their head]
who have twice tampered with the succession would do so a
third time, if occasion required it ;' and Mr. Hennessy, who is
all for King James, writes of the defeat by Sarsfield of 'the
Whig usurper at Limerick.'

The 'alliance' is by both assumed to have blossomed and
borne fruit in the time of Mr. Pitt. From 'the benignant
policy of Charles I.,' Mr. Disraeli passed, in 1844, to that of
' Mr. Pitt, the last of Tory statesmen,' who proposed ' measures for the settlement of Ireland, which, had they been agreed
to by Parliament, would have saved Ireland from her present
condition ;' and Mr. Hennessy is at pains to make out that
Pitt's leaning towards the Roman Catholics of Ireland was the
result of natural friendliness and affection for their religious
system. He repudiates 'the language of O'Connell' imputing
fear as the moving power with the Tory statesman, and, to his
own mind, satisfactorily rebuts this 'language' by the demonstration, 'that it was not fear that actuated Pitt in making the
concessions which O'Connell says conciliated the Catholics and
separated them from the Republicans, is evident from the fact,
that at the very time he was maturing and carrying his plans of
Emancipation he was refusing to repeal the Test Act, that pressed
only on the Protestant Dissenters.' Now, I have no intention
of disputing the alliance between Pitt and the Catholics ; I am
much of the late Lord Derby's opinion, that Tories and Catholics
are ' natural allies ;' I am much of Mr. Disraeli's opinion, that he
and his friends are, in regard to the Roman Catholic religion, 'the
natural allies of the Irish people ;'[1] but my 'historical conscience' demands that the 'heedless rhetoric' of Mr. Disraeli's
Roman Catholic disciple shall not pass uncorrected ; and I

[1] _Speech on Ireland_, Feb. 16, 1844.

must enforce my denial of Mr. Hennessy's assertion that ' Pitt was really moved by his genuine friendship' for the Roman Catholic body.

Mr. Froude tells us that Burke's 'advice to Pitt, his advice to the world, was to save his countrymen from the revolutionary tempter by restoring to them the privileges of citizenship;' that the prelates by whom 'the Catholic Committee in Dublin had hitherto submitted to be guided,' 'terrified at the aspect of France, were inclined to the English connection ;' and further, that, in 1790, 'confident in Pitt's disposition towards them, the Catholic prelates published a letter condemning revolutionary principles.' Now what was Mr. Pitt's disposition ? Mr. Froude[1] says that, ' in the well-disposed, loyal, and pious Catholics, he was hoping to find a Conservative element to cool the revolutionary fever.' But we have the best evidence of Pitt's disposition in the letters from his colleague, Dundas, to the Lord-Lieutenant of Ireland. Dundas wrote that the Ministers wished only 'that the Protestants should decide for themselves how far a slight concession might safely be made;' and he added, in a 'most private' communication,[2] which has eluded Mr. Hennessy's eye—

'I have nothing further to say, except that I and all His Majesty's Ministers have some reason to complain of the spirit and temper which have manifested themselves among our friends in Ireland in this business. If they had made no advances to us in the matter, we should have left it to their own judgment. But all through the summer and autumn they were expressing their fears to us of a union between the Catholics and the Dissenters. They asked for our opinion, and we gave it. What motive could we have, except an anxious concern for the security of the Irish Establishment? Whether we are right or wrong, time will show ; but there is no imaginable reason why this opinion should have been received with jealousy.

'Mr. Pitt concurs in everything I have said. He and I have not a shade of difference in our opinion.'

This at once ruins Mr. Hennessy's argument as to Pitt's friendship, while it exposes the true motive of Pitt's action.

[1] *English in Ireland*, vol. iii., p. 59.
[2] *English in Ireland*, vol. iii., p. 43.

He must have been 'moved by his genuine friendship,' Mr.
Hennessy contends, because, while he was promoting Catholic
Emancipation, he was refusing to abolish the Test Act. But I
have made it clear that the sense of justice did not enter into
his calculations. He indulged in a 'flirtation'—to use the
word of the Viceroy of the time—with the Catholics, because,
as that high functionary wrote, 'it is good policy that the
Catholics should be attached to the English Government,' and
because he wished to baffle the Dissenters, from whom he had
no scruple in withholding justice, by maintaining the Test Act.

I have said that Mr. Hennessy appears as a Catholic Rip
van Winkle ; that, fortunately for his organization, to the heat
of the tropics has not been superadded the torrid atmosphere
of religious controversy, which has blown like a sirocco over
Europe. Take, for example, his innocent reference, as 'a
student of history' following 'the growth of Mr. Pitt's sentiments
respecting the Catholics,' to the application made by
that Minister 'to the Universities on the Continent for those
authoritative expositions of Catholic principles with which he
showed that his clients were the best friends of order and of
a Conservative Monarchy.' What were these 'authoritative
expositions'? Mr. Froude tells us, in the volume from which
I have already quoted—

'Pitt sought the opinion of the Universities of France and Spain on the
charges generally alleged against Catholics—that their allegiance to their
Sovereign was subordinate to their allegiance to the Pope,' etc. . . . 'The
Universities had unanimously disavowed doctrines which they declared at
once inhuman and un-Christian ; and, on the strength of the disavowal, the
British Parliament repealed the Penal Acts of William for England and
Scotland, and restored to the Catholics the free use of their chapels, and
re-admitted them to the magistracy.'

Mr. Gladstone has reminded us, in his 'Expostulation,' that a
similar proceeding was adopted in the current century, when
Catholic Emancipation in England was the question of the
day ; and he has recorded the 'declaration,' in 1826, of the
Vicars Apostolic—

'That the allegiance which Catholics hold to be due and are bound to pay to their Sovereign and to the civil authority of the State is perfect and undivided.'

He has also quoted the Bishops' 'Pastoral Address to the Clergy and Laity of the Roman Catholic Church in Ireland,' in Art. xi. of which——

'They declare, on oath, their belief that it is not an article of the Catholic faith, neither are they thereby required to believe that the Pope is infallible.'

Now, from Mr. Pope Hennessy asleep in the tropics, let us turn to the Tory Catholic in the present Parliament, and see how the opinions of the party bear upon these 'expositions.' Lord Robert Montagu, a recent convert, now occupies the place of Mr. Pope Hennessy; and this callow, candid Catholic, has, in reply to Mr. Gladstone, expounded the Tory Catholic creed, both political and religious.[1] 'We,' says the Tory Catholic party of the present, 'owe the strictest allegiance to the Queen, and yield to no subject of her realms in loyalty ; we also owe the same to the Pope ; because the one power is subordinate to the other, just as the end of the State is subordinate to the end of the Church, and as the body is subordinate to the soul ;'——'thus the civil society which has the care of one end is subordinate to the society which looks after the other end ; '——' and so the State is subordinate to the Church.' 'Kings must be subordinate to the Sovereign Pontiff,' says the Tory Catholic of this day, and 'in all questions of disputed jurisdiction between Church and State, the head of the Church must overrule the government of the State ;' and it is 'not,' as Mr. Gladstone thinks, 'an "exorbitant claim," but most rational ; nay, a necessity wherever there is not to be a chaos,' that the principles of the Papal Church should recognise in the Pontiff 'the right to determine the province of his own rights.'

No doubt Mr. Hennessy thinks the thing was better done in

---

[1] *Expostulation in Extremis.* By Lord Robert Montagu, M.P. 1874.

his time, and perhaps it is a pity that he took to practising instead of preaching the art of government. But much has happened since he quitted Parliament, and Lord Robert Montagu is, I can assure Mr. Hennessy, quite in the fashion of the day. Lord Robert would deride, if he were aware of it, the opinion of the Universities which reported to Mr. Pitt. He tells us that our 'vaunt and glory in England is' that we have a '*limited* monarchy,' and he implies that the Pope is the proper limiting power. He says a king 'cannot be prevented from falling into the practice of tyranny, except he is regarded as subordinate to a superior authority. . . . Such a Supreme Ruler has been provided by our Lord. He is the ruler of the Universal Commonwealth—of the Catholic Church.' Yet something more has happened since the former Tory Catholic party in Parliament accepted a Colonial Governorship. This king of kings—this infirm and aged man who had far less acquaintance with the world (of which he beheld only a few leagues) than the Seyyid or the Shah—this Pope became infallible. Against that assumption of all Catholic authority, the illustrious statesman who was lately Prime Minister [Mr. Gladstone] issued an eloquent and powerful 'Expostulation,' and the line of our inquiry now leads us to consider how are the relations of the two great political parties with the Catholics affected by the new definition of this dogma.

The cardinal principle of Liberal policy is that the people are the supreme ultimate authority of a State ; and therefore Liberals are the natural allies of those who seek to be relieved from any questionable disability which prevents their participation in this power. The Liberal political creed teaches that civilization is concurrent, if not synonymous, with the extension and the proper exercise of civil rights ; and instead of declaring with Mr. Disraeli,[1] 'If government is not divine, it is nothing,' a Liberal is disposed to say : 'If government is not human, it is nothing.' It is because Lord Beaconsfield

[1] *Speech on the Irish Church*, April 3, 1868.

believes that[1] 'an intelligent age will never discard the divine right of government,' that he is a 'natural ally' of Roman Catholics. The Catholic power has been by the Vatican Decrees constituted an absolutism, a despotism, so changed in character that even Liberal Catholics cannot bend the knee to its yoke; how much, then, is it altered in the eyes of Liberal politicians who are not Catholics? Mr. Hennessy is not yet awake to all this, and I strongly recommend him to study the recent writings of the most acute of the princes of his Church—of that eminent prelate whose policy he has had the presumption to condemn, though the name of Cardinal Manning is never mentioned in his paper. No one has laboured with more skill or with greater success than Cardinal Manning to prove that the Vatican Decrees have not altered the status of the Papacy. But he has failed, because he cannot deny the existence of a vast body of opinion in his Church, which formerly recognised a different authority in the Pope from that which his Holiness now claims. Contesting the view of his 'brother,' Mgr. Maret, expressed in 'Du Conseil Général et la Paix Religieuse,' that 'no judgments are certainly *ex cathedrâ* except when the Pontiff acts with the concurrence of the Bishops,' Cardinal Manning wrote,[2] 'The Ultramontane opinion is simply this, that the Pontifi's teaching *ex cathedrâ* in faith or morals is infallible. In this there are no shades or moderation. It is simply ay or no.'

This is the Ultramontane faith, which except a man believe, he cannot partake in the most sacred offices of the Roman Catholic Church. But it was not always so, and I hold Cardinal Manning to have admitted this, indirectly in his laboured arguments against 'the Gallican idea,' and directly in his Pastoral Letter of a recent year (1875), in which he says: 'We are now told that the civil powers of the world can hold no relations with a Pope who is infallible. No account is, however,

---

[1] *Speech on the Irish Church*, April 3, 1868.
[2] *Postscript to Pastoral of* 1869.

given of the fact that the civil powers have hitherto been in concord and amity for a thousand years with an infallible Church.' There is just the difference ; the justification of Mr. Gladstone's ' Expostulation.' The government of the Church has, by a revolution, been changed into the government of the Pope. Perhaps we may measure the difference most accurately by regarding the conduct of Pitt in 1791, and of the House of Lords Committee in 1825, and by reflecting how absurd it would appear, were Lord Beaconsfield to address inquiries to the Universities of France and Spain, or to interrogate Irish prelates for ' authoritative expositions ' of the Vatican policy. The response of the Universities, like that of Bishop Doyle, was in flat contradiction to the Ultramontane doctrine. The Pope of our day is infallible, and he dared to trample on the primary duty of the German or any other State—that of compelling obedience to its laws—in publicly declaring—

' To all whom it may concern, as also to the whole Catholic world, that those [Falck] laws are null and void, as being utterly opposed to the Divine Constitution of the Church. For it is not the powerful of this world that the Lord has placed over the Bishops of the Church, in all that concerns His holy ministry, but St. Peter, to whom He entrusted not only His lambs, but also His sheep, to feed.' [1]

No Liberal can be in ' natural alliance ' with a power making invasive claims of this sort. It would be the reduction of infallibility to absurdity for the Pope to pretend that the German Government, by imprisoning a bishop for contumacy against laws of the State, deprives him of the spiritual quality, whatever that may be, of episcopacy. The punishment, the severity of which I deplore, relates to the misuse, in regard to the law of the State, of functions and authority which he exercises from and in the buildings of the State. The supremacy of the civil power over any particular religious denomination in all that affects the law, the property, or any disposition of the income, of the State, is, as I have said in other words, the cardinal

---

[1] *Encyclical Letter to Archbishops and Bishops of Prussia*, Feb., 1875.

principle of Liberalism; and, inasmuch as Vaticanism invades
this principle in the most uncompromising manner, there can
be no 'natural alliance' of Catholics with the Liberal party.
There can be fortuitous alliance, as there has been, but every
step by which the Catholic, in a State like ours, advances to
religious liberty and equality, diminishes the possible duration
of a common policy with the Liberal party.   Mr. Hennessy's
contention is that it has been a mistaken course for the Catholics
ever to co-operate with the Liberal party.   They might, he
argues, have trusted for enfranchisement to the friendship or
self-interest of the Tory party, which would have sought them
as allies against Radicalism.   With regard to religious equality,
he indicates that in helping the Liberal party to convert the
remainder of the Irish Church property to secular uses, they
lost, for the time, at least, their chance of furthering the more
profitable Tory policy of concurrent endowment, and Mr.
Hennessy is evidently of opinion that, if the Catholics will
only return and remain faithful to their 'natural alliance,'
something of this sort may yet be theirs.   He blames the
Irish Catholic policy which helped to drive 'the Prelates of
the Anglican Church from the House of Lords;' he extols the
Tory support of the measure which, in 1774, secured tithes to
the Roman Catholic clergy of Canada; he lauds Charles II.,
but has no words of praise for George III., who 'refused to
allow Pitt to complete emancipation and to establish concurrent
endowment' in Ireland.

The tactics of the Tories will be to strengthen the 'natural
alliance,' and to sever the Catholics from the Liberal party by
dangling before their eyes the possibility of a reversion to this
policy.   The present Premier [Lord Beaconsfield] in 1844
commended Pitt's policy, and affirmed that it would have
'settled the Church Question;' in 1868 he vindicated the
proposal to grant a charter to a Roman Catholic University,
in affirming that 'in Ireland the wise policy is to create and
not to destroy, and to strengthen Protestant institutions by

being just to the Roman Catholics.'[1] In the same speech he
suggested, as superior to Mr. Gladstone's policy, the introduction of ' measures which would have elevated the status of the
unendowed clergy of Ireland, and so softened and terminated
those feelings of inequality.' He even argued that ' the principle of property would be vindicated in a much higher degree
by the principle of restitution [of Church property to Roman
Catholics], and so it might be contended that there was no
violation of property at all.' This, however, we—and the
Catholics—must remember was said in his place as Prime
Minister *before* the crushing defeat of the Conservative party
in the election which carried Mr. Gladstone to power in 1868.
After that event we find the policy of Pitt, of Mr. Hennessy,
and, I believe, of Mr. Disraeli also, placed quite in the back-
ground. The people of the United Kingdom, and especially
the Conservative borough-voters had in many places fought
to the cry of ' No Popery ! '

At this point, then, we shall do well to inquire what is the
strength, and what the weakness, of the undoubted ' natural
alliance ' between the Tory party and the Catholics. The
strength is the innate Conservatism of the two bodies, a
strength which brings them into close and continual alliance
in all the Catholic States of the world ; the weakness lies in
the fact that two eminently Conservative classes—the shopkeepers and farmers of England and Scotland—are also the
most obstinately Protestant. The alliance is therefore ' natural '
rather than ' kindly.' We have seen Lord North in 1774
trying to strengthen himself against the Liberal policy by
endowing the Roman Catholic clergy of Canada ; Pitt pur-
suing the same idea, and for the same motives, in 1791 ; and
Disraeli in 1844 and 1868 labouring to detach the Catholics
from the Liberal party by suggesting concurrent endowment as
preferable to religious equality. The ' natural alliance ' always
endures ; the co-operation or the kindliness between English

---

[1] Speech on Irish Church, April 3, 1868.

Conservatives and Catholics depends upon whether the Catholic demand menaces any institution dear to the superior strength of Protestant ascendancy in the Conservative party. Lately the two parties found a wide common ground of action, and in several English boroughs the Roman Catholics in 1874 gave decisive aid to Conservative candidates because of their concurrence upon the great question of education. Mr. Hennessy points with glee to the occasion when—

'The powerful party of the Church of England, and the small but compact party of Catholics in England, made an open alliance on the 8th April, 1870, in St. James's Hall, when the Duke of Norfolk and the Marquis of Salisbury, the Duke of Northumberland and the Chairman of the Catholic School Committee, Lord Sandon, Mr. Beresford Hope, and a crowded meeting of the leaders of both Churches, assembled in support of religious education. They voted together at the Parliamentary elections in 1874, and they can now be seen every week assisting each other most cordially at the School Boards.'

There they sit, and there they will continue in ' natural alliance.' In Ireland, the alliance will probably be strengthened by the suggestion of concurrent endowment rather than secularisation, when the surplus property of the Irish Church comes to be dealt with. There is perhaps no rock ahead in the way of the alliance in Ireland, except the great stumbling-block of Home Rule. Mr. Hennessy, with the political agility natural to one who has quitted the arena of politics for more healthy intercourse with barbarous people, jumps lightly over it, and writes of Mr. Butt as the leader of the ' Irish Catholic party.' It is only a Catholic party in so far as Home Rule would give ascendancy to the Catholics in an Irish Parliament, and it would be in alliance with the Liberal party if ever that party should promote a policy of decentralization in the direction of Home Rule.

It remains only to consider how the great question of Disestablishment would affect the ' natural alliance ' of Tories and Catholics in this island. But for this question, the alliance would certainly endure and grow stronger every day : will it last when the superior status of the Church of England is

seriously menaced—when the disendowment of Romanizing
clergy is the demand of angry Churchmen, when religious
equality is the cry of the Nonconformist, and loudest perhaps
of those Dissenters who, for respectability's sake, and to be all
things to all men, have feigned acquiescence in the existence
of the Establishment? The Conservative party, prizing the
Establishment infinitely above the Catholic alliance, would
then repeat with approval the nonsense which Mr. Disraeli
uttered in 1868, when he defined 'religious equality' as 'that
state of things where a man has complete and perfect enjoyment of his religion, and can uphold and vindicate his
religious privileges in the courts of law.' Yet, perhaps, even
more audacious was his statement on the same occasion that
the Dissenter 'considers himself to be on perfectly equal
terms' with the members of the Establishment. But what
would the Roman Catholic say? Mr. Hennessy would have
him stand by the Church of England, opposing Disestablishment and Disendowment, both or either, as anti-Catholic
policy. He censures the action of the Irish Catholics in 1868;
he declares that the agitation which preceded the passing of
the Irish Church Act 'was not for a Catholic object;' and we
all remember Mr. Gladstone's quotation from the *Osservatore
Romano*, of which Mr. Hennessy speaks as 'the authoritative
Papal organ,' showing that the Pope preferred concurrent
endowment. It is for this that I believe Catholics, both in
England and Ireland, will intrigue and contend, and the
'natural alliance' will lead some at least of the Tory leaders
to look with increasing kindness on the 'levelling up' policy.
Mr. Hennessy reproves Cardinal Manning, among 'the leading
Catholic prelates in England,' for urging Catholic voters to
support Mr. Gladstone as a 'great Liberal statesman' after
'his public announcement that Rome disapproved of his Irish
Church scheme;' and his Eminence has himself denounced
'the desecration of the civil power by the rejection of the
Church,' and 'the impossible theory of a free Church in a free

State.[1]   But then this applies to his own Church, and I cannot affirm that Cardinal Manning would object to Disestablishment if he were assured that would give the Catholics a prospect of concurrent endowment.   The Disestablishment and Dis-endowment of the Irish Protestant Episcopal Church are matters of history, and we are looking to the policy of the future.   Those events ended one of the common aims which united Liberals and Catholics.   The Liberal party and the Catholics are now divorced ; whether they will come together again is very doubtful ; it depends upon the attitude of the Liberal party towards the question of Home Rule in Ireland, and upon the attitude of the Catholics with reference to the policy of Disestablishment in this island.

[1] ' Cæsarism and Ultramontanism,' 1873.

X.

THE RAILWAYS AND THE STATE.

I VENTURE to predict that the Railways of Ireland will be purchased by the State, and that the Railways of England and Scotland will follow the same destiny. It is not unlikely that, in this movement, as in others of no less magnitude, Ireland, from her peculiar circumstances, will lead Great Britain, as she did to the adoption of Catholic Emancipation and of Free Trade. It was in obedience to the demands of Ireland that Mr. Gladstone adopted a policy of Religious Equality which will in due time overspread the United Kingdom, and which has already been so far adopted by both parties in the State that proposals for sectarian endowment are not well received in Parliament, and when new bishops are made there is no attempt to add to the number of 'spiritual' peers. And it was to appease the long-existing warfare of landlord and tenant in Ireland that the same great Minister introduced a Bill for the establishment of tenant right upon the firmest basis, the enactment of which was followed by a revolt of the farmers in Scotland, and by the introduction to the English Parliament of Tenant Right Bills for accomplishing the same object.

On the 29th April, 1873, the House of Commons, on the motion of Lord Claud Hamilton, discussed the purchase of the Irish Railways, and the proposition was negatived by a very large majority. The Prime Minister (Mr. Gladstone), the Chancellor of the Exchequer (Mr. Lowe), the Conservative ex-

Secretary for Ireland (Colonel Wilson-Patten), all spoke against the motion, which, upon a division, was defeated by a majority of 132, the 82 members who voted or paired 'Aye' being, with the exception of nine, Irish members. Yet it is partly upon this division that I found the prediction with which I started. I have not the slightest doubt, from what I have since heard, that the Irish members upon that occasion saw more in Mr. Gladstone's speech than was by himself intended. It is natural with men of the temperament of Mr. Gladstone, when placed in similar circumstances, to speak with a somewhat unreal vehemence, an effort directed to influence their own minds as well as to modify the views of their hearers. I believe Mr. Gladstone, in spite of his speech of April 29th, 1873, to be not unfavourable to the purchase of Railways by the State; I believe him to have been very much more of that opinion at the moment when he was thought to have crushed the expectations of the Irish people, than when he suggested, as I presume he did suggest, the inquiries of Captain Tyler, or than when he permitted Lord Hartington—his subordinate and Chief Secretary for Ireland—to make in 1872 a speech of which the *Times* said that it 'encouraged the wildest hopes in Ireland,' and which the same journal attributed to Lord Hartington's want of skill 'in the management of phrases committing himself to nothing, because their meaning is lost in a haze of words.' Mr. Gladstone is a master of that species of phraseology, yet he did not, Jove-like, throw, as he might easily have done, a cloud over the clear words of the Irish Secretary. But later, in 1873, in the most precise language, he discarded the proposal, and far from showing a readiness to deal with the question of purchase, he made propositions in support of the present system of private ownership. I wish it to be understood that I know nothing directly of the mind of Mr. Gladstone in the matter; but this I know, that throughout his career he has been faithful to the principle that free locomotion is one of the concerns of Government; that in public and in private he has always manifested the closest, deepest interest in all that would promote the most easy and economical circulation within the United Kingdom. As a young legislator, he interested himself in passing the Act of 1844, which gave the Government power to purchase Railways under certain circumstances ; as a railway shareholder, he bade his directors 'stick to the democracy,' a policy which they have not followed, and I believe that as a Minister in the plenitude of power, he thought in the year 1872 of taking the Irish Railways. Perhaps he was afterwards advised that the experiment in Ireland would not be successful, and that it need not be dissociated from a similar project in Great Britain.

I cannot doubt that Mr. Gladstone is very strongly impressed by the unanimity of the Irish people in this matter. He resists the Home Rule movement in Ireland because he is confident that separation would not be for the benefit of the sister island. But neither he nor any honest man can withstand a unanimous demand from the Irish people referring to a matter of strictly internal concern, not inimical to general laws, and of which they profess themselves willing to bear the financial hazard. Mr. Gladstone cannot have even a shadow of doubt that if Ireland were ruled by a native Parliament, a Bill for the purchase of the Railways would become law in the first Session of that body, and this being so, his conscience would not exonerate him in permanently withstanding the demand of the Irish people for such a transaction. Such a veto would be a striking addition to that oppressive policy recorded in the past history of Ireland, of which no one has spoken with more indignant abhorrence, and would vastly strengthen if it did not entirely justify the 'Nationalist' demands of the Home Rule party. We who oppose, or who are passive in regard to Home Rule, must of course satisfy ourselves upon one point ; we must be sure that the internal affairs of Ireland do not suffer, but are rather benefited by the Union ; and if Irishmen are unanimous upon any measure of

P

strictly local character, if they are moreover prepared to bear
its burdens ; and if we cannot reasonably allege that its enactment would be prejudicial to the general government, we are
bound to remember that our functions are in strict justice and
honour limited merely to considering whether it fulfils these
conditions, and whether it is an act which in the best judgment
of the Irish people would be undertaken if Great Britain did
not practically—just as much as when Poyning's Law was in
force—exercise a veto upon the Bills of Irish members. I
believe that this sense of duty and justice does animate
Mr. Gladstone, and I have a strong conviction that the
contrast between the speech of the Irish Secretary (Lord
Hartington) in 1872, and that of the Prime Minister (Mr.
Gladstone) in 1873, is to be ascribed to the great advance
which in that interval the question of the purchase of the
Railways by the State made in England, and to the conviction
entertained by the most judicious promoters of that undertaking that it would be inexpedient, and would not tend to
promote the purchase in Great Britain, if experiment were
made where it would be least profitable—in Ireland.

We hear a great deal of nonsense talked about the functions
of government, and some people seem to imagine that we are
retrograding from an ideal standard. I entertain a quite opposite opinion. I think that, in spite of much ignorance and of
much interested opposition, we are arriving at a truer knowledge than has ever yet been practised of the proper domain
of government. The earliest idea of government was the
infallibility of some wholly personal will, and still the Sultan or
the Shah could venture from mere caprice to put a barber or a
mule-driver at the head of affairs in their respective States ;
then it was held that the State should possess a monopoly of
religious truth, a function which has met with successful resistance, and which, though its shadow survives in the institutions
of several States, is practically abolished in Europe. It has
been held to be a function of government to secure in a

population the distinction of certain classes by privilege, and this too seems to be fading away. · But it has never been doubted by those minds which are the beacons of progress, and popular experience has only served to strengthen the conviction, that it is a function of government to assert by the authority of law, the equality, in regard to life and property, of the weak with the strong ; it has never been doubted that it is the duty ᷑ of Government to secure for the people the means of inter-communication.

When Railways were established it was assumed that they would operate as auxiliaries to the traffic upon the turnpike roads ; it was the idea of some that none but 'carriage people' would use the new mode of travelling, and that each person would have his own vehicle upon the Railway, his private carriage being also adapted to the road.   It was never dreamt that Railways would become the highways of the country in the sense which we see accomplished.   Who, except some eccentric tourist on wheels, or one of some dozen fanatical believers in the good old days of posting, or one of a few commercial travellers with a taste for horseflesh, now travels over a hundred miles of highroad in England ?   The thing is quite abolished.   Practically the only means of communication between the great towns are the Railways ; and the Government, from the earliest con-struction to the very recent enactment of the Railways and Canals Traffic Act, has by a mass of legislation admitted and accepted the function of securing for the people the best facili-ties for intercommunication upon these iron roads.   That this is a proper function of Government cannot be questioned ; our internal traffic being virtually limited to the existing Railways, Government is bound to take care, as one of the most vital necessities of the State, not only that the best means of inter-communication are afforded, but that these could not be given with greater advantage to the public.

There is no exit from this position.   The country between London and Manchester, or between Dublin and Belfast, might

as well be infested with brigands, or even occupied by hostile
armies, as the Railways remain in the power of those who,
through bad management or conflicting interests, impede or
forbid traffic.   One-half the errors in regard to progress which
are made by Governments, arise from a mistaken estimate of
the losses consequent upon bad laws or misgovernment.   All
good men are averse from war, but few understand that the
waste and ruin of war are inconsiderable in comparison with
the waste and the ruin which is perpetrated in times of peace by
error and ignorance.   How trifling, for example, is the loss of life
in battle compared with that which is due to neglect of sanitary
laws !   If Lord Derby is right, and I firmly believe he is correct
in saying that the agricultural produce of the country might be
doubled, and if I am right in assuming that our laws and customs relating to the inheritance, the transfer, the settlement,
and the entail of land, form the chief material obstacle to this
increase, then clearly, from an economic point of view, the
ravaging of this country for twelve months by 100,000 Germans
would be a preferable evil to the continuance of these laws and
customs.   If, putting ourselves in the position of Spain, those
were *our* Railways which were impeded by attacks of robber
bands, nobody would question that it was a function of Government to keep the Railways open, and, at any cost to the State,
to attack and disperse those who hindered the traffic of the
country.   And can it be denied that this duty does pertain to
the civil power in the State when the obstructions are caused
by interests which the civil power could satisfy and harmonise ?
The only question would be whether, in the exercise of this
authority, there would be any improper invasion of the rights
of citizens, and whether such action would result in permanent
benefit to the community.

Before proceeding to discuss some of the evils of the present
Railway system, it would be well to dismiss one fallacy which
is found alike in the arguments of those who favour and those
who are adverse to purchase by the State.   Mr. Martin, an

intelligent advocate of purchase, apparently supposes it is a
'logically true' argument which asserts that if the State takes
the Railways it must also 'own and manage the cabs and
omnibuses' as well as 'the harbours and lines of steamers.'
The Statistical Society seem to have accepted this argument,
which, it appears to me, is very incorrect. If the State take
the Railways it is because the Railways exist and can only
be worked as a monopoly. There is no analogy whatever
between the cabs and omnibuses, the steamers and the Railways. There is no suggestion of an absolute monopoly of
wheel traffic in the streets; still less can there be a monopoly
of service at sea. It by no means follows logically that if the
State take the Railways it should therefore take the cabs and
omnibuses. If there were but one track in the sea from Liverpool to New York, in which the ships of but one company
were allowed to proceed, then only would the 'logical' comparison be established. But there are as many tracks in the
sea as there are ships; there are as many courses in the streets
as there are cabs and omnibuses; there is no logical connection whatever between arguments relating to a road which is
monopolised and a road which is free not only to all comers
but to every description of conveyance. The same error was
apparent in the very illogical speech which Mr. Goldsmid made
against the proposal put forward by Lord Claud Hamilton.
He actually appeared to suppose that the transfer of the Railways was not to be thought of because some of the Railway
companies possessed hotels, some docks, others steamboats, and
so on. Whoever possesses the North-Western Railway has a
monopoly of the most direct and indispensable route between
the two chief centres of the English population in Middlesex
and in Lancashire. Monopolies are invariably, and obviously
must be, to some extent controlled by the Government, but
the question as to dealing with the railway monopoly is not in
the least complicated by the fact that this or that Railway has
accessories which form no part of any monopoly. The Govern-

ment would have no greater difficulty in leasing the Great
Western Hotel than they have in regard to receiving the
ground-rent of the Reform Club; and with reference to the
delivery of goods by cart, or of the conveyance of passengers
and goods by sea, while it is likely that these things would be
best performed by a service in close connection with the Railways, this is by no means a necessary consequence, and in
neither case could there be, as upon the Railway, a monopoly
of transit or delivery.

The Railways of this country were formed in disunion, and
their formation was burdened by the ignorance and the disgraceful rapacity of the landowning and the governing class
which has benefited so enormously by their construction. The
Railway history of England would show that Norman barons
could defeat a popular right in the first half of the nineteenth
century almost as easily as in the twelfth. In no country have
I seen personal as opposed to public rights carried with so
high a hand as in England. One of the ancient highways of
the country passed before the house of a noble marquis whose
deer-park stretched wide and far in the rear of his mansion.
A town of ancient date and busy population stood by the wayside nestled under the shadow of the great house. Powerful
as ever Norman baron was over the obsequious county, this
nobleman obtained permission to cut off the stream of life—
to turn the highway before it entered the town, and condemned travellers by that road for all time to make a *détour* of
a mile round the outskirts of his park. I remember when in
Russia I thought it very cruel that the letter of a Polish
soldier addressed to his mother should be detained because it
was not addressed in the official Sclavonic language. But I
have met with something of the same sort in England. It is
not many years since a noble Postmaster-General, having resolved that it was an impertinence on the part of an eminently
respectable population to call their new town by a name
which formed a part of his title, decreed that all letters so

addressed should be delayed in delivery by an unnecessary circuit. The same interest worked in the same direction—the overwhelming power of the landed interest has led in this country to an excess of cost in the construction of Railways which really forms a considerable part of the difficulty in regard to purchase. In another paper contained in this volume (Free Trade in Land), I have estimated this excess at £100,000,000, upon the basis of a calculation made by a very eminent authority, the late Mr. Joseph Locke, C.E. A certain share of this excessive cost, amounting to about 20 per cent., has been occasioned by the rivalry of competing schemes. If it had not been for this needless cost, partly the result of disunion, railway shareholders would have been at present receiving a very handsome return for their investment. It is, I am disposed to think, a very moderate estimate which places this wasteful, inequitable, and unnecessary expenditure in the construction of our Railways, at £6,000 a mile. Even with such a deduction, the cost would appear vastly in excess of that of any continental system.

Official returns show that the average cost of construction in France has been £25,000 per mile against £39,000 in England ; of this excess of £13,000 per mile, I think £6,000 at least is fairly chargeable to the difference of our system. This, upon 13,000 miles of railway, would represent a total loss of £78,000,000. But this does not represent the measure of the defective economy of our system, though it is more than one-sixth of the total sum expended in the construction of railways in the United Kingdom. Of this defective economy, Bradshaw's Railway Map is the best illustration that I know of. The main highways of the kingdom, may be shown to have been curved this way and that way in deference to the opposition of some short-sighted but powerful landowner. It is of course evident that all highway improvements are fraught with pecuniary benefit to the property to which they give approach. Instead of receiving large sums by way of compensation, it would have been a very reasonable contribution on the part of the great majority of landowners had they given the land required for the Railways. I know no more signal example of how much greater is the advantage of the property owners than that of the constructors of such improvements than the results of the temporary abolition of the Southwark Bridge penny toll. The number of foot-passengers over Southwark Bridge paying a penny toll was 257,616 during six months. By way of experiment the toll was taken off, and though it might be supposed that the public would not, without years of habit, regard this as a free bridge, yet the number of foot passengers rose during the six months of freedom from toll to 2,359,312. There is a moral in this fact applicable to Railway companies and Railway fares.

Comparison is often made with the Railways of Belgium, and it is assumed that rates which are profitable in that State would, with the same traffic, produce similar results in England. This is, of course, incorrect, for while the average cost per mile of the Belgian lines has been about £14,000, the average expenditure per mile of railway in the United Kingdom on the 31st December, 1871, was no less than £35,943. The causes of this excessive cost are not solely due to our extravagant methods of conveyance and transfer of land, or to the greater value of the soil, of labour, and materials in England. It must not be forgotten that for the most part the north of Europe is a level plain, while in England the country is very uneven and difficult. Any argument drawn from the Belgian system must be taken for no more than it is worth. If our Railways had been constructed at the same nominal cost as those of Belgium, a net income of £10,500,000 would suffice to pay a dividend of 5 per cent. upon the total capital : but in 1871 a net profit in the United Kingdom of £24,475,512 was not sufficient to pay more than 4·68 per cent. upon our Railway capital, then amounting to £552,682,107. This vast sum is the *nominal* cost of the

Railways of the United Kingdom. But it would be a great mistake to suppose that any such sum has ever been received by the companies from the stock and shareholders. We have no means of ascertaining with precision what proportion of the stocks and loans and nominal values of shares which make this gigantic total has been actually paid, but there have been many issues greatly below par, and the cost of construction of many lines has been paid for in stock subsequently put upon the market at rates which, though yielding large profits to contractors, were greatly beneath par value. The issue by the Metropolitan District Railway Company of £1,500,000 of Preference Stock at £68, is an instance of the former, while the history of the London, Chatham, and Dover Railway would supply striking examples of the latter. The profits upon this capital are very unequal. In 1871—the year of greatest prosperity, unblemished by the rising price of coal and labour, which neutralised the increase of traffic in 1872—no interest whatever was paid upon 8,139,701 of Preference Stock, and of the £230,250,152 of Ordinary Stock 31½ millions received no dividends whatever. Of the remaining Ordinary Stock—

4½ millions	received dividends of less than 1 per cent.							
10½	„	„	„	from 1 to a fraction under 2 per cent.				
18	„	„	„	„ 2 to nearly 3 per cent.				
8¼	„	„	„	„ 3	„	4 per cent.		
26	„	„	„	„ 4	„	5	„	
30	„	„	„	„ 5	„	6	„	
9½	„	„	„	„ 6	„	7	„	
66	„	„	„	„ 7	„	8	„	
2	„	„	„	„ 8	„	9	„	
17½	„	„	„	„ 9	„	10	„	
2	„	„	„	„ 10	„	11	„	
½ million	„	„	„ 11	„	12	„		
3 millions	„	„	„ 12	„	13	„		
¼ million	„	„	of 13 per cent.					
198								

The profits of Railways are not very large. The Railways Act which was passed in 1844 provided that the

Ordinary Stocks of Railways constructed after the passing of that measure, could be purchased in 1866 and subsequently at twenty-five years' purchase, the price being definitely fixed only in the case of those lines which should have paid a dividend of 10 per cent. for three years ; if they were paying less than that, the price was to be settled by arbitration. At the time of the passing of the Act (1844), it seemed that the profits of Railways would in thirty years become enormous. In a paper read by Mr. Martin before the Statistical Society, in 1873, he quoted the following list of prices, at which the shares mentioned were selling in the autumn of 1845 :—

	Paid.	Price per Share.
	£	£
Great North of England . .	100	217
Grand Junction	100	242
Liverpool and Manchester . .	100	217
London and Birmingham . .	100	222
London and Croydon . . .	13	25
Manchester and Leeds . .	76	215
Manchester and Birmingham .	40	90
North Union	100	225
Stockton and Darlington . .	100	275

This was at a time when Railways existed in comparative isolation, before the Railway war broke out in which the waste of treasure was probably equal to that incurred in the Crimean struggle against Russia.   But now the age of conflict has, we may say, passed, and for years a process of consolidation has been going on.   Not a single one of the companies named in the above table has now a separate existence, and these are only nine among hundreds which are no longer to be found in the lists of the Stock Exchange.   The railway history of the past thirty years is, as the late Mr. Graves said, ' but one long list of absorptions and amalgamations.'   Some thirty of the defunct organisms have passed into the mighty system of the London and North-Western Railway; the Lancashire and Yorkshire Railway is made up of five or six extinct companies, and upwards of three hundred and fifty companies have been reduced to twenty-eight. Sated with the spoils of war, the survivors of the Railway men of 1846 have become wealthy proprietors and directors, and the ground being for the most part occupied, they have turned their arms against the public instead of against each other. Amalgamation is only part of the policy which has been pursued; the more interesting matter for the people has been the agreement as to rates which the Railways have generally established for their mutual benefit. But this latter is a subject which we shall pursue at a later stage of the argument. Here we are concerned with amalgamation and the progress it has made and is making towards that practical monopoly which Railway managers tell us to fear if it should pass into our own hands.

When, in 1871, two of the largest Railways in this country stood ready to knock at the doors of Parliament with a request to be united, the public took alarm, forbade the banns, and a *conseil de famille,* in the shape of Lords and Commons, was assembled to consider whether in this union of the London and North-Western and the Lancashire and Yorkshire Railways might not be discerned the dreadful consummation of monopoly. The mileage of the two is almost equal to that of all the Railways of Ireland; their united capital is almost thrice that of all the Irish Railways; they connect the two great centres of population in England, and, with the Caledonian Railway, embrace the chief seats of trade in the island. What is that of which Parliament was fearful? These Railroads are governed by sagacious men; they know that amalgamation will produce great economies. The North-Western was very much afraid of losing the hand of the Lancashire Railway, which the Midland would have been very ready to seize. And why? Because, Acts of Parliament notwithstanding, Railway companies have within the admitted limits of their rates power to turn the trade

of the country this way and that way at pleasure.   Fearful of
the spectre of monopoly, the Joint Committee assembled, and
what was the panacea offered by the most experienced witnesses ?   Sir Edward Watkin bade the nation trust to him ; he
would deliver us from the giant.   Let amalgamation go on, but
preserve competition ; this was the burden of Sir Edward's
counsel.   And how were we to preserve this competition ?   Sir
Edward no doubt means, if he gets the opportunity, to show
us.   He is Chairman of the South-Eastern Railway Company,
Chairman of the Metropolitan Railway Company, and he occupies the same position with regard to the Manchester, Sheffield,
and Lincolnshire Company.   He probably has a notion that
an alliance of the third company with the Midland or the Great
Northern would keep the giant North-Western in order.   He has
himself—perhaps in the interest of the South-Eastern Railway
—been doing battle against monopoly.   He knows what is the
effect of monopoly by comparing the price of coal consumed
by the Manchester and Sheffield Company with the cost of
that used by the South-Eastern Railway.   He has, I believe,
been fighting for years to get cheaper coal-rates for his southern
companies, and perhaps he has an idea that with the help
of the Bridgewater Canal, competition throughout the North-
Western system may be maintained.   Competition has been
the sheet-anchor of the people ; some of them remember when
mad competition gave a ticket to Manchester and back for a
few shillings ; but now they believe they see competition passing away into amalgamation.   Their ' Committees and Commissioners,' says the Report of the Joint Select Committee of
1871, ' have for the last thirty years clung to one form of competition after another ; but it has nevertheless become more
and more evident that competition must fail to do for Railways
what it does for ordinary trade, and that no means have yet
been devised by which competition can be permanently maintained.'   The melancholy tone of this Report must be very
depressing to those who have put their faith in the upholding

of competition. In their despair, the Committee, however, recommended the constitution of a Board. Baffled on land, they look to the water, and the first duty relegated to the Board is that of preserving 'the competition which now exists by sea,' where, as we have seen, monopoly is obviously most difficult if not impossible. Further, this Board is 'to give such support as is practicable to competition by canal;' it is to let the public know all about everything; and it is 'to enforce the harmonious working and development of the present Railway and canal systems, so as to produce from them, in the interests of the public and at the same time of the shareholders, the greatest possible amount of profitable work which they are capable of doing.' This was the last utterance of the dying and irresolute Committee, and their Board has been set up. I venture to say that no three men in the country expected less in the way of remedy against the wrong of monopoly, from the action of this tribunal, than the thoroughbred official, the clever railway chairman, and the intelligent lawyer of whom it was composed. What could they do? Their chief business has been to smooth the way of amalgamation, to help the Railway companies to depart farther and farther from the old, vain, blundering ideal of companies fighting with each other for the benefit of the public, whose real want is economy of management and cheap rates of transit for their persons and their goods. I will not deny that the Board has been of some use in this matter. There are still in being a number of small companies and some great ones which it is well should pass out of separate existence. Absorption is their best, their natural and inevitable destiny; and perhaps the companies, with the help of the Railway Commissioners, will manage this business as well among themselves, and with less waste of money, than if the State were the purchaser in so many separate cases.

But what is the virtue in competition which makes it the dear hope of Parliament? It is all very well for Sir Edward Watkin to like competition; but why should the public like it?

What is the meaning of it to them?—what has always been its signification? Waste, of course, and nothing but waste. Are we to rejoice because by virtue of this worn-out idol, two express trains are started, one from Euston Square, and another from King's Cross, at the same hour, both bound for Manchester, neither taking up more than twenty passengers, and neither stopping at more than two or three stations on the road. This is competition, to which, say the Lords and Commons, we have long clung, and which they report is now slipping from our grasp. Are we to feel happy and reassured, to thank Sir Edward Watkin, and be quiet and contented, because, more wasteful still than the express trains at which we have been looking, there are started every day, at the same hour, from Charing Cross and Victoria, continental trains, in close agreement as to fares,—the highest at which the two Companies think the public will consent to travel,—which rush to Dover; the two trains having no more passengers than could be conveyed in one? This is competition, and its exposition accounts for high fares and low dividends. The Board, influenced, no doubt, by such views as those which Sir Edward Watkin has put forth, may try to realize the old ideal by a masterly combination of Railways; and perhaps competition may yet contrive to prevent the southern railways from getting coal at a reasonably cheap rate. Is that to the public advantage? Of course not. The Board has doubtless done all that is possible to facilitate intercommunication between the allied systems, though I suspect that the Committee of the Railway Clearing House has been the more authoritative tribunal. But the Commissioners cannot reduce the army of watchmen and accountants, which is one of the drawbacks of the cherished system of competition. Few have written with greater prescience upon the relations of the Railways and the State than Mr. Arthur Williams,[1] and he speaks of 'the delay, expense, and inconvenience arising from the divided ownership of rolling

---

[1] *The Appropriation of the Railways by the State.* (Stanford, 1869.)

stock.' One of the elements of competition is 'the daily history of each carriage, waggon, tarpaulin or other covering that passes off its own line on to a strange line.' Well may Mr. Williams say, 'There is something painfully ludicrous in this imposing array of 300 number-takers and 600 clerks, all engaged in posting up the daily and even hourly history of the carriages and vans which appear 700,000 times, and of the tarpaulins which appear 140,000 times, on foreign lines during the year.'

What else does this competition, which the Joint Committee was so anxious to preserve, and which, in a more dignified and therefore less dependent and more selfish degree, the new Board has laboured to keep from death—what else does it display? It produces some 2,500 directors, most of them dummies, pawns of the chairman or managing director, whose salaries, amounting, say to £300,000 a year, are necessary because of the divided ownership of the Railways. The Secretary of the London and North-Western Railway ought to be as good a judge as any practical man of the value of amalgamation in point of economy, and Mr. C. E. Stewart, who for twenty-five years held that position, estimated that if competition ceased upon the Railways, and if they were all to belong 'to one proprietor, whether to a company or to the Crown,' the saving which must result would be at least equal to 10 per cent. upon the gross earnings. Mr. Graves, the late member for Liverpool, who was also a practical man, and who, as I well know, never delivered an opinion in public, except after laborious consideration, was of opinion that a reduction of not less than 25 per cent. from the present amount of the working expenses would be accomplished by transfer of the Railways to the State. Upon the earnings of 1871 Mr. Stewart's calculation would give us a saving of £4,710,755, and upon the working expenses of the same year Mr. Graves's estimate would yield £5,658,011. But financial economy is not the only sacrifice we make to obtain this chimera of competition. We permit the erection of bars and barriers, compared with which all the turnpikes that ever demanded our sixpences, but not the hours of our day, were as nothing. Lord Claud Hamilton's account of the progress of the Belfast mail, which on the down journey stops two hours, and on the up route one hour and a half, might be matched by reference to the delays which beset the traveller on every cross railroad journey in England where the lines belong to different companies. Is it not plain that competition is itself an evil—a source of waste, and therefore of loss? Monopoly—that is, beneficent monopoly—is what the interests of the public require. But there can be only one beneficent monopoly; self-interest or public-interest must rule, and the people are not safe in the hands of companies or of a single company. Competition is only a less evil than private monopoly. The State should allow neither to rule the roads of the country.

In Athens and in Madrid, I have heard statesmen of Greece and Spain, embarrassed at the approach of an elected king, discuss the question whether he was to rule or to govern. There was a good deal of puzzled and involved argument, much of the sort that one has heard in England as to whether the State should trade or govern in the matter of the Railways. The State has made an attempt at what may be called governing in the establishment of the Board of Commissioners. As to what will be the ultimate fate of that Board, I entirely agree with the *Quarterly Reviewer*, who predicted 'a final triumph for the Railway interests.' Let any one who holds a contrary opinion peruse the scornful—not to say rude—letters which a Railway Chairman addressed to a late President of the Board of Trade; let him study the indignant speech which Mr. Bancroft, acting Chairman of the North-Western Railway at a half-yearly meeting, fired off against the Bill by which the Board was constituted. If these gentlemen had been licensed victuallers, addressing 'Bruce' at eleven o'clock on Saturday night, they could hardly have been more vituperative. Under the Board, amalgamation has made progress, the value of Railway property has risen, the Companies have become more powerful, and the agitation for transfer to the State has slumbered.

There is no instance of such a transaction as this purchase would be; but, in approaching the arguments of those who oppose the transfer, I am struck by their weakness. I cannot find a single point which offers any stout resistance in the way of reasoning. One of two things appears to me certain— either all the ability of the country is on the side of transfer, or ability can furnish no weighty reasons to the contrary. Avowing myself an advocate of State control in this matter, I shall endeavour to deal with all the arguments put forward on the other side; and first, I am surprised to find that we are warned against the example of France. In that country the main lines were laid down and partly constructed by the Government, which was subsequently, by the inaction of its lessees, dragged into assisting in the formation of the branch lines. No doubt there was financial error in this, though not to the extent of £100,000,000, which we have seen was the sum expended in excess in this country; but France has very important advantages which we do not enjoy: she has trunk lines, not warped hither and thither, as ours are, to avoid the ignorant opposition of this town council or that nobleman, who wish now to have the railway for a neighbour; and instead of facing, as we do, the prospect of a permanent monopoly, to which we must succumb or with which we must deal, France is looking forward to the reversion of railway property worth at least £400,000,000. If she wishes to purchase, she has to deal with concessionaires whose leases have in some cases but sixty years to run. What has been done in Belgium is still more interesting. There we have seen among a dense population State control and private ownership working side by side; and, says Mr. Williams, 'It is clear from the evidence of M. Fassieux, Director-General of Posts and Railways in Belgium, that even those lines which have been constructed and worked by private companies on concessions for long terms—a very different thing* from a mere lease—are not worked or managed so carefully with reference to the convenience of the public as those lines which are owned and worked by the State.' 'The public,' says M. Fassieux, ' prefers the management of the State.' The State Railways, too, —and this is a very striking fact—' though working at much lower rates than any of the private companies, except one, net a much larger profit than the latter.' ' This,' adds Mr. Williams, 'is only a natural consequence of united, central, and responsible management.'

The question, therefore, as to the possibility of the management of Railways by the State with success and even popularity may be taken as settled. I do not propose to tarry on the objection advanced against the trading character of the operation. I regard the work of the Railways as only a magnified postage system : the carriage of men and women, of boxes and bales, differs only in degree from that of letters and packets ; as to the business of the State, it is evidently as lawful to do one as to do the other. There is one form of objection which should not be overlooked : I refer to the general reference which is made to the position of certain opponents as a guarantee of their authority. No one has greater respect than I have for the permanent officers— the managers and secretaries—of our Railway system. But it is just because they are good managers that they are wholly unfit to decide the main question. These gentlemen are all men—great men—of detail ; they may properly and most usefully be called upon to give evidence, and we must take their speeches as such, on the matter. But—to adopt a phrase of Mr. Bright's—the first twelve men who pass through Temple Bar are probably more competent to decide the main question. Specialists, particularly while they are still working in their own groove, have always a tendency to see none but their own side of the matter. These officers are specialists, and would make just as good servants of the State as they do of any company. Of this useful body none is more eminent than Mr. Allport, whose speech in 1873 against the purchase of the Railways by the State, affords an opportunity of studying many of these objections in their most practical form. One of the first subjects touched upon by this experienced railway manager was that of accidents, and he did all he could to show that in the year 1871 no fewer than 1,042 males and 84 females smashed and burnt or otherwise killed themselves in connection with Railways. There appears to be no room in Mr. Allport's calculations for fault on the part of the management, and diligent search is only rewarded by something like an intimation that the Board of Trade Inspectors may have had a hand in these deaths. But where Mr. Allport unconsciously proved how beneficial would be State control in regard to accidents, was in his reference to the block and interlocking systems as means of prevention. In one part of his speech, he suggested that such preventive means are bad, because men would naturally 'take less care with the block system than they would without it;' and in another he said that the Midland Company were spending £60,000 a year upon one of these means for the avoidance of accidents, and £20,000 a year on the other, and he admitted that this large expenditure was but a portion of what was requisite to make these systems universal upon the Midland Railway. Was there ever anything so illogical ? Did Mr. Allport mean us to understand that he was expending £80,000 a year in deference to an idle whim expressed by officers whom the Railway companies are constantly proclaiming have no authority whatever ? Of course not. The value of the block and interlocking systems is universally recognised, and they have only been partially established as the direct consequence of the verdicts of the Board of Trade Inspectors, laying time after time the death of passengers at the door of the Board-room, as resulting from neglect to adopt such means of prevention. There can be no doubt that the traffic management of English Railways is generally very admirable ; and if lives are now and then sacrificed to regard for economy in wages and works, no one ought to wonder when they regard the exigencies of shareholders. When Colonel Yolland once told the Great Western Railway Company that the safety of the public demanded the expenditure of £100, which they had withheld, he indicated what is common enough in Railway annals. When in fire and smoke and darkness, passengers were killed in the Clayton Hill Tunnel accident, and Captain Tyler attributed the disaster to its obvious cause—the non-adoption of the telegraphic system, the Brighton Board, with their eyes and their hopes fixed on a surplus, doubted the efficacy of the telegraphic system, as taking responsibility from drivers. No intelligent manager has, I believe, in his own mind any doubt as to the value of the telegraphic system ; what he is disposed to do about it is what Mr. Allport said he was doing—adopt it in part ; spend some thousands a year in prevention, and then calculate that to do the work thoroughly would cost a very large further sum, and that therefore it is as well perhaps to go on without it, and to take the chance of accidents. But who can suppose that the State would be permitted thus to play happy-go-lucky with the lives of the people ? Talking to engine-drivers, I have often heard them narrate their 'narrow shaves' and 'near goes'—risks which would have made many passengers start with horror had they known that such were not unfrequent incidents in the career of a night mail. This is the system of education which Mr. Allport commended as making men take care of themselves. But let a meeting of engine-drivers be called, and ask them what is best for their wives and children and for the passengers ; or let them vote by ballot—block system or no block-system,—and if the companies acted on that result, the Railway Inspectors would have no more need to urge the adoption of these costly but imperatively needed provisions. With the Railways under State control we should not only have the advantage of the universal adoption of such preventive measures, but by eliminating competition a frequent cause of accidents would be avoided.

Mr. Allport used the political objection, though not to the fullest extent. He feared having 300,000 men under Government, and we will present him with the argument that to obtain votes in a division the Secretary of the Treasury X might promise the construction of a Railway for which there was no proper demand. I confess that neither of these arguments alarms me. The influence of Government over *employés* diminishes as the number employed increases, and is practically abolished by the operation of the ballot. Mr. Allport said there were 12,000 *employés* of the Midland Railway Company resident in Derby. No doubt it was to win the favour of this class that Mr. Bass engaged in paper war, with whom— the Government? No—with the Chairman of the Midland Railway Company, who himself sat, *not* for Derby, but for Gloucester. Sir Edward Watkin is a great Railway potentate. But even before the introduction of the ballot he was at times unfortunate in his attempts to win a seat in Parliament. We do not find that the large employers of labour command the votes of their 'hands.' Think of the Lancashire, and Yorkshire, and Midland boroughs—by whom are they represented? The largest employer in a town is but rarely the man who represents that place in the House of Commons. The Railway interest is certainly strong enough in Parliament, but it does not get there by the votes of *employés* so much as through the activity of those who are but indirectly associated with the railroads. Was it ever supposed that the thousands of Post Office officials in London have been 'influenced' in their votes at an election? In the good old times, when they were comparatively few, coercion was, where they had a vote, certainly practised; but that is now a thing of the past.

I hold the opinion that the safety of the State demands in

these days the largest proper co-operation on the part of its members, and that the State in accepting a transfer of the Railways would be doing just what Mr. Allport thinks it is undoing. He believes he is an instrument of what he calls 'self-government,' to which he attributes England's greatness. I think that by transfer to the State the Manager of the Midland Railway would for the first time become an instrument of self-government. Against one evil I feel sure he and his brother-managers hold that we are in any case secure ; they have no more fear that any Lord Dundreary will be appointed to their places than to the Judicial Bench. They know very well that Railway managers must be made, not born, and that to secure the proper administration of patronage Parliament would only need to be careful that the pay of each class in the service was properly graduated, and that when no special training is requisite the emolument should not be unduly attractive. I regard this fear of Government suborning the vote of 300,000 Railway *employés* as ridiculous. Would any First Lord of the Admiralty like to stake his official existence upon a *plébiscite* in the navy, or any Secretary of State for War upon the vote of the army ? Both may have done well, yet any ex-Minister of Marine or War might perhaps get a larger vote. It would be suicidal for a Minister in the face of a penny and halfpenny press to choose Railway porters chiefly with reference to their politics ; but were he so foolish, it must be remembered that his appointments are few ; the vote which he would need is that of those who owe him nothing, and who for obvious reasons are sometimes disaffected towards the Minister in office. I admit that the evil of State jobbery is far greater than that of company jobbery ; yet both are evils, and the former is more easily detected, while the other secretly spreads the germs of corruption. It would, I fear, be impossible to deny that there are cases of bribery in the affairs of the State, but every one at all acquainted with the concerns of Government will support me in asserting that they are few and isolated. On the other side, I am told by those who know, that in public companies it is far otherwise ; that the half-a-crown for which a porter crowds other passengers in order that an Eton schoolboy may spread his small limbs and puff his cigar over six first-class seats, is but a type of the bribery which, under the name of commission, passes current in higher ranks of the commercial world. The public of course regard this as a matter of purely domestic concern ; it is no affair of theirs ; but would they be so indifferent if the Railways were their own ? Have they not taken to Co-operative Stores partly because they wished to checkmate the system so common among tradesmen of ' tipping ' their household servants ? Were they not greatly excited when an Admiralty clerk was arraigned for accepting a bribe of a few pounds ? How is it that we never hear of such a case in this Railway business of £600,000,000 capital, which men like Mr. Allport regard as too big for the State to handle ? Is any one so silly as to answer that it is because frauds do not occur ? Is it not the truth that they are not exposed because being private concerns they do not interest the public and the press ? Is not the tone of public morality endangered because it is not the interest of every one to hunt out these briberies, which no one suggests extend to the Telegraph Service or to the Post Office ? With what implacable zeal public opinion would hunt down a Government telegraph clerk who was detected in a fraudulent use of messages, and how comparatively languid is the public interest in a defaulting cashier of a Railway Company. What other engine have we of sufficient force against misuse of power ? When I was a child, Deans and Chapters sold leases of Cathedral estates right and left, many of their transactions being highly scandalous. To what is the change due in their case ? Their successors have still some few powers of this sort ; they do not pretend to a fuller knowledge of theology ; the improvement is accounted for by the fact that, as Mr. Gladstone said of the Governors of Endowed Charities, 'men are not angels and archangels, and they need looking after.' We cannot have local government upon Railways because, where fitly managed, Railways are not local; they are coextensive with the limits of the island, and cannot be most effectively used in sections. For which reason I hold that they fall properly within the domain and function of the general government of the State.

Regarding the money question as one of the simplest, I propose to leave it to the last. The policy of taking the Railways is really a more difficult matter to determine than the payment, and against the policy one of the strongest objections raised by so-called practical men has reference to rates. Experts who are doubtful as to their own position are prone to hurl stupendous figures at the heads of their opponents when their stock of arguments is exhausted, and Mr. Allport accordingly brought out his myriad rates on the Midland as a climax. 'How was the Government to deal with all that?' This is not a very strong obstacle, seeing that it only needs competency to suppose that the State is as able as the Midland Railway Company. The transfer of the Railways, though it may be held to involve changes in the scale of rates which would tend to diminish their number, need not imply any alteration in the booking system. If the State obtained possession of the Railways, it might happen that some day uniform rates would be adopted as in regard to postage; but that is no necessary part of the matter, and I shall assume that, speaking generally, the system of booking both for passengers and goods would remain as at present. Yet this view, though it settles Mr. Allport's reference to the matter of rates, by no means exhausts the whole subject. Many men of much experience in regard to Railways see in the probable extinction of differential rates the chief hindrance to the transfer. Let us take in illustration of this alleged difficulty the circumstances of the three ports—Liverpool,

Hull, and Hartlepool. The Railway companies now, for their
own interest, facilitate a competition, say between Hull and
Liverpool, in regard to the supply of Manchester, and Hull
and Hartlepool in meeting the wants of the London market.
They find, we will assume, that it answers their purpose—that
it assists the development of traffic to charge the same rates
for the conveyance of certain goods from Hull and from
Liverpool to Manchester, though the distance to the eastern
port is nearly three times that to the great port on the Mersey.
They contend that this policy is full of benefit; that, to the
great advantage of the people of Manchester and to the port
of Hull, it enables the latter to enter into competition with
Liverpool, which would be impossible if a fixed uniform
mileage rate were imposed. Similarly, with reference to
London, the metropolis is, they say, relieved from the danger
of monopoly at certain ports by the counteracting policy of the
Railway companies, which places a shipper or an importer in
regard to the supply of the metropolis in an equally good
position, whether he makes for Hartlepool or for the nearer
port of Hull. It is contended, and I concur in the contention,
that under a system of State management it would be difficult
if not impossible to maintain these differential rates arranged
on no system whatever. Each in their own interest, the people
of the ports would agitate for fixed, intelligible, and systematic
rates, and they would not be content with, nor would the
Government maintain, the method by which Railway directors
now manage the business of the ports with a single eye to the
present or ultimate advantage of their lines. The Hull people
would say that if Government made the same charge from
Hull and from Hartlepool to London, the Hull importers were
unfairly burdened with the cost of carriage for the longer
distance from the northern port, and rates of charge wholly
free from the present aspect of caprice would have to be
settled. And it is undeniable that the adoption of rates more
equitable with regard to distance would confer upon the

shipper to the nearer port that which would be equal to freedom from an import duty, and that by so much the price of commodities might be raised against the consumers.

This argument is to my mind by far the most powerful objection of a practical character which can be raised against the transfer of the Railways, and I hope those who generally dissent from my conclusions will admit that I have endeavoured to state it with candour and precision. I have never yet met with it in print, and I think it is amply deserving of a full discussion. I conceive it possible that some day passengers and goods may travel by railway as letters and parcels do by post, at one uniform rate—the same whether they be going thirty miles or three hundred. It is obvious that this would settle at once the question of differential rates and their consequences at the ports. I will venture to say that until this is accomplished we shall never have really 'free trade' within England. But for the present we must put such plans out of our thoughts as only embarrassing and hindering the solution of the problem. Yet we must make some advance in this direction, and if the Railways become the property of the State it would perhaps be necessary to impose mileage or 'zone' rates, steadily diminishing as the distance increased, and we should have to meet the complaints of those who paid short, and therefore more expensive rates, with demonstration that such a policy was a necessity of any general system of intercommunication ; we should show them that the senders of letters from one part of London to another, bear for the commonwealth, and for their own occasional advantage, the extra cost of transmitting letters for longer distances, and we should adduce the fact that once the goods are loaded and upon the rail, the actual cost per mile of their conveyance very rapidly diminishes with the increase of distance. I think that in this manner the difficulty as to rates might be overcome.

The money question appears to me to involve the strongest argument in favour of the transfer, because the improvement and increase in value of the property appears to be certain and considerable. Within a few years the recent augmentation in value of Railway Stock may be very moderately estimated at £60,000,000, and we see in comparing the estimates of earlier writers on this subject with the figures which are now brought forth, that had the transfer been effected seven or eight years ago the National Debt might already have been reduced by many millions. For example, Mr. Arthur Williams in 1869, when North-Western Stock was quoted at 117, assumed that the owner would be perfectly satisfied to accept in exchange a Government annuity of £5 1s. 6d., or £145 in cash. Since then we have seen this Stock selling in open market for £160, and we have heard the Chairman, when a dividend had been declared equal to £7 15s. for the year, expressing a confident hope that the profits of the undertaking would never fall below that amount.

But it will be said that this prospective increment in value is entirely the property of the shareholders, and that is a proposition from which I shall not dissent. I can, however, only infer their estimate of this increment from the price at which Stock in times of conspicuous absence of pressure is sold in open market, just as, with regard to land, I can only infer its value in like circumstances. If land is required for the common-wealth, it is taken by power of Act of Parliament at a liberal estimate of the price which it would fetch if sold by auction. Then, I may be asked, why not take the Land as well as the Railways, and pocket for the State the increment of value in both cases? Undoubtedly such a course may be recommended, but I do not think it is expedient, desirable, or even feasible, because the subdivision of the land, which I hope to see greatly increased, tends rather to diversity than uniformity of value; and while value, which is due to situation and other advantages, is fairly determined in private contract by the eager self-interest of the seller, equity would demand, if the State were the owner, that each parcel, however small,

should be let by public competition, a business which I think
would elude the checks which public supervision must maintain
upon the operations of officers of the State.

With regard to the Railways, I do not find on reviewing the
daily list of quotations that there is any lack of regard for the
possibilities of improvement. To-day men buy and sell, and
for years past they have bought and sold, the Ordinary Stock of
the Metropolitan District Railway, and of the London, Chatham,
and Dover Railway, at considerable prices. Yet even now there
is no certainty of dividend upon these Stocks for years to come.
Other Stocks would show a similar dealing in great expectations, and surely shareholders—of whom it may not be imper-
tinent to say that I am one in regard to each of the Railways
I have mentioned—would have no right to complain if the
highest market value of their property within the last five years
were taken as the price at which, with an addition for compulsory sale, they might be transferred by authority of Parliament. But before we can fix a price in a Government Stock
at which transfer might equitably be enforced, we must inquire
what are the expectations of income from such Railway investments. And if we turn to the Railway Stocks which are
most steady in regard to dividends, and if we look to periods
when public opinion has been most settled and most hopeful
with regard to the future improvement of the property, we find
that 5 per cent. is indicated. This, then, I think, would afford
a fair basis for the transfer. Suppose the highest official price
of Chatham and Dover Ordinary Stock, now quoted at 23, to
have been 30 within the last three years, the shareholder might,
I think, with justice, be compelled to accept £50 in a Three per
Cent. Stock, and that in nine cases out of ten he would be a
holder at those terms I have no doubt whatever. With regard
to the Preference and Debenture Stock and Loans it would
seem fair to offer Stock in each case to the value of the income
guaranteed. In the case of those Stocks upon which interest
is not paid, the earnings of the companies being insufficient,

the transfer might be arranged upon the basis of the highest quoted price, as in the case of the Ordinary Stocks, the expected income being that fixed by the railway company.

Thus, in addition to receiving the highest price at which their Shares and Stocks have been quoted in a time of great prosperity, the proprietors would obtain, by way of compensation for compulsory transfer, the improved security of Government Stock. At this rate the State would give about £266 in Three per Cent. Stock for £100 ordinary Stock of the London and North-Western Railway ; and while the eight millions odd of the Chatham and Dover Ordinary Stock would stand in this Stock at four millions, the thirty millions odd of the London and North-Western Ordinary Stock would figure at about eighty millions. It would take long to determine precisely the annual charge which at this rate of purchase the State would incur. But we know that the Railways distributed in 1871 about £24,475,512 of profits, and that upon the £230,000,000 of Ordinary Stock, of which thirty-one and a half millions received no dividend at all, this sum gave an average of 5·07 per cent. ; and without prolonging this already too extended article, I may assert this much—that if the transfer were made under the conditions which have been suggested, a certain profit would accrue if only the average of the saving estimated by Mr. Graves and Mr. Stewart as resulting from united management were accomplished. That is a reckoning which does not include the prospects of the future, the certain increase in the value of the State monopoly of Railway traffic ; the advantage to trade and personal intercourse which must result from abolition of the barriers which have been erected by company against company, and board against board. I have left myself no room to speak of the Department, the Council, and the districts in which I should propose to reorganize the Railways as the property of the State.

XI.

THE INTOXICATING LIQUORS QUESTION.

BEYOND the necessary provision for the nutriment of the body, and the renewal of its tissues, the great requirement of vital heat presses upon people with increasing force as the situation of their country declines from the equator. And there can be no doubt, for we have the fact before our eyes, that, wisely or unwisely, this demand is largely supplied by the use of fermented Liquors. Therefore, we are not surprised to find drunkenness, as a national feature, follow climatic or zone conditions. We know it must be so. If the British are not the most drunken people upon earth, we may be sure that is a disgrace they share with the North Germans, the Scandinavians, the Russians, the peoples of Northern Asia and America.

Climatic or zone conditions are marked with other features. A friend of mine, who is an occasional reader of the organ of the Licensed Victuallers in the London Press, once asked me,—'How is it,' said he, 'that the English are earnestly Protestant and sensually intemperate?' 'Consider,' I answered. 'Cast your thoughts round the world, and you will find that the zone of drunkenness is also that of religious liberty and of the sacred, Protestant right of private judgment.' The hardy races, whose weakness is alcohol, exhibit their mental strength in resistance to superstition. Both are fostered by the same circumstances; but how different: one a miserable craving for unnatural heat of the body; the other an inspiration of the spiritual life ; for, it is incontestably and securely true that Protestantism has been the parent of religious liberty, and that in exalting the right and duty of private judgment, in renouncing the mediatorial influence of saints and priests, it has promoted individuality and progress, and the true conception of spiritual duty. Who are the most temperate people of Western Europe ? Need we ask ? Should we be surprised to find that they are the most southern, the nearest to the sun, the gay people of Andalusia, the people of Xeres— whose sherry, with a large addition of brandy, we drink so freely ? Their own drink is mostly water. In their towns, they have, it is true, no Metropolitan Drinking Fountain Association, but there the water-sellers with their monotonous cry, ' *agua*, *agua !* ' do a good trade. They send us largely of the fermented fruit of their sunbeams ; for themselves, there is heat enough to be had from their unbrandied wine, from chocolate and coffee.

Again, in the East, we may ask the same question, and shall receive a similar answer. The Turks are the least drunken and the most southern. Even in the temperate zone we observe slighter variations of climate affecting the disposition. The evidence is unanimous that in the United States of America the effect of Liquor is greater than when taken in this country. I have heard a very eminent American say that the only difference he finds between New York and London is that here he can take wine at dinner with impunity ; and English tourists in America seem to view the Niagara Falls with fewer expressions of wonder, and with less desire to communicate the facts of the phenomenon, than when they behold the long and pure array of glasses for iced water and the absence of wine bottles at the dinner tables of the American hotels. In a debate upon the Permissive Bill, Mr. F. S. Powell said : ' In America such was the invigorating character of their translucent atmosphere, that but little desire was felt for intoxicating drinks. The amount of spirituous liquors which was drunk in this country with impunity would produce powerful intoxication in America.'

I do not bring forward geographical arguments to excuse the vice of drunkenness in our country ; and, as my conclusions will show, I do not gather from the influence of climate, and therefore, in a less degree, of race, upon the consumption of Liquor, that as Mr. Bruce (now Lord Aberdare) once put the matter, the advocates of the Permissive Bill are setting themselves 'against what appeared to be a law of nature—that is, a desire for stimulants.' I merely assert and explain that which is indeed a very obvious fact, that the craving for Liquor which has the power of intoxication is, from climatic conditions, probably strongest in this country, where geographical position and the course of the Gulf Stream produce during many months of the year a damp, chill air, for which, with the bulk of the population, the favourite counteractive is fermented and heating drink.

But we have dwelt long enough upon the influence of climate ; let us henceforth confine our attention to the taxation, the sale, and the consumption of Liquor, as all this may be seen within the limits of the United Kingdom. And as that is the very groundwork, and, with many statesmen, the initial thought in regard to legislation, let us first look at the contribution which the consumption of Liquor makes to the revenue. It would be the height of folly to ignore the extent to which a people like the English regard themselves as slaves to whatever 'is,' in reference to their national income. There could hardly be a greater contradiction than between our professions of duty relative to the civilisation, through the conquest, of the East, and our official vindication of the opium traffic. We have gone, year after year—our mouths stuffed with fine phrases concerning the whole duty of man— pushing our way, with a sword in one hand and poppy juice in the other ; the real object being, not the propagation of sound morality, nor the extermination of the people by the sword, but the sale of opium for the advantage of our planters and of our Indian revenue. It is well to bear this in mind before one looks at the income which is derived from the drinking propensities of our fellow-countrymen. A glance is sufficient to convince us of one extremely important fact, which is this ;—that the legislature has at no time regarded the consumption of Liquor as a necessity of life. When the Committee over which Mr. Charles Villiers presided took evidence upon the question more than twenty-five years ago, men who had been actively engaged in the temperance movement in Ireland produced figures which showed conclusively that the decline in the consumption of Liquor had led to a vast increase in the sale of those elements of the breakfast-table which were then very highly taxed, but upon which, as alleged necessaries of life, the taxation has been greatly reduced, and which the public welfare demands should as soon as possible be made free altogether from taxation. Those who maintain that Liquor is not only the quickest producing agent of vital heat, but that it is necessary food, have not found in the common sense of the people an affirmative response ; for the enormous taxation levied upon Liquor —under which denomination, for the purposes of our present argument, we will include beers, wines, and spirits—could only have been retained upon the universal admission that its habitual consumption is not a requirement of life, that it is in fact, like armorial bearings, an unnecessary matter which may be very heavily taxed, without giving its consumers any right to complain. Nay, more than this ; have not our ears grown dull, from often repetition, to the unctuous lament of Chancellors of the Exchequer, who seem to feel that, although the taxation of Liquor is only a matter of fiscal concern—no one has ventured to rally English electors with the cry of 'cheap gin !'—they ought not to take the millions stained with blood, and ruin, and harlotry, and sloth, without

R

muttering a few words of apology as they sweep the year's gains into the public purse, before they are shot out upon the sea of expenditure?

I shall not look farther back than the commencement of the century with reference to the duties which have been levied upon Liquor; the chief purpose of such a reference being to show the influence of taxation upon consumption. We levy duties upon malt, upon wine, and upon spirit. At the beginning of the century the malt duty was 2*s*. 5*d*. per bushel; it is now 2*s*. 8½*d*. At the same period the duties on wine were—on French wines, 10*s*. 2¼*d*. per gallon, and on other kinds, 6*s*. 9¾*d*. The duty is now 1*s*. per gallon upon wine containing fewer than 26° of proof spirit; 2*s*. 6*d*. per gallon between 26° and 42°; and 3*d*. additional duty for each degree of strength beyond 42°. In 1802 the average duty upon spirits was 6*s*. 1*d*. per gallon; it is now 10*s*. 1*d*. Of these duties on Liquor, which produce one-third of the entire revenue of the country, the malt-tax has been most often attacked, and most near to falling. I think the malt-tax is a bad tax. Lord Russell said in 1846: 'If I were Prime Minister, when protection to agriculture was abolished the first tax I would repeal would be the malt-tax.' Mr. Charles Villiers said in 1839, that 'all those who were injured by the operation of the corn laws would be willing—nay, would be anxious—to get rid of the malt-tax.' Mr. Cobden said in 1864: 'It has often occurred to me to compare the case of the British agriculturist—who, after raising a bushel of barley, is compelled to pay a tax of 60 per cent. before he is permitted to convert it into a beverage for his own consumption —with what I have seen in foreign countries, and I can really call to mind nothing so hard and unreasonable. I am quite sure that the cultivators of vineyards and the growers of olives in France and Italy would never tolerate such treatment of their wine and oil.' This may be very apt, but it is not so apt as would have been a comparison between the farmer's inability to make his own malt with a similar disability in regard to the manufacture of spirits. Is it not just as hard that he should not be allowed to distil a glass of alcohol from his barley, as that he should not be permitted to convert his barley into malt? And if he were free to distil and flavour whisky, why should he be protected against the competition of the foreigner, to the disadvantage of his neighbour the tradesman, by the imposition of a duty on foreign spirits? We must be careful how we reply to these questions, for thereby hang no less than £25,000,000 of taxation. I cannot see how, with our present expenditure, a Chancellor of the Exchequer could spare the six millions derived from the malt-tax, and I cannot find reasons for repealing that duty which do not apply, at least in some degree, to the home-made spirit duties producing £12,500,000; to the £5,000,000 raised from foreign spirits; and to the wine duties, which yield more than £1,500,000 to the revenue.

I think it is not to be doubted that the consumption of beer would be increased by the repeal of the malt-tax, and it is probable that the great evil of adulteration would be lessened. The beer of foreign countries, where no such duty is levied, is undoubtedly purer and less intoxicating than that mixture, so often impregnated with tobacco-juice, *cocculus indicus, nux vomica*, grains of paradise, and too much salt, which passes by the name of beer among the poor of England. We are a beer-drinking people, but it will surprise many to learn that we do not, in the reign of Queen Victoria, consume one-half as much beer per head of the population, as we did in the reign of Queen Anne. The average consumption of malt per head was —it will be seen from the following table, taken from authentic records—considerably more than twice as great in the middle of the eighteenth century as in that of the nineteenth. From 1740 to 1790 it was—

1740 . . 3·78	1760 . . 4·29	1780 . . 3·94
1750 . . 4·85	1770 . . 3·38	1790 . . 2·57

From 1801 to 1871 it was—

1801	.	.	.	1˙20	1841	.	.	.	1˙35
1811	.	.	.	1˙60	1851	.	.	.	1˙50
1821	.	.	.	1˙38	1861	.	.	.	1˙61
1831	.	.	.	1˙63	1871	.	.	.	1˙72

John Barleycorn is from this point of view less powerful in the nineteenth than in the preceding century—and why? He was greatly upset by John Chinaman. I think the fact is indisputable. In the time of the Tudors, beer was taken at every meal; there was a steady drinking from breakfast to supper. As compared with that time, the draught per head of Malt Liquor has declined more than one-half, otherwise there could not have been the enormous consumption of tea. The British people now consume very nearly 4 lb. of tea per head per annum, an amount which has steadily progressed, while the consumption per head of malt has been all but stationary. This fact is interesting, if only because it shows that it is possible, by the introduction of new drinks and by legislation, to change the bibulous habits of a people.

With reference to the wine duties, which yield no very considerable sum to the revenue, it cannot be said that they press severely upon the people. Indeed, our legislation on this subject seems generally to have had rather a political than an economic significance, and the next change is likely to be advocated upon similar grounds. The absurd treaty concluded in 1703, and known by the name of its noble negotiator as the Methuen Treaty, is not an unfair indication of arrangements which had anything for their object but free trade. England engaged by that bond, which remained in force until 1831, to levy on the wines of France duties higher by 50 per cent. than those charged upon the wines of the Peninsula; and the consumption of French wines, which never under that treaty exceeded 500,000 gallons in any one year, has since, under Mr. Gladstone's shilling duty, amounted to nearly 5,000,000 gallons; so that in regard to French wines, a shilling duty is now as productive to the revenue as the ten-shilling duty, which, under the Methuen Treaty, was imposed at the commencement of the century.

The taxation upon spirits is a matter, so far as the revenue is concerned, of the very gravest importance, for the annual income thus derived is not less than £18,000,000. In regard to all excisable Liquors, we have abundant and convincing evidence of the effect of duties upon consumption. I will mention but one. In 1800, a duty of 11s. 1d. on foreign spirits produced £1,382,718. Forty years later, the duty was raised to the immense charge of £1 2s. 10d. per gallon, and the sum collected, amounting to £1,354,079, was nearly 180 per cent. under that which would have been received had the 'duty-paid' consumption per head remained unaltered. High duties of course lead to smuggling, to illicit manufacture, and to adulteration as well as to abstinence. I believe that the last evil, that of adulteration, is now as rampant as were the two former evils at the commencement of the century. It cannot be doubted that smuggling and illicit distillation then provided a large flow of alcohol upon which no duty was ever paid. The first was especially the practice of England and Scotland ; the second of Ireland. Very striking evidence as to Ireland is given in the reports of the Inland Revenue department, from which we find that in the year ending March 31st, 1866, the convictions for illicit distillation were as follow :—

England.	Scotland.	Ireland.
41.	11.	3,557.

There is no question that even in Ireland this unlawful practice is fast following the decline of smuggling into this island. Adulteration, far more noxious to the health, and therefore ultimately to the purse of the community, is far more safe and easy. It cannot be doubted that a duty of 600 per cent. will produce such malpractices. Yet in spite of all this, the income from the spirit duties steadily increases ; it is looked upon as the financial barometer of our prosperity; and as no one appears to doubt that one-half of the consumption is certainly injurious, because taken by persons already more or less inebriated, it follows that to an amount equal to the present cost of the Navy we take toll of drunkenness. Lord Derby's friend, who said of the year 1872, 'We have drunk ourselves out of the American debt,' put the truth in sober language. The only serious evil which seems to arise from the high spirit duties is that of adulteration, and I am not disposed to think it a sufficient ground for diminishing the charge. Rigid, scrupulous, and persevering inspection is a remedy for the evil of adulteration, to be followed by severe punishment in detected cases. So far as the interests of temperance are concerned, there can be no doubt that these are promoted by the imposition of high rates. We shall see, when we pass to consider the sale of Liquor, that all restrictions upon the traffic have the effect of diminishing drunkenness.

The position of Liquor in regard to the revenue is not so much the subject of dispute as the sale of Liquor, and the control which may be exercised over the trade. No reasonable persons can entertain any doubt as to the right of a State to make regulations affecting any or all trades ; and that the Liquor trade has long been regarded as one specially liable to restricting regulations, it is easy to prove. An Act of the 5 and 6 Edward VI., after reciting 'the intolerable hurts and troubles to the commonwealth of this realm that daily grew and increased through the abuses and disorders had and used in common ale-houses and other houses called "tippling houses," ' provided that none should keep an ale-house without a licence from two justices of the peace. Licences were issued on payment of duty in the reign of Queen Anne. In 1736, a special licence was imposed on retailers of spirits, and the punishment for non-payment of penalty was committal to the House of Correction for two months, and at 'his or her' discharge to be 'stript naked from the middle upwards, and to be whipt until his or her body be bloody.' From that time to the present, the control of the trade has never been abandoned ; it has always been regarded as a traffic which must be carefully limited. And there can be no doubt that this control has had reference to the possible hurtfulness of the trade to the social well-being of the people. The licence fees have not simply been demanded as revenue, but rather as caution money, virtually in order that any disreputable house for the sale of Liquor might be closed by the shortest possible process.

That control of the Liquor trade has always existed within the memory of this generation need not be shown ; it is a plain fact within common knowledge. Perhaps there is no one more remarkable among the many anomalies of English life than that under a system of permissive prohibition—for the control of the magistrates amounts to nothing less—there should have grown up an interest so vast upon a security, legally, though not practically, so precarious. The goodwill of such a public-house as the Royal Oak in Bayswater, or the Elephant and Castle on the other side of the river, would probably sell for many thousands of pounds, and it is no uncommon thing for a man, on taking a lease of such premises, to expend £10,000 or £15,000 upon a reconstruction, in perfect confidence that the tenure of the licence, which is the chief element in the value of his lease, will not be disturbed. A home trade which sells to the value of £100,000,000 must engage a vast amount of capital, and we are not without an estimate of that which is employed in the manufacture and sale of Liquor. There are about 140,000 public and beer-houses in the kingdom, of which 10,000 are in the London district ; and, adopting the estimate of the brewers' advocate, setting them at £300 each in the country and £1,500 in London, their trade value would amount to £54,000,000.

There is no reason to doubt the accuracy of calculations which
place the sum involved in the trades associated with the
supply of these houses,—in debts, in tenants' capital, etc.,—
at nearly twice as much more, and thus we get a sight of an
interest probably as powerful as any in the country, because so
thoroughly diffused among the people and so single-minded in
its object.   'Liquor knows no politics,' said an American
statesman, and we have had and shall have abundant con-
firmation of the opinion in this country.   The doctrine has
moreover been notoriously proclaimed by licensed victuallers
in every direction.   The Manchester and Salford Association
unanimously confirmed the report which pledged them 'to
vote as one man, regardless of political party,' and the
publicans acted in 1874 upon that platform.

It was against this trade, so united, so powerful, that Mr.
Bruce launched his famous Intoxicating Liquors (Licensing)
Bill, by which it was proposed to issue two classes of certificates ; one to the publican—in lieu of the three licences for
beer, wine and spirits ; and one to the beer-house keeper, with
other privileges of sale than those he now possesses.   Every
seller must have taken out one of these licences, with—if his
house was well conducted—a ten years' title to renewal, after
which he would be subject to refusal where the public-houses
were too numerous, or to the risks of competition in tendering
for a new certificate.   We need not recall to mind the storm
which that Bill evoked.   'Confiscation' was the cry of the
Liquor-sellers, and they drove the Bill from Parliament.   The
Quarterly Review, like other organs of the Tory party, eager
to make political capital out of a blunder so culpable, because
the attempt was so ill-advised, said of the measure, that,
'stimulated by an insane desire of notoriety, or pricked by
furies in the shape of Welsh teetotalers, the unfortunate Home
Secretary, taking counsel, as is said, with some agent of a
London brewery and with some abstainers in his own office,
put forth the Bill.'   Such was its ribald epitaph, and after

labouring another twelve months, the same department produced the Bill of 1872, which, in its enacted form, dealt with
adulteration, penalties for drunkenness, police inspection, hours
of closing, and valuation for licences—the main provision
being that outside London—wherein the hours for opening
and closing were fixed at five A.M. and midnight, with special
exceptions granted under certain conditions by the Chief
Commissioner of Police—the licensing justices should be
empowered to alter the hour of opening from six A.M. to five
or seven, and the hour of closing from eleven P.M. to ten or
twelve ; on Sunday, the hour of closing from ten P.M. to nine
or eleven. This is what its ingenious inventor denominated
an 'elastic system.' Mr. Disraeli called it 'helter-skelter legislation,' but his nickname conveyed no moral reprobation.
'Elastic' legislation upon a subject which, in the opinion of
all, is closely connected with the increase of crime, is worse
than 'helter-skelter.' It would be 'elastic' legislation to
decree that a man convicted of embezzlement might be sen-
tenced to two years' imprisonment or to receive for two years
a pension equivalent to the sum he had succeeded in convert-
ing to his own use. 'Elastic' legislation is a deliberate and
cowardly betrayal of the functions of Parliament.

By the comments which that Act drew forth, we find the
ground strewed with fallacies, and in none was fallacy more
apparent than in those resounding sentences with which Sir
William Harcourt spiced the wine of his electors and fellow-
Druids at Oxford. Such men do not, we must believe, consciously betray their higher instincts, do not consciously yield
their *esprit* to be, as it were, the gases in their tipsy neighbours'
wine. Yet Sir William Harcourt's well-known speech at Oxford
on the Licensing Act was of the stuff that fills a wind-bag ;
it collapses at a single prick. If he had made free trade in
Liquor—freedom for all hours and in all places—the basis of
his argument, that would have been substantial. If he had
sought to liberate the trade from the network of enactments—

forty since 1736—in which it is involved, that would have been logical. If, adopting the words of a great wit, he had said : 'There has been in all Governments a great deal of absurd canting about intoxication. The best plan is to let the people drink what they like, wear what they like, and to make no sumptuary laws for the belly and the back;' that would have been intelligible. But he did nothing of the sort. The Act which he stood up to abuse had conferred 'elastic' powers with reference to the hours of closing ; it found the hours of closing already fixed by enactments against which this younger Druid had not a word to say. Looking to what existed before the Act of 1872, Sir William Harcourt commenced his speech by saying there was 'no cause for legislative interference at all, unless perhaps in respect of certain alterations in the system of licensing.' Again he said : 'I can see no justification for interfering with the hours of closing at all,' admitting that the pre-existing hours—*i.e.*, the average of those of the 'elastic' and obnoxious Act—were not a subject for complaint. It was upon this infirm flooring—strong enough, perhaps, for Oxford Druids—that Sir William Harcourt reared his speech and made his talk of nightcaps and of the adjustment of such head-gear by the members of Mr. Gladstone's Government. It was upon this illogical basis that he stood up to declaim against restrictive legislation and 'grandmotherly government.' The maintainer of highly restrictive hours as they were defined in 1871, the maintainer of the permissive prohibitory powers of the licensing justices as they have existed and have been exercised ever since Sir William Harcourt heard of the powers of a justice of the peace, called upon the Liberal party to divorce themselves from 'restrictive legislation,' said it was no legitimate child of theirs, and expressed a desire to 'argue it out.' Sir William Harcourt can be grandly logical when he pleases, and seeing the fallacy of his 'night-cap' talk at Oxford, he may develop into that position which Mr. Lowe seems disposed to take up, and become an advocate of free trade in the sale of Liquor. Let him be warned in time. Let him ponder upon what was the condition of a neighbouring country—of Sweden—under a system virtually of free trade, and mark how it has improved under a *régime* of careful restriction. It does not lie in Sir William Harcourt's mouth to deny the possibilities of restriction so far as they have reference to the decrease of drunkenness, for he has gone farther than I am prepared to go in that direction; he has by implication contradicted all the evidence as to the alleged failure of the Maine Liquor Law; he has gone beyond Neal Dow himself. Sir William Harcourt has said to his constituents at Oxford: 'You might, of course, make it impossible for any man to get anything to drink, and then, of course, no man could be drunk.' Believing this, if he looks to Sweden he will be less liable to fall into the enormous error of free trade in Liquor. We have the high authority of a leading Scotch journal for the opinion that twenty years ago Sweden was 'probably' a more drunken country than Scotland. In both, spirits, not beer, form the intoxicating medium. In Sweden, every landowner was allowed to distil spirits for domestic use on payment of a nominal licensing fee, and every burgher in any town could become a publican without a licence. More than twenty years ago, the Diet appointed a committee, which in its report avowed that 'seldom, if ever, has a conviction so generally or unequivocally been pronounced with regard to the necessity of rigorous measures against the physical, economical, and moral ruin with which the immoderate use of spirits threatens the nation. A cry has burst forth from the hearts of the people, appealing to all who have influence—a prayer for deliverance from a scourge which previous legislation has planted and nourished,' and an Act for the regulation and sale of Liquor, imposing statutory restrictions upon the traffic in spirits—beer is there unimportant as an intoxicating Liquor —was immediately passed. By the Swedish law it is now conditional on a publican's certificate that he should also sell food.   In boroughs, the councils; in rural districts, the magistrates, decide on applications for additional licences, which are reported to the Governor of the district, who can allow or disallow, but cannot add to the number to be granted.   The sale is prohibited after ten P.M. on week-days, and more strictly on Sundays; drink debts are irrecoverable at law, and it is forbidden to sell Liquor to drunken (*ofver-lastad*) persons, as it is also to turn such persons out of the house without some one to provide for their safety in the street.   The licences are tenable—on good behaviour—for three years, and the new certificates are publicly sold, the purchase-money being retained for municipal purposes.   Now Sir William Harcourt, who believes that you may make such laws that 'no man could be drunk,' will not be surprised to learn that this advance in Sweden from free trade to severe restriction has effected a great reduction in the number of persons fined for drunkenness, and that the number of cases of *delirium tremens* has been diminished by one-third.

The Gothenburg system, which, upon the earnest recommendation of Mr. Chamberlain, was provisionally accepted by the Town Council of Birmingham, and discussed in Parliament, is based upon this law.   And, as we have seen, the Swedish law offers peculiar facilities for its operation.   Every third year all licences are in the market, and, under these circumstances, a company which could bid £20,000 a year for the monopoly in the provincial town of Gothenburg, is not likely to find many competitors.   The Company, or *Bolag*, of Gothenburg, had, as Mr. Chamberlain pointedly states, 'no vested interests to deal with.'   The Company has accomplished great results, not merely in the 'enormous profits' which have been realised for the benefit of the municipal revenue, but in regard to the decline of drunkenness.   So conspicuous has been the advance of temperance in Gothenburg that the attention of the capital has been attracted, and a Special Committee of the municipality of Stockholm have recommended the adoption of the Gothenburg system. 'The Committee selected as periods for comparison the twelve years 1851—1862, and an equal period, embracing the years 1863—1874, in the first of which there were three years of good harvests and trade, seven average, and two bad ; and in the second, two good, seven average, and three bad. They find that the proportion of drunkenness to the population increased about 5 per cent. in the latter period. But a similar comparison in the case of Gothenburg shows a diminution of drunkenness of more than 50 per cent. in the second period of twelve years, during ten of which the new system has been in operation.'

Mr. Chamberlain did not fail to perceive that the circumstances of an English town are very different from those of Gothenburg ; that here we have to deal with a 'vested interest' at the corner of every street ; and he declined to lay down any plan of compensation. He proposed that this should be settled by Parliament. In my opinion, the Gothenburg system is impracticable in this country. It has been proposed to 'nationalise' the land, and that visionary scheme is defeated by the same argument which may be used to show that the municipalisation of the public-houses is impracticable. It may be asserted that it is impossible to carry on with profit the business of any great class whose proprietary and trade interests have to be paid for at fair and normal rates of purchase and compensation. The Gothenburg system is recommended because, under that system, the sale of Liquor would not be pressed by self-interest. There might be some successes in the way of economy of management, but these could not equal the loss of profit due to the subtraction of the personal interest of the publican. Yet he would have to be compensated, not only for the loss of all profits—those made from the soddened drunkard as well as from sober thirst—but beyond this, he must have, and would be entitled to, compensation for disturbance. Bearing a load of this sort, it would be long before the community would drink themselves clear of debt. Even Birmingham is not so philanthropic as to be prepared for a great deficit; and I think it easy to show that profit, which could accrue only through a vast extension of the town, is vaguely remote, if not impossible.

Leaving that aspect of the question, I pass to the side of Mr. Lowe in maintaining that the Birmingham Corporation has no proper business in this matter. If Liquor was a necessity of municipal life, if it was a commodity which did not admit of retail competition, and if all the Birmingham townsfolk required but one sort and quality—if in these conditions it resembled Gas and Water, then I should advocate the monopoly. There is, too, an essential difference between Scandinavian and English society, which appears to have escaped the notice even of so shrewd an observer as Mr. Chamberlain. Because he has done so much for the good cause of public education in England, and is so sincere and so earnest an opponent of the Church Establishment, I am the more surprised that in attempting to transplant the Gothenburg system, he appeared to have taken no note of the difference of soil. The religious basis of society in Sweden is a dead level of uniformity, and the acts of authority, whether religious or secular, royal or local, are not questioned at every step. It would, however, be unfair not to state that Mr. Chamberlain put forth all the objections he could think of to his proposal, and that Mr. Lowe in his comment, published in the *Fortnightly Review*, did not do justice to them. Mr. Lowe said he was 'not much moved by the objection that it is wrong to enter into the Liquor trade, which appears to us just as legitimate as any other.' No one supposed he would be moved at all by any such objection. Yet it is one, the great force of which Mr. Chamberlain fully appreciates, and it would weigh heavily with a large class of English people. It is heard in Sweden, where Mr. Chamberlain told us that 'the profits made by the *Bolag*, and now devoted to public uses, are enormous, and the financial success of the undertaking has actually formed part of the indictment brought against it by the more extreme advocates of temperance.' Again, Mr. Lowe was scarcely justified in assuming that the Permissive Bill is only a measure for the suppression of the Liquor traffic, and on that ground to ask, 'Will Mr. Chamberlain consent to relieve the rates of the town by the profits of a traffic for the forcible suppression of which he is, we understand, prepared to vote?' But it must be admitted that Mr. Lowe's criticism was on the whole very successful in its work of destruction. He might have convicted himself of an acceptance of fallacy, such as he alleged against Mr. Chamberlain, had he gone farther in the direction to which he leans—that of free trade in Liquor.

But, indeed, free trade in Liquor is not the demand of any considerable party in any State. In England, we have seen a provisional executive committee of the United . Trades Association of Licensed Victuallers inviting the whole trade to a national council upon quite a different platform. 'Anxious,' their manifesto ran, 'to conform ourselves to, and even to promote, legislation for the regulation of our trade.' And in no place do we observe any well-grounded denial of the benefits of restriction, as enforced by recent legislation. To refer once more to Sir William Harcourt, we have found him assuming at Oxford that the whole population passes every evening in public-houses, and proceeds to tie on night-caps when driven from those haunts. The Secretary of the Manchester Licensed Victuallers' Association gave similar testimony; but it appeared that while Sir William Harcourt's language won for himself an abiding place in the hearts of Oxford vestrymen, this gentleman lived high in the clouds, where the setting sun is visible long after the sight of it is denied to the earthly scene of his labours. He said that 'if the new Act had done anything, it sent them home to bed like good boys, and in some places' (? clouds, or the Secretary's fancy) 'in the summer months

before the sun had gone down.' Indeed, although I am not
about to conclude with a recommendation of the Maine
Liquor Law, I have only less doubt than Sir William
Harcourt has naïvely expressed, that it is possible to make
men sober by Act of Parliament. Look at the operation of
that law as described by those who go to report what they
call its failure! No one can question the sincerity of Mr.
Justin M'Carthy's evidence against the Maine Law, as given
in the *Fortnightly Review* during the summer of 1871. But
for my own part, I wish to go no farther than his pages for
testimony to its considerable success. Mr. M'Carthy is almost
as illogical as Sir William Harcourt. He, it seems, with
the best intentions, gets a friend or two to show him the trick
of how to get spirits in a town where the sale is prohibited,
and then says the law does nothing. In one part of the town
Mr. M'Carthy was surprised to see bottles containing spirits
exhibited for sale; 'in other streets,' he says, 'my friend
pointed me out various houses where, he assured me, drink
could just as easily be procured.' Elsewhere he says : 'My
friend asked the young man behind the counter, in a low tone,
whether he had anything to drink.' Mr. M'Carthy ranged,
'for hours one evening,' the lower quarters of Portland,
frequented by seamen, and saw 'nothing particularly riotous.'
The Mayor told him, 'The present permissive law is about
as good as could well be devised.' The Deputy-Marshal of
Portland held the same opinion. 'The practice of the police
is to prosecute the seller of drink to a man found drunk in the
streets.' 'The trouble is always with the foreigners.' Mr.
M'Carthy thinks Mr. Thomas Hughes's evidence as to the
success of the law in preventing the sale of spirits was owing
to his not understanding the trick of how to find it ; acknow-
ledging the very great influence of the law in saying that
if Mr. Hughes had known that '"sample room," and other
such names and titles,' meant Liquor, he would not have
searched for wine and ale without finding it. In fact, I look

upon Mr. Justin M'Carthy as an unconscious Balaam, who, evidently possessed with a call to curse the Maine Liquor Law, unwittingly bears strong testimony in the opposite direction ; and Mr. Mundella's argument, which is bound in the same volume with Mr. M'Carthy's, is very much of the same sort. The clever Member for Sheffield had been to look at Massachusetts, and 'he would be very sorry to see the want of respect for law which he saw in the New England States.' Now, Mr. Mundella has not been a 'home-keeping youth,' and has not 'homely wit' ; he knows the Continent, and has some personal acquaintance with Nottingham 'lambs' and with Sheffield 'blades.' Can he tell us of any part of the earth where the respect for law is so widely manifested as in those New England States? To find their equal in that respect he will have at all events to name a country of which I know nothing.

I will confine the few remarks I have yet to make to the laws regulating the Liquor traffic in this country, and to the changes which it appears desirable should be introduced for the promotion of temperance. I shall not deal with the blunders in the 'helter-skelter' compilation by a thousand hands in both Houses of the Act of 1872, nor with the paltry gratifications which have been paid by the party in power for the support of the Liquor trade in 1874. I will not take upon me to decide whether the valuation clauses mean what they say, or something different, nor deliver myself of an opinion as to how the sale of Liquor at fairs was regulated by that Act. I entirely approve of the increased gravity which was given to the offence of the public exhibition of drunkenness, and would gladly see strengthened the powers to detect and the punishments inflicted in regard to adulteration. The only points to which I shall refer are the licensing authority, the investment of the publican, and the control of the trade by the community.

We may consider it established from what has gone before

S

that to the State pertains both the right and the duty of interference—of regulation in regard to this traffic.   We have seen
that this is admitted by the friends and even the representatives of the trade ; and, of course, such interference can have
but one object and one justification—that it is well aimed at,
and is successful in preventing the immoderate use of intoxicating drinks, and therefore in reducing the vice and evil of
drunkenness.   This being the object of control, it would be
difficult—indeed it seems to be impossible—to mention any
subject of greater importance to the people.   It concerns the
social and civil life of every one of them ; not precisely in the
same way that the due administration of justice affects them,
but rather as sanitary regulations, the neglect of which will
favour the outbreak of epidemic disease.   The State, century
after century, has made the sale of drink a monopoly, a share
in which it grants to certain persons on certain conditions of
locality, character, and payment.   At the present time, while
the extension of this monopoly is determined by local authority, the scanty income from it, rendered to any but private
persons, is centralised in the Inland Revenue department, and
such of the profits of the enormously valuable monopoly as
are taken for the commonwealth—say from somewhat drunken
Glasgow—are shared equally by the heavily rated inhabitants
of that town with the total abstainer in some lightly taxed
village of the south.   I think this is a part of the subject
which needs further consideration.   But let us first examine
the claim of the local authority to which the power of
extending this monopoly is conceded—I mean the licensing
justices.   I wish to speak with all the personal respect they
deserve of the unpaid magistrates.   For several successive
generations, I know not for how many, my fathers have been
licensing justices, and I have certainly no inborn dislike to
the class.   Yet I think their functions involve much injustice.
I will set aside their ignorance of law, which is often grossly
manifested ; but it is neither just nor wise, nor will it long

be thought tolerable, that men who represent nothing but property,—whose qualification is the possession of property,—should sit as judge and jury to try, in many cases without appeal, offences against the rights of property. Prince Bismarck has contended against very similar feudal privileges in Germany. Here and there only do they endure. Here and there only is it a fact that the possession of land or the rental of a house of certain pretensions is the qualification for a rural justice ; and here and there only is it a fact that the possession of an estate by a man of fair public character implies elevation to the seat of justice. In boroughs, the matter is a little different, but certainly not more advantageous to the public service. There the only difference is that we have less land and more license. I have watched the intrigues by which in this or that borough the nomination by the Lord Chancellor has been secured, and have observed that when it has not distinct and undoubted reference to Brewster Sessions—with regard to which, in utter ignorance of the borough, of course the Chancellor is blinded—it is usually a matter of party, of mere political colour. It is not to hands thus qualified and thus chosen that the people of any town can safely commit the regulation of a valuable monopoly, any more than they would delegate the functions of their Local Board or Board of Guardians to such a body. Mr. Bruce began higher than this in his Liquor legislation ; he slid downwards at the bidding of Parliament. Of course it was culpable in him to propose, and in Parliament to enact, ' elastic ' legislation, and we cannot be surprised that many scandals and much irritation occurred in consequence ; scandals, of which, perhaps, the case of the magistrates of a borough granting a special licence in a postprandial session for the continuance of their own mayoralty dinner was the most truly typical. It is abundantly clear that the power vested in licensing justices is not given to them from any conviction of their absolute fitness, but rather because, for certain reasons which are not fully stated, it is not thought desirable that it should be given to those who with full consent possess nearly all other local authority—the ratepayers.

Why have not the people control over this monopoly ?   In the Licensing Bill of 1872, Mr. Bruce proposed in the case where there was already more than one licence to 1,500 of the population, up to 3,000, and one for every subsequent 1,000 in towns ; and where in other districts there was more than one licence for every 600 inhabitants, that a majority of three-fifths of the ratepayers should have power to forbid the grant-ing of any new licence ; and in the Bill of 1872, with reference to hours of opening and closing, Mr. Bruce was prepared to give to locally elected bodies the 'elastic' powers which were afterwards conferred exclusively upon the justices. Yet in spite of this strong evidence of disposition to do justice to the inhabitants' claim of control, it is yet unaccomplished.   I repeat, Why is this ?   This denial is made, we are told, out of regard for the vested interests of the Liquor trade, and for the desires—which we may also call the vested interests—of the public-house-going portion of the community, whose facilities for obtaining intoxicating drink would, it is supposed, be endangered if the granting of licences were controlled by the ratepayers.   So that if we wish with general consent to accede to this claim for popular control, we have only to consider by what means, if any, the alleged immemorial concurrent and certificated rights of those connected with the Liquor trade, and those who are its customers, can be secured against oppres-sion or unjust extinction.   All the arguments resisting such control based upon comparison of the effects of similar regula-tions upon trades or manufactures which are not already, and have not been within present memory, the subject of such control, are unworthy of attention.   There is and can be 'nothing in it.'   If the trade is—as everybody admits—a fit subject for control, and for regulation of hours of sale, it is a fit subject for contraction.   It is absurd to take any other position. Parliament has refused to give the ratepayers control out of regard for the interests of the Liquor trade and of the consumers, freely admitting the evils inseparable from free traffic by maintaining a strict system of control, with a menace, in case of bad behaviour, of confiscation. At present, the licensing justices have a permissive prohibitory power, protected by their leaning to the interests of property, by public opinion, and by the indefinite power of the Lord Chancellor and the lords-lieutenant to add to their numbers. Can we not give to the interests which would be at stake, if the ratepayers' vote elected a Licensing Board, quite as efficient security? We can say that the sale of Liquor shall not be prohibited in any district but by the vote of a clear majority of two-thirds of the ratepayers, and we can require that within brief periods the sanction of that vote should be renewed. 'What tyranny!' say the 'rob-a-poor-man-of-his-beer' party. Yet they say nothing concerning the fate of a population of hundreds of thousands of their 'own flesh and blood' who, simply because they cannot obtain a local majority, or it may be a parliamentary majority, to do them justice, are compelled to drink liquid sewage. If I must die of drink, I would rather be killed by adulterated gin than by Thames water containing Windsor sewage and the washings of the highly-manured lands of the Thames basin. I think the millions who are drinking poisoned water—in London as in rural districts, because a majority resist, or are apathetic in regard to the establishment of an efficient local authority—deserve at least as much attention as the possible fate of this hypothetical minority of protestors against the very improbable stoppage of the public sale close to their homes of any fermented drink. But I would add something more than the requirement of a vast majority to protect this minority, and this I should propose to accomplish by a due regard for the interests of the licensed victuallers. I have never been able to support the Permissive Bill because I will not deny the publican's claim to compensation for the extinction of his

business on any other conditions than those assigned in his
certificate. I think the claim of the publicans, in such a case,
to compensation is quite as good as that of the proctors, and
better than that of military officers to over-over-regulation
prices as a consequence of the abolition of Purchase in the
Army. The country is full—too full—of evidences of the
sense of security in which their outlay has been made, and
if it were not unjust it would be highly unwise, in effecting
any moral improvement, to allow that it should be leavened
by any sense of injustice. Mr. Bruce himself said, in 1870 :
' It would be very unjust to deprive those engaged in that
[the Liquor] trade of their right to sell without giving compensation. . . . The publicans were encouraged by Parliament
to make those investments, and they should not be deprived
of the value of those investments.'

´ I think that the ratepayers' control of the Liquor traffic
might be at once assumed, but that there should be no power
of depriving a well-conducted house of a licence except by
compensation, the amount to be settled in the ordinary way.
Yet it is evident that in an increasing community where there
was a disposition thus further to restrict the monopoly of sale,
the value of all existing licences would rise ; and this consideration brings us to the matter of the Licence Rent, which
I believe Mr. Bruce once thought of imposing in addition to
the cost of the certificates. With the exception of a small
charge for certificates, paid to the Inland Revenue department,
the Licence Rent should always belong to the local authority,
and this charge, which should be imposed upon the fair rateable
value of the premises, ought to be proportionately raised every
ten years, if, upon the publication of the census, it was found
that the relation between the number of licences and of
inhabitants had altered in favour of the holders of the
monopoly of sale. It would only be just that this Licence
Rent should, together with the cost of Inland Revenue certificates, be equal to the difference between the value of the

premises for other occupation and their value as a licensed public-house ; the landlord having clearly no claim whatever to a value conferred upon the premises by a share in a public monopoly granted to his tenant. These Licence Rents might be passed to the receipts of the municipality in reduction of their ordinary expenditure, or set apart to accumulate a fund for the extinction of licences where that was thought desirable. The ratepayers' control would thus be weighted with a heavy responsibility. The elected Licensing Board would be cautious how they granted new licences which would reduce the Licence Rent they received from existing houses, and to the holders of which they must pay compensation if they desired the extinction of their business. The Liquor-selling part of the population desire no stronger protection against the power of two-thirds of their fellow-inhabitants, if those, together with their votes, are prepared to pay their share of the value of all licences in the district. The evil which could arouse a community to such an action must indeed be enormous. I have endeavoured to prove, as I firmly believe, that such a policy of extinguishing the traffic must involve very considerable pecuniary sacrifice, which could not be wholly avoided by adoption of the Gothenburg system. The Permissive Bill would, I think, become a practical measure if to it were added clauses such as have been sketched, altering the system of licensing, imposing—besides the Excise licence—a Rent belonging to the local authority, and providing compensation.

'Rather free than sober!' Thus spake the Anglican-Hibernian Bishop of Peterborough, and long will Dr. Magee's words be rung in our ears. It seems to me hardly more difficult to resist a feeling of contempt for a drunkard than for a sober man who is not a free man. To be sober is to be free ; to be intemperate is to be a slave. This agitation has bred fanatics on both sides. Egged on one by the other, they prove the most astounding things, to the immense satisfaction of themselves and their followers. If Mr. Bass does

not exactly write a new *Ebrietatis Encomium,* he now and
then does all that figures can accomplish to show that people
do not drink enough.   While one party expends real vigour
in the curious task of proving that wine is not commended in
the Bible, the other dilates upon ‘ the intercourse and recreation of the public-house ;’ and Scotland is racked with doubt
concerning the great sacramental controversy, entitled ‘Wine
or Must ?’ which is to determine whether a teetotaler can be
compelled, on pain of loss of Church membership, to sip the
cup of wine when he demands the unfermented must.   But
above and beyond all the fanaticism, all the selfishness, and
all the strife, rests the sad truth, which I despair of putting
more forcibly, and more hopefully, than did Mr. Bright when
he said :   ‘ If we could subtract from the ignorance, the
poverty, the suffering, the sickness, and the crime which are
now witnessed among us, the ignorance, the poverty, the
suffering, the sickness, and the crime which are caused by one
single, but the most prevalent, habit or vice of drinking
needlessly, which destroys the body and mind, and home and
family, do we not all feel that this country would be so
changed, and so changed for the better, that it would be
almost impossible for us to know it again ?   Let me, then,
in conclusion, say what it is upon my heart to say, what I
know to be true, what I have felt every hour of my life when I
have been discussing great questions affecting the condition
of the working classes—let me say this to all the people, that
it is by the combination of a wise Government and a virtuous
people, and not otherwise—mark that—that we might hope
to make some steps to that blessed time when there shall be
“ no complaining in our streets,” and when “ our garners may
be full, affording all manner of store.” ’

[1] Speech of the Right Hon. J. Bright, at Birmingham, January, 1870.

XII.

TEMPORARY EMPLOYMENT IN CASUAL DISTRESS.

THE indigent poor, for whom the legal machinery of relief exists, do not, in ordinary times, comprise many of the working class, in which I include those regularly attached to any trade or manufacture, with some special instruction in its operations. But the vast capital, which, in the United Kingdom, is applied to productive industry, will sometimes over-reach the demand for the products of a particular branch of this manifold labour, and so occasionally necessitate the partial or complete suspension of that employment, causing a large number of the workpeople to become dependent upon legal or charitable relief for the necessaries of life. A partial cessation of demand in any trade may be caused by an out-break of war, in which our country is neutral, an occurrence which no human prescience can foretell; and in any one of our great towns such an event may cause a thousand able-bodied men to be suddenly deprived of their ordinary employment. In such a case, it is obviously the interest of all to keep the men upon the place of their labour, ready to resume their productive industry.

Their strength and skill form a valuable portion of the capital of the country. If they are forced to migrate to other localities, and pressed by hunger to find employment in less valuable industry than that to which they have educated themselves, there is to them an individual loss, and there is national loss also, for the skill of a working man is his capital, and a part of the national capital, just as much as any sum of money which his employer has lodged at his banker's. If the man degrade his skill or loses it through long-continued rough labour, so that he never can resume his customary work, an ignorant waste has been committed which it is our present purpose to avoid, by suggesting the means of providing local labour to be undertaken during and only so long as the stoppage of production in any trade shall continue.

I am of opinion that we shall never see that improvement in the position of the working classes which is the most urgent demand of our time, till labour is placed by its own efforts and those of its enlightened friends in such a position at home as to counteract the charms of emigration. I am not of course alluding to the emigration of individuals who have peculiar taste or fitness for colonial life, but of that indiscriminate emigration which has been carried on and which many have regarded with inconsiderate delight. For emigration, whether patronised or voluntary, is national blood-letting of a doubtful and possibly of a dangerous character. I have observed that 'assisted' emigration, which supplements a working man's savings with a grant, deprives the country of the very flower of the operative class, and takes from that class those bright examples of thrift and prudence—of careful management and good household economy —whose presence in this country confers far wider benefits upon humanity than any to be gained by their expatriation.

Voluntary emigration, which it should be our aim to counteract by elevating and improving the life of labour at home, has been letting out the life-blood of the nation and leaving behind that which is less vital and healthy. I will venture to exhibit this fact in its darkest colours by a reference to that part of the United Kingdom where emigration has been most general—comparing the two census years 1851 and

1861 ; and it will be seen how—by the 'deportation of the able-bodied only—the proportion of deaf and dumb, of blind, of insane, of the idiotic, and of the lame and decrepit had increased in Ireland :—

PROPORTION TO POPULATION.

	1851.			1861.
Deaf and Dumb ...	... 1 to 1,265 ...		...	1 to 1,026
Blind	... 1 to 864 ...		...	1 to 843
Insane	... 1 to 1,291 ...		...	1 to 1,821
Idiotic ... ... '	... 1 to 1,336 ...		...	1 to 825
Lame and Decrepit	... 1 to 1,498 ...		...	1 to 1,408

I contend that it is in the highest degree dangerous to the vital interests of the country to regard emigration as the ever-ready panacea for distress. What our working classes most stand in need of is education and that economy in the affairs of common life which we trust will be its result. But if this is only to lead to the departure of such as are most success-ful in the acquisition, England, in bestowing this education, will be performing an act of duty—righteous and too long delayed—but suicidal. Therefore, it is our aim in considering this subject of employment during seasons of temporary distress, to make such provision as will not render the life of labour less attractive, and to counteract the invitation of friends across the Atlantic and at the antipodes.

It is a good symptom of moral health, that working men thus accidentally deprived of employment, by causes which they could neither foresee nor control, should be unwilling to apply to guardians of the poor for relief ; because they are in want of *wages*, not *alms*, and the Poor Law was not in-tended to supply wages, and cannot afford wages without danger of great disturbance of industry. The intention of the Poor Law and its customary duty, is to provide for the relief of the 'residuum' ;—of that most unfortunate class of persons which is in a condition of chronic indigence, often the result of a vicious and intemperate life ; often the fault-less consequence of naturally feeble intellect left without a kindly effort towards development. But the more general cause of application for Poor Law relief is sickness, incurable disease, and old age, when work is impossible. In all these causes, except the first, no shame should attach to the receipt of Poor Law relief. Such are entitled by right to the pittance which the law awards them, and, often present at its bestowal, I have grieved deeply to feel the necessity for its insufficiency, in regard to the provision of comfort.

But it is not likely that a working man, in full possession of active and skilful faculties, whose rapidly increasing family, it may be, has prevented any saving, would not feel shame at being classed with such incapables. His pride in his strength and his ability, so useful to himself and his country, revolts at such association. I visited hundreds of poor homes in Lancashire during the Cotton Famine distress, and I can say confidently that the nearest approach to starvation among that immense population was in those cases where pride strove with want, unwilling to demand relief from the Poor Law, which I am bound to admit was always extended with readiness and consideration. What bankruptcy is to the solvent, honourable men of the commercial class, pauperism is to the best of the working class—a surrender of that which can never be regained. But the French proverb, *ce n'est que le premier pas qui coute*, is never more true than in this matter, and I observed in Lancashire, how that once ' th' relief' was accepted, the proud independence not seldom ceased to appear wounded, and that the same people who had displayed so honourable a resistance, would often prefer the 2*s.* or 3*s.* per head of charitable relief which allowed them to lie in bed half the day, rather than five or six times the amount in wages, to be earned only by regular and steady labour. It is therefore most desirable for their sake and for the wider interests of the community, to keep the operatives and workmen suffering temporary distress from seeking the relief of the Poor Law. The Poor

Law has done all that is possible to prevent idleness by demanding an outdoor-labour 'test' of every able-bodied man who receives relief out of the workhouse. It is the function of guardians to prevent starvation, not to promote employment, and they cannot pay wages, or compete with employers. The health of a man with a wife and a family of six children will demand from them at least 12s. per week as the barest sum upon which their life can be maintained ; but a single man, equally valuable in respect of his labour, may be equally well preserved against starvation with a weekly allowance of 3s. 6d.

Guardians of the poor cannot undertake productive industry without effecting much harm. If they engage the distressed workpeople in the particular trade to which they are accustomed, their stock would further diminish the value of those, the too great accumulation of which has been the cause of distress. And if, with operatives quite unaccustomed to the work, they undertook the production of goods foreign to the area of their jurisdiction, they could not compete with the skilled producers of such articles, and they must sell their badly made goods at a loss, making up the wages of the poor out of the rates. So that in any case, if guardians undertook productive labour, they must supplement the payment with Poor Law relief. Probably, they would be displacing labour in another locality, creating elsewhere an equivalent amount of pauperism, and thus doubling the extent of distress. Moreover it would be necessary under such a system to guarantee a minimum of wages, which would be given alike to idle and diligent, and if these wages approximated to those which rewarded independent labour—as perhaps they would in the case of men with large families—the guardians would find themselves permanently charged with an immense population, growing with embarrassing rapidity, the value of whose labour would decline until, by the bankruptcy of the Union and their inability any longer to supplement the insufficient earnings of the people, the system collapsed with a disaster—— and famine and pestilence, the natural remedies of economic error, made ghastly claim to interference.

Therefore in the test of indigence, the guardians of the poor, as well as all voluntary associations formed for relief of distress, have experienced great difficulty in providing employment even for ordinary times, but, in extraordinary seasons, such as it is my purpose to deal with, they have wholly failed to meet the occasion. It must excite surprise in the minds of those who have not given much consideration to the subject, to hear that besides stone-breaking and oakum-picking there are no employments extensively used for the 'test' of indigence. And this is the more unfortunate, because it would not be possible to mention any two kinds of labour more painful to unpractised hands. Well do I remember seeing the blistered hands of hundreds of cotton operatives who could scarcely bear to touch the stone hammer for three weeks after they commenced the labour; and bleeding fingers with broken nails are always the painful result of inexperienced attempts at oakum-picking. Labouring with a spade or pickaxe; quarrying and loading stone, or even the work of roughly squaring stone, does not 'jar' the hands so cruelly as the task of breaking stones for road-mending, and there is no labour which has so exclusively bad, so peculiarly criminal a reputation as picking oakum, and I think, from a good deal of observation, there is none which men so much dislike. Such labour is used as task work—little or no encouragement is given to break or pick a larger quantity. The man breaks a yard of stones or picks so many pounds' weight of oakum, and then he is entitled to a pauper's sustenance.

Labour of this sort is intended to prevent demoralisation, in which it fails completely. I do not say that it is useless, but I am certainly of opinion that when applied to unfortunate working men it promotes demoralisation by degrading labour. If the best and most intelligent motive of labour, the completion of some work worthy of the labourer, or the acquisition of wages proportioned to the skill and strength expended, be not fulfilled—if the uninteresting, uncongenial, and unrecompensed task is compulsorily imposed, the workman—if he be a true workman—is degraded.

But it is not uncommon for even a more demoralising system than this to be practised with the victims of temporary distress. Yet a worse method is the requirement of work for so much time, perhaps one day a week, in consideration of the relief afforded. I have several times watched such schools of idleness. This system of labour is, I think, more injurious than total and declared abstinence from work, because it destroys, in the mind of the working man, any ideas he may have formed as to the dignity of labour, and positively teaches him idleness—a teaching and a habit much more easily acquired than thrown off. In order to make my meaning more clear, I will relate the operation of Relief Committees in two of the towns of Lancashire, during the Cotton Famine, which, being unwilling to dispense the money entrusted to them without some requirement of labour, undertook at fair rates of payment earthworks of the simplest description ; in one place, the easy formation, in a sandy soil, of roads upon a field of building land ; in the other, the removal of a large heap of dirt—both works admirably adapted for the employment of unskilled labour. I watched the men, talking, lying in their barrows, taking a long rest between every exertion, and desired the local officers in charge of the works to communicate to me the results upon completion. By the figures they sent me, I found that if, upon the road-forming, the men had received only their daily earnings, each would have been paid with less than $\frac{3}{4}d.$ a day, and that the dirt-heap, for the removal of which the other Relief Committee received from the landowner the just price of £17 7s. was not cleared away for less than £476 6s. 6d.; in other words, the Committee undertook the work at 2d. per cubic yard, and its execution cost them twenty-four times as much, or 4s. per cubic yard.

Upon the subject of the production by public authorities of saleable commodities, it is useful to regard the results of prison labour. I wish to give the Directors of our Convict Prisons great praise for the manner in which they have endeavoured to make the compulsory labour of prisoners remunerative. For the first time, in the not far-reaching history of prison economy, an English prison of the largest dimensions may be said to have paid its cost to the country in the year 1867. The convict prison at Chatham, employing a daily average of 990 men, incurred expenses, during that year, amounting to £35,315 18s. During the same period, the value of the prisoners' labour, taken upon schedules approved by the Admiralty and the War Department, amounted to £40,898 7s. 0½d.; so that the total sum earned by the convicts at Chatham, during the year 1867, exceeded by the amount of £5,582 8s. 11½d. the expenditure for their food, clothing, and all the necessarily heavy cost of their training and supervision.

This is a very important fact, and although convicts have no connection with the class we are especially considering, yet it has this association with our subject, that even under penal compulsion this great result was never attained until the introduction of the 'mark' system, by which prisoners are encouraged to work for the reward of privileges and small gratuities which are found to act as sufficient incentives to labour. The history of this success was told in the Report of the Governor of Chatham Prison, and in the following words :—

'A large number of the convicts, whose labour has been classed under this head (Admiralty Works), have been employed in the different descriptions of work connected with the manufacture of bricks on a large scale ; upwards of 17,000,000 bricks were made by them during the season.'

But in the employment of the indigent poor, no such productive labour can be undertaken with a view of giving the men, during the suspension of their proper trade, a fair day's pay for a day's work. If guardians of the poor undertook the manufacture of bricks, they would certainly fail in making them at a profit if they paid distressed men the usual rate of wages ; and the brick-makers in the union, whose stocks would be depreciated in value by the guardians pressing their bricks upon the market, would be taxed as ratepayers to assist the guardians in producing bricks to their own further ruin, and so on in all trades.

Stone-breaking and oakum-picking are adopted simply as the basest occupations and for no other reason. But the supply of broken stones or of oakum may be too great, and it is obvious that these degrading employments, though they may be fitted for a 'test' with tramps and vagabonds, are not suited for the class now under our consideration. I think it follows from these premises that the labour of such men must be employed upon works of *public utility*, in actual relation with the improvement of that which I will call the national freehold. They cannot be employed in connection with their own trade, for it is the stoppage of that trade which has reduced them to want. I have shown that as men working for wages they must not invade the area of any other industry under the protection of the guardians or any local authority. If they produce anything in their own trade, they defer the time when they may resume their customary employment, and if they attempt another, the operatives and workmen of that trade have to be taxed to supplement their inexperience. But if, by works of land-drainage, they can give the soil greater fertility—if, by providing for the storage of water, they benefit the health and convenience of communities and promote the fertilisation of crops in dry seasons—if, by shortening, levelling,

T

and improving highways, they can lessen the difficulties of intercommunication and the cost of carriage—if, by reclaiming land from wastes, and swamps, and shores, they can increase the area of cultivation—if, by the execution of house-drainage and sewerage works they can promote health and strength, cleanliness and self-respect ;—if, by these and many other such useful works, they can earn wages, these wide fields of labour are open to them, and when they resume their customary industry, after assisting in such undertakings, they can look with pride upon the useful works their hands have accomplished.

I have now, I hope I may be allowed to say, narrowed the subject so far as to make it plain : 1st. That in seasons of temporary distress, it is unadvisable to promote emigration. 2nd. That the production of saleable commodities cannot be undertaken. 3rd. That in any employment of persons so accidentally reduced to indigence, it is absolutely necessary to provide such labour as that at which they can earn *wages* sufficient for their maintenance. 4th. That no more than the proper value of their labour should be given in payment for the execution of such work. 5th. That the labour of indigent persons during periods of temporary distress, employed by guardians of the poor or any other local and corporate authority, must be confined to works which will come under the denomination of '*public utility,*' or '*sanitary improvement.*'

These words are extracted from Mr. Charles Villiers' Public Works (Manufacturing Districts) Act, 1863, and the plan I propose and recommend for the employment of the poor during seasons of temporary distress, is founded upon my experience in the administration of that Act. And generally successful as that Act was in operation, I must say that it could not possibly have been introduced among a population less fitted for outdoor labour. Accustomed to work in mills, purposely kept at a high temperature, the cotton operatives are men of soft skin and loose muscles—the last that would be chosen for handling a pickaxe or a shovel. By that measure, and by a subsequent Act of 1864, a sum of £2,000,000 was devoted to such works, my connection with which, commencing in 1863, was not terminated until the beginning of 1867.

During each year that the works were in progress I made more than two hundred official inspections, and after they had been a few weeks on the ground I could never distinguish factory operatives from 'skilled' men. Their faces reddened, their muscles strengthened, and their whole frames were invigorated by the labour. I have seen cotton operatives delighting in their quickly acquired skill in the construction of sewers, using the levelling staves and 'boning rods' with complete understanding of those appliances ; and I do not think that land-draining could be better executed than some work I saw performed mainly by the labour of cotton operatives both in Lancashire and Derbyshire. If it be admitted that only works of 'public utility and sanitary improvement' can properly be undertaken, and I am in a position to show that under a system of employment which—in conjunction with my friend Mr. Rawlinson—I watched, and with every detail of which I am thoroughly acquainted, nearly 4,000 cotton operatives, than whom no men could be more unfit for such labour, found employment upon the works, and that their average earnings, at fairly measured piece-work, were more than 12s. 6d. per week,—it seems sufficient to explain the operation of such a system and how it can be made of universal application.

This is what I intend to do, proposing such amendments as my experience suggests ; and some of these will have especial reference to bringing the provisions of a Public Works Act more quickly and easily into operation than was accomplished during the Cotton Famine .

I would propose that a Public Works Act should be passed, applicable to the United Kingdom, limiting to £2,000,000 the annual sum which the Treasury should be empowered to pay to the Public Works Loan Commissioners for the purposes of the Act ;—the special consent of Parliament being obtained if any further sum was required in any one year. I think it is desirable that a Minister should be directly responsible for the reorganised business of the existing Public Works Loan Commission ; but so long as that remains without a chief directly subject to parliamentary control, the advances for the purposes of the Act should be made by the Public Works Loan Commissioners, upon orders bearing the seal of the Poor Law Board and the signature of the President of that Board for the time being.

As a matter of detail, it would be desirable that printed forms of these orders should be kept in readiness at the office of the Board, and printed deeds of security at the office of the Public Works Loan Commissioners, in order to reduce as much as possible the cost to the local authorities of obtaining loans, and to avoid delay in passing the moneys to their account. We found in practice, that delay and expense were caused by the local authorities having to deal with two public offices, and it would undoubtedly be desirable to concentrate all the business of the loans under one department.

Loans should be made to any Local Board acting under the Local Government Act 1858—to any local authorities in-vested with powers of town government and rating under any local Act, by whatever name such local authority may be called—to any commissioners or body of persons, or any other authority having power to levy rates for general or special purposes, and to any guardians of the poor who have authority to borrow.

No previous limitation of borrowing powers, by any local Act, should affect the claim of any local authority to borrow under the Public Works Act a sum equal to one year's rateable value of the property assessable within the district, or parish, or place, in respect of which the loan is applied for. Any local authority having borrowed to this full amount may again mortgage their rates and obtain a further loan, an equal amount of the original loan being already repaid.

The cost to the Government of the money advanced under the provisions of the Public Works (Manufacturing Districts) Act 1863, was 3¼ per cent., the rate of interest charged upon the advances being 3½ per cent. per annum. If this advantage of ¼ per cent. can be maintained, it should be applied to the cost of inspection—to which I will refer hereafter, and the surplus in reduction of the costs of the mortgage deeds, so that as nearly as possible the charge of 3½ per cent. per annum for interest should represent the total expense to the local authorities.

The repayment of the loans under the provisions of the Public Works (Manufacturing Districts) Act 1863, was by thirty equal instalments of principal, the annually diminishing interest being added. I think that a better plan would be to calculate principal and interest together, in which case the annual payment for thirty years of about 5 per cent. upon the total amount of the loan would pay off both principal and interest, with the advantage to the local authorities of paying an equal sum every year.

The security for the loans would be upon mortgage of the rates of the city, borough, district, parish, or township in respect of which the loan was applied for, including 'any property of which the local authority was possessed in that locality.

It would be requisite that the works proposed to be undertaken should be of *public utility* or *sanitary improvement*, and the expediency of granting loans would be determined by the department charged with the administration of the Act, the Minister at the head of such department being responsible for the loans, the grant of which would in every case bear his signature as authority for the advance of money.

The loans must be exclusively devoted to the actual works in respect of which such sanction is given.

The money would be advanced in such instalments as the department charged with the administration of the Act thought proper to sanction, and the payment of any instalment might be postponed or withheld on notice being given by the department to the local authority, that the works were not being proceeded with in conformity with the plan proposed.

But the department should have power to sanction alteration of plans on the advice of their inspectors, being at the same time free from all responsibility in respect to the design and execution of the works, which, together with the requisite superintendence, would be entirely committed to the local authorities and their officers.

The Minister presiding over the department should have power to appoint inspectors of public works, whose duty would be to examine the plans, specifications, and estimates, submitted with each application for a loan, and to report upon these to the department ; the inspectors having full power and authority, at all reasonable times, to enter upon and survey the works or the site of the works, and to inspect the accounts of any local authority engaged in the execution of works, or in any expenditure of a loan obtained under the provisions of the Act.

The 7th clause of the Public Works (Manufacturing Districts) Act 1863, abridging the times of notices requisite for the adoption of the Local Government Act, I would entirely incorporate.

With reference to the sewering, drainage, forming and paving of private streets, I would recommend that every proper facility should be given to local authorities in serving notices upon owners of property, printed forms of such notices being always used, the general plan of the works, together with specifications and estimates, being deposited for examination. In charging the cost of such works to owners of property, the local authority should be empowered to include a fair

percentage of the general expenses for plant and superintendence beyond the actual cost of the works; and the
owners of property should be entitled, at their option, to pay
their debt at once, or with interest at 3¼ per cent. in any
number of years not exceeding thirty.

With the sanction of the department charged with the
administration of the Act, any local authority should have
power to agree with any owner of land, not necessarily within
the area of their jurisdiction, but within the Poor Law Union
within the boundaries of which the local authority was vested,
to undertake works of improvement, the proprietor repaying
their expenditure, with interest at the rate of 3½ per cent. in
thirty (or less at his option) annual instalments.

Where such owner has but a limited estate, he should have
power by deed to charge the cost of such improvement works
upon the inheritance of the property, a certificate of one of the
inspectors of public works being attached to such deed, certi-
fying that the works had been duly executed, and that the
charge upon the estate is warranted by the improvement which
has been effected.

In case of the guardians of any union undertaking public
works in any part of their union, they must resolve at a
meeting, after special notice in writing sent to every elected
and every *ex-officio* guardian, that the execution of the proposed works would promote the health or the convenience
of the inhabitants of such place, and the cost of the works
must be charged upon the place in which the money is
expended; and if in two or more places, then in proportion
to the outlay in each place. The guardians may appoint a
committee, of which the elected guardian or guardians, and any
resident magistrates, should be *ex-officio* members, delegating
to it full power to direct and carry on the works.

There is no city, or town, or district in the kingdom in
which there is no need for the execution of works of public
utility and sanitary improvement. Many are wholly without

sewers, or only supplied with old drains which are nothing better than poisonous cesspools ; many have no other water supply but from polluted wells ; many draw their contaminated supply from brooks full of sewage and other impurities ; in many, old streets are badly paved, and new, or by-streets, are impassable in winter, the surfaces covered with putrid filth thrown out from the houses ; scarcely a river-bed is properly and periodically cleansed of the accumulations brought by storms, which, obstructed by the bridges and buildings of towns, are usually deposited in their neighbourhood.

It may be said, that near every town there are undrained lands injuriously affecting the health of the population, the fertility of which would be greatly increased by drainage. Upon the public highways there are, in every direction, hills which might be levelled and valleys filled up with great benefit to the public convenience and reduction from the cost of cartage.   I could mention two places where every farmer, in a wagon-journey of six miles to the railway, has to send two extra horses, merely for three hundred yards of rising ground, which, with an expenditure of £200, might be made as easy as the remainder of the road.

The permanent works of highway improvement executed in several rural parishes under the provisions of the Public Works (Manufacturing Districts) Act 1863, effected a saving of 50 per cent. of the highway rates, the cost of repairs, including the annual sum due on account of repayment of the loans, being permanently reduced by that percentage.

About 68 per cent. of the sum advanced under the provisions of that Act was applied to the execution of sewerage, drainage, road and street works.

In the execution of sewerage works in the Borough of Stockport, out of 200 men employed, 160 were cotton operatives, who earned wages averaging 15s. 8d. per man per week.

In the borough of Bolton, in digging a reservoir for water supply, out of 336 men employed, 280 were cotton operatives, whose average weekly earnings were 12s. 7d. per man.

In the Union of Glossop, where, through the Board of Guardians, Lord Edward Howard (now Lord Howard of Glossop,) expended £20,000 in reclaiming land, in land-drainage and water-works, more than 400 cotton operatives were employed, whose average weekly earnings exceeded 12s. for each man ; and the expenditure of this large sum, upon the completion of all the works, was found to be thus proportioned for every pound : labour, 13s. 11¾d. ; materials, 3s. 2¼d. ; team work, 1s. 11¼d. ; plant and materials, 10¾d.

These are but fair samples of what was accomplished in very many of the ninety places in which works were undertaken under the provisions of the Public Works (Manufacturing Districts) Act 1863.

The works executed under such an Act are all of so beneficial a character that their commencement before the occurrence of distress, or their completion after it has passed away, are thoroughly advantageous and satisfactory. With reference to works executed in the Union of Macclesfield, the Clerk to the Board of Guardians wrote : ' It is a striking fact that in one street in particular, where fever always more or less existed, and where the labours of the Union surgeon were in constant requisition, no sooner had the main sewer passed each range of houses and provided for the surface and house drainage, than the fever abated, and finally there was not a single case in the street, an event previously unknown in the experience of the relieving officer, and this too at a time when the local relief committee was in full action, providing for destitution, which generally under other circumstances is the precursor of fever and other contagious diseases.'

It would be desirable that the department charged with the administration of the Act should issue instructions and suggestions for the execution of works, drawn up by the inspectors, pointing out the most improved methods of designing and carrying out works of sewerage, house and land drainage, water-supply, and with reference to other public works ; these printed suggestions to be always had on application to the department. During the administration of the Public Works (Manufacturing Districts) Act 1863, the local authorities readily adopted the resident inspector's suggestions, and in dealings with ninety local authorities nothing occurred to endanger the cordial co-operation of any one of them with the Government. The local authorities were always glad to avail themselves of his advice, partly because it was gratuitous and presumably independent.

In order to bring the Act quickly into operation upon the occurrence of sudden distress, local authorities should be advised to prepare and keep in readiness plans and estimates of such public works as they could undertake, preferring those which would afford most employment for unskilled labour.

At the commencement of operations, it would generally be necessary to supplement the earnings of unskilled men for a 'training' of four weeks. From the first, they should be employed upon measured or piece-work, and to the married men with families a small supplementary allowance might be given during this period. After four weeks' training, able-bodied men will be able to earn fair wages, and those who do not, being able-bodied, should be discharged from the public works and left to seek Poor Law relief.

The same men who, when employed by the Relief Committee to which I have referred, were loitering, lying on their barrows, and earning less than $\frac{3}{4}d$. a day, earned more than 12s. each in the first week they were engaged upon piece-work under the provisions of the Public Works (Manufacturing Districts) Act 1863.

The execution of the works should be entirely under local superintendence, the Government Inspectors having no authority to direct their progress. The unskilled men should be divided into gangs with a skilled man at the head of each gang. After a month's experience, and sometimes much less, the cotton operatives 'ganged' themselves, with one of themselves for leader, and I have heard men who earned less than $\frac{1}{4}d$. a day upon the 'make-work' system scold one of their gang for losing a moment's time by laying down his shovel to speak to a friend. Such is the effect of working for wages upon piece-work.

The formation of public parks or cemeteries affords very much opportunity for the employment of unskilled labour. The cotton operatives of Oldham laid out a public park in the neighbourhood of that borough, and I have many times heard them allude with pride to their share in the labour of such or such a part of that ornamental and useful work.

The weakly and aged men, who are capable of work, may be provided with employment under cover in bad weather, in preparing materials for the abler-bodied.

Charitable committees may very usefully co-operate with local authorities by providing warm clothing and thick boots for men engaged upon public works, and assisting those who from sickness are not capable of such labour. But it has been found impracticable for any voluntary association to undertake the execution of public works, because such a body cannot enter into binding contracts, having no sufficient corporate existence, and the individual members refuse to be personally responsible. Such committees may also very beneficially co-operate by establishing schools for the men who cannot find employment on the works, and night schools for those so employed, encouraging the former with gratuities sufficient for their maintenance, according to their progress in the school, and the latter with smaller gratuities for their fewer hours of study.

They may also establish schools for boys whose fathers are distressed by the suspension of their customary work, and schools, with sewing-schools attached to them, for women and girls who are able to attend, always accompanied, for both, with instruction in household economy—in cooking, washing linen, in general cleanliness and good order. For want of such training, I have seen in the 'pig-tubs' of poor cotton operatives such good food wasted, as in the houses of their employers would never be thrown away.

It is probable that in any other county than Lancashire a much larger sum would have been applied for, to be expended in land drainage ; but agriculture is nowhere more neglected than in the cotton district. About four hundred miles of main sewers and drains were laid, and an equal length of road and street works undertaken and completed.

There can be no doubt that the advantage of obtaining money for the execution of public works at the rate of 3½ per cent., and upon such easy terms of repayment, would conduce greatly to the sanitary improvement of the country, and would ensure applications for loans being made in times of distress, when it may be anticipated that local authorities would be anxious to prevent the emigration or the pauperisation of unfortunate operatives and workmen, and also to avoid the heavy poor-rates with which they must otherwise be charged.

XIII.

A REPLY TO CASSANDRA.

BECALMED in the vessel of State, I was suddenly alarmed by a cry of 'Rocks ahead!' and on looking up in a tranquil time, I felt tempted to say, 'It is only Mr. Greg,' and to resume a careless attitude. I remember to have heard Thackeray tell how that once on leaving London for Brighton he purchased a number of a cheap publication called 'Mysteries of the Court,' which was not calculated to sanctify the memory of His Majesty King George IV. Seven years afterwards, when about to re-travel the same journey, he bought another number of the mysterious issue, and to his surprise he found His Majesty 'still at it.' I have no hope whatever of detaching Mr. Greg from his favourite *rôle ;* he is always pointing to 'rocks ahead'; according to him there are, there always will be, 'rocks ahead.' But now he appears as a seer as well as an economist and as a politician. We must not suppose that his cry is simply that of an amateur, spying distant rocks, the mere sight of which of course bodes no danger. It is not as a simple traveller that Mr. Greg must be regarded ; he is Cassandra—Cassandra beloved and maltreated by the gods ; Cassandra heard and disregarded by inferior creatures.

I may be thought presumptuous if I attempt a reply to communications of this sort ; our Cassandra's eyesight is so superior to that of ordinary mortals. These 'rocks' are visible, but only 'to an observant and forecasting mind.' 'Englishmen never did look far before them ; but,' says our

Cassandra, ' I will signalise those dangers which I seem to see coming.' It may well be thought audacious for one who has no pretensions to prophecy to look straight in the face of superior wisdom of this sort and smile with assured confidence and contradiction. Mr. Greg having, however, brought the rocks within the range of common sight, we may pause to look at them with him. They are three, and are labelled :—

   1. The political supremacy of the working classes.

   2. The approaching industrial decline of England.

   3. The divorce of the Intelligence of the country from its Religion.

As I do not intend to devote three articles to a reply, I cannot equal Mr. Greg in expansiveness of argument. But I should not have taken up my pen if I did not feel that within the narrower limits to which I subject myself I could make it plain that Mr. Greg's arguments and statistics are confused, inconsequent, contradictory, and based upon error : and I shall not fully attain my end if I do not still further discredit as political guides the members of the school of which he is a distinguished professor, whose critical and intellectual eminence is ever vainly seeking the public ear, which is ever heedless, because these gentlemen display their incapacity in parading their belief that there is something magical and recondite about human progress—something which they alone can guide and fashion, which they only can impart and interpret—a doctrine at which humanity has laughed success-fully through all the ages of its history. One of their funda-mental errors is that which we may see lurking around the first of Mr. Greg's ' rocks,' and it concerns the distribution of political power. They have habitually and always viewed the diffusion of power with suspicion and dislike. For my own part, I have always looked upon men of this school as would-be members of an oligarchy, which, if it held supremacy, would drive me into revolt, probably sooner than any other tyranny. Hating all oligarchies, I should decidedly prefer a feudal oligarchy to one based upon self-sufficient intellect. There would surely be more of human nature in the former, and that is an excellent quality in rulers.

The diffusion of political power affects all matters of State ; and if our Cassandra would not admit the right of men and women to a directly representative share in the government which they support by the payment of taxes, and to whose laws they are prepared to render obedience, then I shall not fear to fall back upon the inferior ground of expediency. I will go on to show that this diffusion of power is indispensable to the welfare of the people, to the enactment of just laws, though we shall observe by the way that it is not only in the attainment of their right as citizens, but in its civilising influences, that this diffusion is also valuable. I shall be prepared to contend that the truest path of civilisation, and one which has never led a nation to ruin, is to be found in the extension of civil rights, and that the country most civilised is that in which the largest proportion of the population is able in absolute freedom to perform the political duties of citizenship. We must be aware that there are at least two other definitions of civilisation, and that our Cassandras would perhaps talk of what they call 'culture,' and mourn the decline of culture as an evidence of the decay of civilisation. Now I am far from saying that they themselves are without—no honest-minded teacher is without—real value and function in the State. Mental culture is their proper work and duty ; and though some trim their minds into strange and uncouth shapes, resembling 'cultured' garden shrubs of the Georgian *régime*, and others force their intellect to unnatural and unwholesome growth, while all suffer more or less from narrowness, from the seclusion necessary to such culture, or, I should say, from the exclusion of human infection, yet these evils are infinitely preferable to the diseases incident to many callings, and may to some extent at least be counteracted. These Cassandras will say, perhaps, that the spread of civilisation cannot be con-

current with the diffusion of political power because of the
decline of culture, which they allege is a consequence of that
diffusion, forgetting that under such circumstances culture does
not decline, but only appears to do so because of the large
number of persons, hitherto without its ken, who are suddenly
brought, not to the possession of culture, but within the sphere
of its influence.   I cannot say whether our present Cassandra
would regard my view of civilisation as more 'unlearned' and
vulgar than that third position, which, mistaking cause for
effect, looks up to civilisation as a huge and beneficent idol
whose head is the steam-engine, with the electric telegraph for
brain ; whose body is stuffed with paper money, with steam-
ships for hands, and whose legs are a compound of railways
and tramways.   It is not this or that ; a State is civilised in
which the people are powerful, not for a moment but as a
permanent force ;   and they are unlike the despot or the
oligarchy in this—that they can only be powerful where the
reign of law is supreme, and where their intelligent sense of
self-interest guarantees the security of property and the maintenance of order.

Accepting, then, what Mr. Greg calls the 'Revolution of
1867,' as due to the highest interests of the country, and its
consequence, the numerical superiority of the lower classes in
the electorate, we have to consider whether the avowed bases
of Cassandra's warnings are substantial.   We cannot be too
thankful for this change in the *modus operandi* of prophetesses,
though it may well be doubted if their reputation would have
survived had they in earlier ages made public all the grounds of
their dicta.   But here we must pause for a moment to supply
an omission which is very conspicuous in Mr. Greg's papers.
Perhaps Cassandra, scanning the horizon, scorns to look back
upon 'folly at the helm,' but while I profess small reverence for
prophetesses, I will say that if I took to the business myself—
and I am sure it is a very alluring profession, though its gains
are tenably reduced—I should certainly prepare my judgments

by a careful study of the past. I want to know what we are to lose by the alleged 'political supremacy of the lower classes;' I want to know what we have gained by the prolonged political supremacy of the upper classes. As to our country and its institutions, I believe I am at least as much of a Conservative as Mr. Greg ; but from his arguments it would appear that he finds in the statesmanship and in the laws of the past something quite opposite to that which I see in them.

The 'concise' and 'succinct' statements from the *Quarterly Review*, quoted by Cassandra, were, I believe, written by Mr. Greg, and these would seem to assert as a fact that the golden age of English history, in Mr. Greg's view, lies somewhere behind 1832. This appears marvellous, but it is at least intelligible. One way of refuting the assertion that we are going to ruin because of 'the political supremacy of the lower classes,' is to show that the extension of the franchise has been followed by universal improvement. There is to me something of incomprehensible self-delusion in a passage like this : ' Previous to 1832, in those old times when England was so great and paramount a nation, when we were so proud of our institutions when we were so exceptionally free.' I doubt if there is one among the teeming millions in those 'lower classes' of whom Mr. Greg writes with such superb patronage, who, if he or she were asked for an opinion on English history, would give one so intrinsically ignorant, so blind, so mistaken, so utterly incorrect as this, which Mr. Greg reproduces with something like paternal pride. The period of his eulogy was a time when from the profligate monarch on the throne to the knavish pauper 'on the rounds,' corruption and disregard of right rise as it were in a wall behind us. The Ministers, little more decorous than those of a former time, bribed only with patronage ; the Bishops, Deans, and Chapters trafficked for their own advantage in leases of Church lands ; in the Army, purchase ruled where nepotism did not ; in the Navy, the people were robbed by the appointment and payment of the infant sons and nephews of

U

those who had power, many years before the vessels to which
they were nominated could be launched ; the Civil Service was
filled with the creatures of the governing class ; trade was
embarrassed by protective duties, designed to benefit the landed
interest ; the penal code was brutal and bloody ; the foreign
policy of England was rude, ignorant, and flagrantly extravagant;
the people at large—'when *we* were so proud of our institutions '—were, as our agricultural labourers yet remain, the most
miserable in Europe.   In every one of these matters there has
been improvement, which I contend is chiefly due to the incor-
poration of the people in the government of the country.

It is well for the reputation of men like Mr. Greg, that they
are not tempted to set forth the national blessings of those
'good old times.'   Change had been slow in the 150 years
which preceded 1832, and it may be worth while to glance at
what Lord Macaulay has said of England in 1685, when 'the
finest of the houses in Bath, then a place of fashion,' resembled
'the lowest rag-shops and pot-houses of Ratcliffe Highway,'
when between the north and south of London there was no
communication save 'a single line of irregular arches, garnished
after a fashion worthy of the naked barbarians of Dahomey,
with scores of mouldering heads, which impeded the navigation
of the river.'   'If,' wrote Lord Macaulay (who died when London
was almost mean and miserable, compared with its present
condition), 'if,' said that historian, 'the most fashionable parts
of the capital could be placed before us, such as they then were,
we should be disgusted by their squalid appearance, and
poisoned by their noisome atmosphere.'   Then as now there
were Cassandras, who looked with fear upon the increase of
wages.   In 1680, a Mr. John Basset, M.P. for Barnstaple,
remarked that the high wages paid in this country made it
impossible for our textures to maintain competition with the
produce of Indian looms.   'An English mechanic,' he said,
'instead of slaving like a native of Bengal for a piece of copper,
exacted a shilling a day!'   How wisely Macaulay censured

shallow reference to old times when he wrote : ' It is now the fashion to place the golden age of England in times when noble-men were destitute of comforts the want of which would be intolerable to a modern footman, when farmers and shopkeepers breakfasted on loaves the very sight of which would raise a riot in a modern workhouse, when to have a clean shirt once a week was a privilege reserved for the higher class of gentry, when men died faster in the purest country air than they now die in the most pestilential lanes of our towns, and when men died faster in the lanes of our towns than they now die on the coast of Guiana. We, too, shall in our turn be outstripped, and in our turn be envied. It may well be in the twentieth century that the peasant of Dorsetshire may think himself miserably paid with twenty shillings a week ; that the carpenter at Greenwich may receive ten shillings a day ; that labouring men may be as little used to dine without meat as they are now to eat rye bread ; that sanitary, police, and medical discoveries may have added several more years to the average length of human life : that numerous comforts and luxuries which are now unknown (or confined to a few), may be within the reach of every diligent and thrifty working man. And yet it may then be the mode to talk of the reign of Queen Victoria as the time when England was truly merry England, when all classes were bound together by brotherly sympathy, when the rich did not grind the faces of the poor, and when the poor did not envy the splendour of the rich.'

Why are we in ' vital ' peril because of the numerical supre-macy of the lower classes in the electorate ? It is not difficult to find the soft spot to which Cassandra's warnings are directed. She says : ' In round numbers the population of this kingdom may be divided into *eight* millions of persons who hold realised property of some sort, and *twenty-four* millions who hold no property, but subsist by the labour of their hands. These twenty-four millions, or the householders among them, who may be reckoned at one-fifth, have now votes, or will have very shortly, or may have when they please, and they can, therefore, when they please, outvote and overpower the householders among the eight millions, who may be reckoned at one-fourth. That is, to put it broadly, there are, or may be, and soon will be, *five* millions of poor electors against *two* millions of well-to-do electors.' The allegation is that these five millions of men will wreck the ship ; that they will put their backs together and form a rock upon which the vessel that bears our Cassandra and ourselves must be broken. Why should this be ? Why should 5,000,000 combine to ruin their country, and 2,000,000 to save it ? Because the majority are stupid ? Who says they are stupid ? Cassandra. Ought not we, having by the hypothesis, nothing but the good of the country at heart,—ought not we to promote the desire of the many to foster by honest legislation the diffusion of property? Is it not because we feel the concentration of property to be dangerous that we need the influence of these 5,000,000 electors to render property more assured ? Property cannot be so secure when its ownership is confined to a small minority, as when proprietorship is diffused. Have the few shown the most intelligent appreciation of the position ? No well-informed person, thoroughly acquainted with the population of other lands, will dare to say, in the face of facts, that the people of England are happier, that they have more self-respect, that they are wiser, and more thrifty and prosperous. Mr. Greg, in a manner which is to my thinking odiously pharisaical, is 'satisfied' that 'properly trained, properly led, properly dealt with, they would make out and out the best Proletariat in the world.' Mr. Greg, 'repudiating with infinite disgust' anything like flattery, is graciously willing to admit that our lower classes are on the whole 'more intelligent, more fair, more sober-minded, and, but for their drinking propensities, more respectable than those of most other lands.' My opinion is not so favourable ; I am inclined to think that the mass of the people of England, while they possess unequalled natural capacity for government, are inferior in the points Mr.

Greg mentions to the working classes of most other lands, and that for their defects we have to blame such false guides as this Cassandra, whose idea of a proletariat is closely akin to *l'idée Napoléonienne*, and who deprecates their partnership in national affairs very much in the manner with which a head master would refuse the voice of the first form on the question of holidays. The truth is that Mr. Greg's ideas have had their day, and that the real peril of this country is now seen to be, not the participation of the labouring classes in the work of governing, not the diffusion of property, but its restriction, due to the supposed but mistaken self-interest of the extremely small class to which in this country alone the possession of real property in the agricultural soil is confined. The interest of the masses in the hands of representatives elected solely by the upper classes has been disregarded. We need no other proof of this than the repetition of Lord Derby's statement, that the produce of the country might be doubled. I have had some personal acquaintance with the people of every European State, and I never conceal my opinion that my own countrymen and women are not the most happy. They do not want money, but they lack that self-control which nothing that I have observed will make general except the potential possession of property in land, and the desire to accumulate savings, which the careful possession of property of any sort engenders. And that now they are entrusted with the suffrage, they will, with that cautious, prudent nature which is their inalienable birth-right, set to work to remedy the peculiar evils under which they have laboured, owing to the long reign of privilege in this country, is my earnest and confident hope. Their first act was full of promise, and refutes at a stroke whole pages of Cassandra's argument. Compulsory education was the first large work of their representatives. They are greatly inferior to the working classes of other lands in that economic and social training which the possession and management of property affords ; and it seems to me that the safety and prosperous progress of our country depend upon the acceptance of legislation which will promote the legitimate diffusion of property.

I wonder that men who have seen the peasants of Prussia, of Saxony, and of Bavaria, perform the greatest national work of the age, and then return, having secured peace, to their fields; who have seen French peasants, after fighting their best to keep their *belle France* from the invader, save the realm from the mad schemes of Parisian workmen, and within a few weeks after they had decreed with their strong arms the maintenance of a Conservative character in their government, lend the State £100,000,000; I wonder, I say, that men who have seen these things remain blind to their lesson. Mr. Greg has to unlearn the error of all men who believe themselves qualified to govern, rather than to serve, the people. He has not a notion what good judges of their own self-interest the people are. He regards them as infants with dangerous tendencies. He would take them out walking in the ways of politics, having first prepared the ground. The paths that lead to foreign affairs they would find labelled ' No thoroughfare—for Diplomatists only,' or ' No road this way.—Keep the Balance of Power.' If they turned their eyes to right or left at home, they would find similar reservations. The questions which affect property and taxation are announced as ' fearfully complex,' and they would be at once warned off from the close preserves of primogeniture, entail, and settlement. In Mr. Greg's school it is held naughty to think that all the children of a family have equal natural claims upon their male parent, and his pupils have to torture their rational powers to ' make believe' that it is for the good of the commonwealth that a testator should be empowered and encouraged to put the largest possible area of land into life-tenure, or virtual mortmain.

The leading principle of Mr. Greg's school is, that politics are non-natural, and that simple ideas in public policy are ruinous and deadly. The proletariat is to obtain the nearest

possible representative of Lord Palmerston, and having placed
him in Downing Street, is evermore to look with awful
admiration and unquestioning respect upon his mysterious
doings.   Yet I doubt if it would be possible for a Foreign
Affairs Committee of working men to make two such blunders
as the jealous opposition to the Suez Canal and the invidious
and untenable exclusion of the Russian navy from the Black
Sea.   Both have been reversed by a Parliament elected since
'the Revolution of 1867,' and none are now heard to lament
the change.   I recall an interview with one of Mr. Greg's
high diplomatists which amused me greatly.   On the eventful
day, in 1870, upon which the Secret Treaty between Benedetti
and Bismarck, concerning Belgium, was published in the *Times*,
I was in the cabinet of the British Ambassador in Berlin.   An
editor of the *Cologne Gazette* had shown me a summary of the
Treaty, which I believe reached the eyes of our Ambassador
by telegraph from London.   He was full of Mr. Greg's ideas.
'Ah,' said he to me, with wonderful *gaucherie*, 'England is
declining ; would you believe it, I have actually received
to-day an application from an English viscount in the capacity
of special correspondent for a *penny* paper, and I dare say
he is paid as well as a secretary of legation!'   I sighed, of
course, at the imminent downfall of my country, and reflected
that possibly special correspondents were the *bêtes noires* of
diplomatists of this sort, whose reputation could hardly sur-
vive the exposition of these ubiquitous observers.   Knowing
what, in Mr. Greg's view, a 'true statesman' is, can we wonder
he should give us as his opinion that 'the very depth of a true
statesman's sagacity, the very forecast of a true statesman's
vision, will alienate from him the sympathies of the average
elector'?   It is wrong, perhaps, to suppose that a prophetess
can be fallible ; but if Cassandra could only know how often
those whom she calls 'true statesmen' have been saved from
terrible errors only by observing and by following the simple
expression of self-interest by the people, she might not perhaps

altogether abandon a *rôle* so interesting, but she would certainly abstain from giving the grounds of her judgment so fully in future. Indeed, one prominent error in Mr. Greg's political ideas is the supposition that his 'lower classes' are unable to see what is good for them because they do not recognise 'fearful complexity' in every question. The undeniable fact is that the nation is the best judge of the self-interest of the nation.

Why does not Mr. Greg bring forward a list of 'vital' errors committed by enfranchised peoples? He is candid, he is intelligent, he is, outside English land and labour, fair and courageous, and he must know that while such errors are hard to find, the shores of the main stream of history are rendered unsightly and horrible with wrecks due to the bad seamanship of those 'true statesmen,' who were a guide unto themselves. He admits that 'for the future our main security will be in the wider diffusion of property, and in all such measures as will facilitate this result,' and yet he is so short-sighted as to mistake the only possible means to that end for a 'rock ahead.' Is there any lesson so patent and so plainly written in history as that the diffusion of property is concurrent with the diffusion of political power? Is it worth while to get one's self up as Cassandra, and to write a book, of which one half is a contradiction of the other half? Mr. Greg and I are at one as to the course which the ship should take—the direction being the diffusion of property. But he throws a boom across the open channel in order to drive the vessel on his 'rock ahead.' He says : 'In a fair fight, unquestionably the Propertied Classes *versus* the Proletariat would have a quick victory now ; they will have an easy victory if they open their eyes and close their ranks in time.' As one who feels that the 'propertied classes' have very important duties in the nation, I pray that they may exhibit no such folly. What can be more absurd than this,—to prescribe diffusion of property, and then to tell the owners that they must close their ranks? That would be a course fraught with peril, and the only satisfaction it could bring would be the justification of Cassandra's warning. The ship would soon be on the rocks. I write this reply because I see that 'the political supremacy of the lower classes' will bring about that 'diffusion of property' which Cassandra admits is our only safety, and which I shall show could be accomplished by no other agency. The history of property is, as any one would expect, a selfish record; its possessors have through all time only consented to laws which promote its diffusion when they were constrained by the supremacy of rising classes. William, England's Conqueror, made large deer forests, and enacted that whoever killed a hart or a hind should be blinded. The chronicle of the time tells us that 'the rich complained and the poor murmured, but he was so sturdy that he recked nought of them. They must will all that the king willed, if they would live and keep their lands.' That was how the king acted when all was his. Then followed the diffusion of property enforced upon King John at Runnymede. Now let us pass on to a time when the owners of land under our present system held unquestioned 'political supremacy'—a time just about two centuries ago. I will make a brief quotation from a paper entitled 'Free Trade in Land,' which is included in this volume :—

'About two hundred years ago the position in which the landowners and the people find themselves to-day was reversed ; the former were mightiest in Parliament. And what did they do ? They found a large taxation levied on the land, of which it is not untrue to say that it was the purchase-money of their estates ; they threw off these feudal dues, and substituted an Act "that the people of England should pay a tax of 1s. 3d. per barrel on their beer and ale," with a proportionate sum on all other liquors sold throughout the kingdom. And it was enacted that a moiety of this tax " shall be settled on the King's Majesty, his heirs and successors, in full recompense and satisfaction for all tenures *in capite* and by knight service, and of the courts of wards and liveries, and all emoluments thereby accruing, and in full satisfaction for all purveyance." This tax was carried in a House of 300 members by a majority of two. Then, again, when a land tax of 4s. in the pound had been imposed, the landowners contrived, in 1697, so to frame the tax (9 Wm. III., c. 10,) that it should not increase with the value of the land, as was at first intended, but should be a fixed annuity without rise in value.'

It must be admitted, I think, that the diffusion of property can only be accomplished by the possession of power to enforce that diffusion, and I have no confidence that the owners of property, even in this enlightened age, would not be ready to follow pilots such as Mr. Greg on to his 'rocks ahead.' If they do not commit suicide by 'closing their ranks,' it will be, I am confident, because such a course would be as ineffective as 'a mop against the comet' in face of 'the political supremacy of the lower classes.' It is time, however, that I should refer to the not less glaring folly of those who suppose or suggest that it is the interest of the 'propertied classes' to 'close their ranks.' The blunder of the majority of those who have held property throughout history has been the assumption that the diffusion of property was synonymous with the impoverishment of themselves. This is Mr. Greg's error both in regard to social and international concerns. How few of the 'propertied classes' have ever comprehended the irrefragable truth that property has this quality—that its volume and value increase, where increase is possible, just in proportion as the ranks of the 'propertied classes' are not 'closed'; in fact, augment as these ranks are extended.

The safety of the British State demands the speedy increase of the 'propertied classes;' not, of course, by the plunder of those now in possession, for that would defeat one of the two objects that we have in view: (1) the better security of property, and (2) the more productive cultivation of land Mr. Greg fears an invasion of the rights of property by (1) a graduated Income Tax; by (2) the imposition of all fiscal burdens upon realised property; by (3) the promotion of Mr. Mill's claim for the 'unearned increment' of land; by (4) the furtherance of such doctrine as that taught by Railway Acts and by the Irish Land Act, which he thinks 'gave up the entire principle of the sacredness of property.' And another class of dangers to issue from this 'political supremacy of the lower classes' is, that they will seek, 'more or less through the instrumentality of legislation,' such things as 'higher wages, shorter hours, more power of dictating conditions of work, and less strictness in the interpretation of contracts.' Of course they will consider their interest. But will they press this to the point of national ruin, of self-immolation ? Of course they will not. Where will they stop ; where should they stop ; to what point does the national interest demand that they shall succeed ? Mr. Greg shall give the answer : 'With the possession of property will come Conservative instincts and disinclination for rash and reckless schemes. It is not in itself a political education, but it forms an excellent basis for it.' Lately I met with curious corroboration of this. Some men, who are members of the Agricultural Labourers' Union, are also interested in the co-operative agricultural scheme of a well-known friend of that method of production, and when the accounts were overlooked the other day, the Union men objected to the high price of labour, in their new capacity as proprietors. Does not this show a way to avoid the 'rock ahead' ? I sail free of apprehension because, through 'the political supremacy of the lower classes,' I see clearly the channel to far greater prosperity than we have ever yet enjoyed, in which, by the instrumentality of good laws, such as will benefit both landowners and landless, by the wider distribution and registered transfer of land, by the encouragement of thrift—that careful fruitful mother of property—the incidence of taxation, direct as well as indirect, will be more general ; the enforcement of contracts will be easy, because of the nearer equality of condition among all classes, and the value of realised property will not only be vastly augmented, but will be guaranteed by millions in place of thousands of owners.

Mr. Greg has really much to discover concerning the classes of whose ignorance he is so certain. He has to learn that which, by their enfranchisement, statesmen of both parties have admitted,—that in all great national causes they are the best

possible jury. It is almost puerile on his part to lead his
followers headforemost on his first 'rock ahead,' by assuming
that the decision of the minute details of administration must
be submitted to the arbitrament of five million voters.
Mr. Greg sees far enough to notice that the degradation of the
House of Commons must ensue if the residuum choose their
members according to the length of their purse. But what he
does not see is that the remedy will come in the same way by
which his 'proletariat' will learn to co-operate in the national
welfare—by the diffusion of property. If the 'propertied
classes' were foolish enough to 'close their ranks,' and to go
on indefinitely as at present, I have no doubt Mr. Greg would
be right in predicting that 'a larger proportion than hitherto
of Ministers, especially of Cabinet Ministers, will in future be
members of the Upper House.' I am so ardently in favour of
associating the 'propertied classes' with the government of the
country, that even if the House of Lords had not the high
qualities which so many of its members possess, I should be
devoted in upholding it ; I should say : Wherever you can
find five hundred men who are owners—though they be only
nominal owners—of one-fifth of the kingdom, place them by all
means in a Senate. But though I am thus steadfast in supporting the hereditary element in our legislature, I think it highly
perilous to rights of property, and a national danger of the
extremest kind, that this can be said of the ownership of our
soil. Of course it would never have happened if the wonderful
wealth of English manufactures had not concentrated so much
of the energy and intelligence of the country upon foreign
trade. But it must not endure. That would be certainly dis-
astrous, not only because it would involve the denial of that
doubling of agricultural production, which, in the opinion of
such a man as Lord Derby, the country might and therefore is
bound to accomplish. Mr. Greg does not yet comprehend that
his first 'rock ahead' is a sure and safe stepping-stone to the
removal of this peril, and no one will gain so much by laws

promoting the diffusion of property as those who are now the owners of property. Thrift, I think, would naturally be very strong in the British character, yet we are the least thrifty of European people. The reason is not far to seek. There is no instance of a frugal people who, to use Mr. Cobden's expression, are divorced from the soil. Mr. Greg must lend a hand to pass such measures as those which I have indicated in 'Free Trade in Land'; by those reforms rather than by others such as have been adopted by less pauperised nations of the Continent, diffusion of property in land must be accomplished, and then the wasteful expenditure of the mass of the people will decline ; then artisans will learn from agriculture, that great teacher of thrift, the value of saving, and the country will be happier, richer, safer because of 'the political supremacy of the lower classes.'

I must deal more briefly with the second 'rock ahead,' which, however, can be disposed of without prolonged or elaborate argument. I do not apprehend that I shall have great difficulty in proving even to Mr. Greg's satisfaction that the 'rock ahead' which he has named 'the approaching industrial exhaustion, or decline of Great Britain,' is a phantom. Mr. Greg has raised a spectre of alarm about the coal supply, which I must not hesitate to say is built up of sensational and arithmetical delusions. The method is simple, and likely to deceive the unwary. He parades the coal-fields of the world, and the glory of them—those which are near the surface as well as those which are deep,—and he compares them with our own in respect to the labour of getting the coal. It has been well known that our main advantage was not only in the position of our seams of coal, and in their proximity to our ports and our mines, but also, and perhaps chiefly, in regard to labour. No figures that Mr. Greg brings forward with regard to labour have any relevancy in comparison with those which I offer to him and his alarmed fellow-passengers in the vessel of State. He quotes Sir Charles Lyell's well-known account of the Pittsburg

seams, and if the inferences which in this and in other places
he apparently wishes us to draw, were really by themselves
accepted, he and all his friends ought, for decency's sake, to
appear much more frightened.   Suppose Mr.' Greg had put
this part of the subject in another form ; suppose, after admitting that labour and population are prime elements in this
question, he had put the matter thus : The population of
England is so much, that of the United States is so much ;
before the square miles of the States become as populous as
those of England, and land ceases to attract from mining, the
population must be nearly *fifty times what it is at present.*
Although the population of the United States has at one time
doubled in a quarter of a century, there are abundant signs in
that country, as in all others, that the rate of increase of population is invariably subject to steady and continuous decline.
I cannot venture to predict the time when the population of
the United States will amount to fifty times its present total,
nor do I think that any amateur Cassandra, with a grain of
self-respect, would ' put a date ' to this problem.   And if ever
it should reach fifty times its present total, it may then be as
disproportioned as at present to the population of these islands.
Yet half the foundation of Mr. Greg's second ' rock ahead ' is
built upon the fallacy of the near approaching equality of condition as regards the coal supply.   In part, also, this ' rock '
stands upon the approaching exhaustion of our own stores.
What I most complain of in Mr. Greg's work is that there is
a fallacious parade of care, with a show of calculation which
is not borne out upon anything like critical examination.   In
this matter, after promising ' most sedulously' that he will
' state no facts or premises that are doubtful,' we find him
writing in the following loose. manner : ' It is obvious that
unless some great check should come to our prosperity and to
our increasing population and manufacturing productiveness,
our annual consumption of coal will go on augmenting, and
will soon reach, not 120 millions of tons yearly, but twice,

thrice, or four times that amount.' Now I want to know why it is 'obvious,' and which is it to be 'soon'—240 or 480 millions ? The climax of this rash and random statement is that the available coal-fields may be worked out in '*a hundred years.*' What is the ground for supposing that our consumption of coal will increase by this arithmetical progression ? I know of none. Surely, if Mr. Greg were himself, and not Cassandra (who of course knew nothing about coal), he would never have piled upon our credulity not only this arithmetical progression, which is of course worthless, but all that plus the native re-sources of all the earth. We are actually asked to contemplate the decline of our coal supply by arithmetical progression, at the same time that we are bade to behold the men of all lands throwing out their own supply and manufacturing their own goods. This 'rock ahead' begins to look very small indeed. It is just the contrary law which governs the whole earth. There is no such thing in real life as increase by arithmetical progression. At our present most extravagant rate of con-sumption it is estimated that the British coal supply will last 1,200 years, and in days when a 99 years' lease is hardly dis-tinguishable in value from a freehold, is the exhaustion of coal a 'rock ahead' visible to 'an observant and forecasting' mind ? We may consider this part of the 'rock' removed.

'But these figures only represent half the facts wherein our danger lies. The essential question is not how soon will our coal be worked out, but how soon will our cheap coal be worked out ?' The answer to this is that our cheap coal is in no danger of being worked out. The recent famine price of coal was not due to the difficulty of getting it, or else the miners' wages would have been forced up by a per-centage closely equivalent to the increase of price. That coal famine was due to a speculative and wholly unreal demand for manufactured iron, which has left the peoples who were pur-chasers of the iron—such as those of the United States and Russia—far more embarrassed by unprofitable expenditure than we were burdened by the coal famine. One result of that period was the opening in North Derbyshire alone of pits which are turning out a supply of 60,000 tons a week, not an atom of which was available before the coal famine. All through Mr. Greg's second paper there runs a palpable fallacy which appears and reappears with curious frequency—a fallacy which may be made very plain merely by asking him to consider that his remarks about cheap coal were written in 1834 instead of 1874. They would have been just as true then as they are now, but what he regards as cheap coal would have seemed to the Cassandra of '34 ruinously dear. He spends page after page upon this point: '*Cheap* coal, we repeat, is obviously and notoriously indispensable to the continuance of our marvellous productions, and how is cheap coal to be secured when every year we have to dive for it deeper and deeper into the bowels of the earth, and to pay higher and higher wages to the miners who produce it?' This would have been just as apposite in '34 as in '74, and if we suppose it written forty years ago, then our day supplies the true answer, and at once the sensational calculations of Mr. Greg's second paper tumble to pieces and fall to worthlessness. Mr. Greg is really the victim of one of the most hoary and inveterate of economic fallacies. There is hardly a simpler mistake to be made in politics than to regard the wealth of one's own country relatively to that of others as the test of prosperity. We are more wealthy in '74 than in '34, not by virtue of the discovery of internal mines of wealth so much as through the increased riches of those who are our customers, our rivals, and neighbours. Coal is relatively as cheap now as it was in '34, and there is no reason to suppose that it will not be relatively as cheap in 1900 as it is at present. The labour that wins it may be rewarded with more money, but it does not follow that the coal is relatively dearer, to the damage of our export business. Mr. Greg has incautiously fallen headlong into the fallacy that the increase of our neighbours must be our undoing, but it would seem that he has decidedly undervalued the progress of economy both in production and in consumption, which are more certain and inevitable in the future than any of his lamentable figures. He quotes Sir W. Armstrong's words, who said : ' Speaking generally of coal consumption in all its branches, there can be little doubt that without carrying economy to its extreme limits, all the effects we now realise from coal could be attained with half the quantity we use.' I could find it in my heart to welcome a ' coal famine,' greatly more prolonged than the last, if it were only to stimulate such economy, for the sake of our atmosphere as much as for the saving of our coal-beds ; and I have no doubt whatever that the event which appears to Mr. Greg as the foretaste of a scarcity which will soon be exhaustion, has in reality, even in its short duration, produced a permanent economy in consumption, the positive value of which has in the years that have since gone by recouped the total extra sum which was paid for coal in that time of artificial scarcity.

We pass now from ' the Exhaustion of Coal ' to ' the Deterioration in the Character of British Labour,' in which by ' character ' Mr. Greg means ' efficiency and conscientiousness.' The general overlying error in this part of Cassandra's warning is in the absurd assumption, from the minor warfare of classes, that the industrial body will commit 'happy despatch' and ruin the country in order to pay the salaries of Trade Union secretaries. No one but a man whose mind was full of conscious condescension to a proletariat could be capable of the mistake involved in this assumption, but Mr. Greg is resolved not to see beyond the array of figures and statements which perhaps will deceive no one but himself. The first point is, ' Does a reduction in the hours of labour involve a corresponding diminution in the produce of that labour ? ' Mr. Greg asserts that those who say, 'No' are theorists. I must be pardoned, therefore, if I state in defence of my claim to be regarded as practical that I have been to a certain extent officially

X

responsible for the labour of 6,000 men in that textile district which is directly affected by the Factory Acts, and I deny, with a knowledge of factories in every town of the cotton manufacturing district, that a reduction in the hours of labour involves a corresponding diminution in the produce of that labour. Mr. Greg does not put the matter fairly. He says that the assertion practically amounts very nearly to this : ' That of two equally able-bodied and well-fed labourers, the one who lays down his spade and wheelbarrow at four o'clock will have done as much work as the one who toils till six o'clock—in fact, that nothing at all is done in the last two hours.' This erroneous statement is only another consequence of Mr. Greg's view *de haut en bas* of the workman, whose labour he thus appraises precisely as that of a machine. The matter can only be rightly regarded as one affecting the man's whole life, and himself as one of the race and nation. If he work, with two intervals for meals, from 6 A.M. to 5 P.M., will he be a better workman and turn out more and better work *through every hour of the day* than if he labour from 6 A.M. to 6 P.M. ? I say that undoubtedly every hour of his day would be more productive, and that where he was not labouring in connection with machinery over the motion of which he had no control, it would very likely happen that he would produce more in the nine than in the ten hours, while it is certain he would be a more healthy, and, probable, that he would become a more intelligent citizen. If a man cannot try this question by uninterrupted daily labour from Good Friday to Christmas Day, he may even get somewhat near the truth by noting how he treats his horses, which are practically his slaves. If Mr. Greg knows anything of horses, he would not think it at all absurd to suppose that the aggregate hours of a horse's working life would number far more if he worked nine than if he worked ten hours a day. I have known many poor farmers, but I never knew one who worked his horses at plough more than eight hours a day. I am quite certain that horses could not drag a plough for ten hours a day with anything like the vigour they possess for eight hours, and as the farmer is the owner of the horses and suffers by their incapacity, illness, or premature death, he does not feel tempted to make the experiment. There must of course be a point at which the advantage of a reduction of hours rapidly diminishes, and again a point at which it ceases to have any benefit in regard to the productiveness of labour and the bodily fitness of the workman. I cannot say whether this natural limit is ten hours or eight hours. It is possible to suppose that for about half the world of labour it is ten hours, and that for the other half, an eight hours' limit is better ; therefore perhaps it is best for the permanent interests of production to fix nine hours as a day's labour.

Of course the increase of the results of labour during shorter hours cannot be great where machinery is the producing agent. Yet there is an increase. Mr. Brassey said in one of his interesting lectures on labour : ' As a general rule it appears that in proportion as the hours of labour are lengthened the rate at which machinery is run is reduced. In Russia, where the longest hours of labour prevail, machinery is run at a slower rate than in any other country in the world.' I agree with Mr. Brassey as to the mode in which the loss occasioned by idle machinery must be recovered. He asks : ' Why should not the machine which never tires be tended by two or three artisans, relieving each other as one watch relieves another on board ship ? ' I am not going to contend that it is under any circumstances possible that the produce of all the factories of Lancashire and Yorkshire would be as large under a nine-hour as under a ten-hour system, but with all his knowledge of ' mules, looms, winding-frames, etc.,' Mr. Greg is apparently not aware how small the difference may become. He does injustice to accuracy in two points. Regarding the human being as a machine, he speaks of 54 or 56 hours with no regard to the national cost and loss from sickness or premature decay ; but I am now dealing with his estimate of the possible results of reduction of hours in the statement that 'some attendants [upon ' mules, looms, winding-frames, etc.'] may no doubt, by greater energy and more unrelaxing vigilance, get as much out of their machines in (say) 54 hours as others will in 56 or 58.' That is four hours ; if I could get Mr. Greg to allow but two more, the case for reduction from 10 to 9 hours would, even in conjunction with machinery, be conceded. What will he say then with regard to the persons, of whom nearly every loom-shed in the cotton and woollen manufacturing districts will furnish examples, who by ' greater energy and more unrelaxing vigilance get as much out of their machine in $40\frac{1}{4}$ hours as others in 54 ' ? The ' three-loomer ' is by no means a phenomenon among Lancashire and Yorkshire lasses ; most women can attend two looms, but not a few can serve three. This class, which simply by superior intelligence and quickness earn half as much again as the majority of women in the same shed, will certainly be more likely to increase with shorter than with longer hours, for their swifter faculties are those which are not extended in a population doomed to severely continued monotony of life, and theirs are precisely those natures which are soonest worn out by unduly prolonged labour. Of course in this argument I am not expressing an opinion in favour of legislation which operates to any extent as a restriction and disability upon one sex, and thus tends to limit its powers of participation in the wages' fund.

In treating of the contention of labour for increased share of profits as bearing upon our national prospects, I think Mr. Greg does the working class great wrong by persevering in one-sided argument. I find throughout his work no appreciation of the fact that in this country, by restrictions which have the force of law, labour is deprived of that more equal partnership with capital which exists in other lands. Why, when in the opinion of great agriculturists and landowners such as Lord Leicester and Lord Derby the food produce of these islands could be doubled,—why should English capital be wasted in purchase of American 'mines' which are metalliferous only on the surface and in the prospectus, and in the purchase of foreign bonds which may be worth only the paper they are printed upon? It is estimated by scientific agriculturists that to produce this increase of food a highly profitable investment of from £500,000,000 to £800,000,000 is requisite, and this sum will never be applied until there is a vast diffusion of property in land, and the use of the best machinery is universal. In Roumania, I have seen ten of Clayton and Shuttleworth's steam threshing-machines in a morning where no farmer held more than twenty acres, and there is nothing to prevent the steam-ploughing of ten farms at a single operation. The real 'rock ahead' is our land system, which the thing that Mr. Greg mistakes for a 'rock ahead' is destined to amend. The diffusion of the ownership of land is the sure means of diffusing the possession of capital; and while capital is less greedy in the distribution of profits when its possession is not confined to the employing class, so labour becomes more appreciative of the sensitive qualities and disposition of capital, of its fearfulness and immediate flight from the neighbourhood of dishonest or irrational power. As compared with continental countries—say with Germany—we are undoubtedly at a disadvantage, because our legislature has proceeded upon the monstrous and absurd notion that it is better for thousands than for millions to have 'a stake in the country.' It is a remarkable testimony to the natural advantages of our country and to the ability of our race (which I believe to be superior to all others in power of industrial production) that we more than hold our own in manufactures against such a people as the Belgians, in spite of the great advantage they possess in the virtual immunity from pauperism and the partial insurance against the fluctuations of industrial employment which their diffused land system affords. In Belgium and in other

European States, the artisans are recruited from agricultural districts in time of great industrial activity, and are in turn absorbed in rural occupations and cared for by the sympathy of agricultural friends and relatives when there is a glut of supply in the manufacturing markets. Mr. Greg fears that 'the political supremacy of the lower classes' will induce them all to live on the poor-rate. I see a time when the owners of property, being then millions instead of hundreds of thousands, will be strong enough to compel stern amendment if not the virtual abolition of our Socialist Poor Law. Although very far removed in the social scale, I believe it to be a fact that primogeniture is the parent of pauperism. We have witnessed a time of great trial in the battles of labour and capital, but these we know are undertaken from a real or supposed self-interest, and it is quite reasonable to promis ourselves that as that sense grows more enlightened and the many become wise as well as powerful, the wars will be fewer and the arbitrations more numerous. This indeed is already everywhere observed.

It is strange that any one should question if working men have gained by the operation of Trade Unions; but of course it is difficult to decide whether they have or have not thereby received a larger aggregate sum in wages. Yet it almost surpasses belief that so clever a man as Mr. Greg should overlook the facility which these Unions have introduced in settling the rate of wages. Mr. Greg must admit it would be absurd to doubt their effect in raising both the net average earnings of the individual workman and the aggregate earnings of the whole body of artisans, if we might assume that their endeavours have always been directed with the utmost sagacity to effect those objects. It would be simply imbecile to question when there are two parties to a distribution of profits, each haggling as to the share which shall be allotted, to the one in respect of his capital and superintendence, and to the other for his labour, that the tendency of advantage is on the side which is most concentrated. But to concentrate the bargaining power of the workmen is not all that the Unions have done. The very first element of successful resistance to an inequitable distribution is the possession of accumulations—the power of waiting. Labour which cannot maintain itself for a time in idleness must be prepared to accept harsh terms, and we have only to suppose that for the most part the Unions have been actuated by a true sense of self-interest to establish incontestably their utility, not only to the workman but to the community which benefits by the results of shorter hours and higher wages —in the improved physical capacity and the higher intelligence of the working classes. And surely there are many most encouraging signs that this improvement is accomplished. I wish I could conscientiously adopt Mr. Greg's silence as to the faults of the capitalist class. Do they not now and then league to limit supply? For my own part, I am more afraid of the sudden action of 'rings' than of Trade Unions. I know of half a dozen village wheelwrights' men who lately quitted the neighbourhood of Exeter, and are now established as skilled miners in North Derbyshire; and from nearly every quarter of England that ogre of Mr. Greg's fancy, the champagne-swilling, dog-fighting collier, is finding competitors. I am sorry that Mr. Greg should make so great a mistake as to put upon artisans and labourers the responsibility for whatever there has been of decline in our national reputation for the conscientiousness of British workmanship. This fault is surely rather to be ascribed to that cardinal evil of our society, which Mr. Greg appears to recognise but will not help to remedy—the aggregation of property. It is the speculative manufacturers and contractors, in too great haste to join the narrow and therefore so envied ranks of 'aristocracy,' who, in order that they may follow the lead in buying estates and riding to hounds, plaster their calico with size, who deliberately steam their workmen in order to make the worse sample of cotton seem better, who make coats of shoddy and knives of iron, who supply guns and powder to our declared enemies, who will only pay for scamped work. No artisan of any country deliberately prefers to do bad work. With artisans trained as ours are, the quality of their labour is mainly a question of materials and superintendence. Mr. Greg twists and turns to their disadvantage and that of his country every circumstance. Let us look at one of his statements. There is none upon which he seems to stand more firmly than that of Belgian competition in the iron trade. It is, I believe, a fact that in the spring of 1874 Belgian iron-masters did secure foreign orders for rails which had been offered to English makers in the first instance, and shortly before I read Mr. Greg's book, in which he prophesies our national ruin partly as a consequence of this occurrence, I met a member of Parliament who is chairman of a large iron company, and we at once began to talk of the reports concerning Belgian competition. He said he had examined some of these Belgian rails, and that he found them of very inferior quality to those of English make. He told me he had no fears whatever concerning Belgian competition [I shall be very glad to give Mr. Greg his name], and that no railway company in the United States which required rails for wear would have purchased such as those from which Mr. Greg infers the downfall of our iron trade. It would be easy to accumulate proofs that the conscientiousness and quality of British labour stand relatively as high as at any period of our history.

But it is not in coal and iron only that, according to Mr. Greg, our trade is to be cut off; on no subject does he make more parade of statement, and upon none is he more lugubrious, than in regard to 'our competitors in various textile fabrics.' Now I shall have written to little purpose if I have not made it clear that in regard to his statements and arguments connected with trade and commerce, Mr. Greg's fundamental error lies in confounding our relative position, which of course declines as other countries approach a higher level of industrial and mechanical industry, with our actual position as regards wealth and comfort in the future. To understand this thoroughly we must make a brief digression into remarks applicable to all trades before we return to deal specifically with Mr. Greg's observations upon the textile industries of the United Kingdom. It appears to me, that in order to fathom the depth of Mr. Greg's mistake, we must obtain his point of view, which I have always regarded as that of a British Imperialist, one with whom the external reputation of the Empire is well-nigh all-important, one who thinks the leaders of the people should be Masters, rather than, as they are, Ministers. I can fancy how hard it is to Mr. Greg to believe in the greatness of his country, when, from a military point of view, he sees her dwarfed from the equal authority she once held, and descended to be of little account upon the Continent of Europe ; and I can well believe that were it not for some lingering echo of ' Rule Britannia,' some vague but hopeful assurance, that if we could no longer assault their inland towns, we could force half the world to keep within their ports, Mr. Greg would not have heart enough to assume the garments of Cassandra. I am sure he could write a well-stocked essay, to show that we have miserably declined since the days of Walcheren and Waterloo. In trade the same theory haunts his mind. No foreigner must make a stocking ; the increase of foreign spindles is deadly ; and as for Belgium daring to increase her export of woollen yarns, it is enough to make Britannia weep and tremble with fears of approaching desolation. Now, regarding ourselves as a trading nation only, having natural advantages, as to climate, soil, insular position, and mineral wealth, it must be a benefit to us, as it is to individual tradesmen, to live among wealthy neighbours. It cannot be to our advantage that those with whom we do business, with whom, in fact, we barter our productions, should continue in a savage or semi-barbarous condition. The quantity of labour which we have to put into an article of commerce, for which some tropical people will most readily give, say, coffee, is but one side of the bargain. The other side is their production of coffee, which becomes more easy as they grow richer and their labour more intelligent and fruitful. It is quite conceivable that increasing wealth, due to the demand of other countries than our own, might enable the coffee-grower to produce two pounds of coffee with the same labour which he formerly bestowed upon the production of one pound. If no one else produced cloth, he must then give us two pounds of coffee for the same piece of cloth which formerly exchanged for one pound. But other people having common wants are also in the market, and let us suppose that their competition keeps down the price of cloth to the old rate of exchange. Then the coffee producer, through the increased wealth of his country, has another pound of coffee to deal with, after the purchase of our cloth ; and, presuming the second pound is for export, he must buy with it something else, to the inevitable advantage of all industrial peoples ; or, if there be nothing else that he wants besides cloth, the price of that commodity must rise. Mr. Greg's error is so patent, so simple, and in so able a man so startling, that one is almost inclined to apologise for setting forth such elementary facts in commercial science by way of refutation. Is it possible he can suppose that 2,000,000 or 20,000,000 of people will exist in any country who because they happen to look at 'happy' England from across the Atlantic or the Channel, and to know something of her mines, and factories, and workshops, will therefore have no thought of mining, of weaving, of fashioning iron and hardware ? We cannot be spinners and weavers for all the world ; we do not feed ourselves ; we cannot even clothe the English-speaking race and the Indian fellow-subjects of England. Time was when we could have clothed and fed ourselves, and Mr. Greg evinces no small desire to do it still, even at the cost of a protectionist policy. Why, in the name of all that is commercial, are we to take alarm because Belgium sends some woollen yarns to this country ? Directly or indirectly she must send something, for she is an importer of British materials and manufactures. She must pay for these in some form or other. Is it any injury to us, whose cotton manufacturers are to a far greater extent engaged in supplying foreign customers than in meeting home demand, that Belgium should pay her debt partly in woollen cloth? and are we in consequence to suppose that Belgium is therefore able to absorb a trade which surpasses the powers of the greatest of industrial nations? There is no people of Europe of whom with any reason it can be asserted that, within any conceivable time, their advantages for manufacturing industry will equal our own. Much that is said of the quarrels between labour and capital is of universal application. We are terribly weighted in the race by the load of pauperism and the cost of strikes, which will never be onerous in countries where the ownership of land is associated with the lower classes. But neither in regard to cheap coal, or iron, or labour, have the nations of Europe at present, or in prospect, advantages equal to our own. Mr. Greg will say this is not so; but if he be right, why, then, is there need to shelter their own industries by heavy protective duties against English manufacturers? If foreign nations could compete with us on equal footing, why do our goods enter those countries, and maintain their place, notwithstanding that they are weighted with heavy duties? If our Cassandra were justified in half her prognostications, we should expect to see no great anxiety on the part of foreign manufacturers to handicap the Englishman in the race. Surely if we are as Mr. Greg represents us, there could be no danger to the manufactures of these rivals and competitors, if we were free to take our goods to Berlin, to Paris, and to Vienna, and there compete with native industry. Has Mr. Greg any doubt what would be the result if trade were free throughout the world? At all events I have none, and in this confident opinion I am supported by that of all the practical men of England who have studied the position of our foreign trade. I will quote the opinion of a large employer in the textile trade, which Mr. Greg regards as menaced with ruin. If there is a practical cotton-spinner in the world, Mr. Hugh

Mason is one ; and is he terrified ?   Mr. Mason says : ' I have
not a particle of fear of ruin to our cotton trade by the adoption of fifty-six hours a week.   Not one of the great powers
could hold its own for a year in cotton manufacture apart from
the high protective duties which prevent the entrance of British
goods.'   We may regard Mr. Mason, in his capacity as Chairman of the Manchester Cotton Supply Association, as the
highest and most conclusive authority ; and we must observe
that he says nothing about export ; he affirms that our competition would kill in one year the home trade of any one of
the great powers of Europe.   Incidentally, in the same letter,
Mr. Hugh Mason touches upon our possession of a permanent
advantage, one which appears wholly to have escaped Mr.
Greg's observation, and one which, happily for us, is inalienable,
and is our absolute and unique possession.   It seems to me
to be a glaring defect in Mr. Greg's argument that he should
have made no allusion to the advantages of our insular position.
' I think it idle,' says Mr. Hugh Mason, ' to talk about foreign
competition, so long as the kingdoms of Europe are divided
into half a dozen vast camps for soldiers, and the claims of
commerce are subordinated to the strife for military glory.'
There is no prospect that this heavy tax upon the industry of
Europe will be removed.   The avoidance of all imminence of
war will not lighten its pressure ; and however confident we
may be that the time will come when there will be a considerable reduction of armaments, we can conceive no period in
which the manhood of Europe will not be largely engaged in
acquiring the art of national defence.

Mr. Greg's second 'rock ahead' is now seen to be nothing
but an inflated canvas painted by himself with mistaken
colours.   Mr. Greg will perhaps take comfort in the reflection
that he is Cassandra, and that Cassandra had no credit however
faithful and accurate might be her predictions.   But, in truth,
such arguments as Mr. Greg puts in her mouth must be tried,
and may be tested by the logic of facts and by the laws of

economic science. I have not, I must admit, demonstrated the insecure foundation of Mr. Greg's arguments more clearly than did a writer in the *Spectator*, who declared that : 'Mr. Greg's error is really closely akin to that old Protectionist fancy that one nation suffers by the development of the resources of other nations, instead of gaining by it. Nothing is more certain, we take it, than that it is for England's national *advantage*, to put it plainly, that she should lose her commercial supremacy, if she loses it by no wasteful blunder of her own, but solely by the legitimate development of such of the resources of other nations as were hitherto unknown or unused.' But I am far from intending to imply that Mr. Greg's labour has been entirely wasted. He does not appear to notice it himself, but he has surely made it clear to others that the diffusion of property by legitimate and well-ordered means is the one thing which more than any other is the need of this country. To strengthen and largely to recruit the Conservative classes, not by such expedients as that recently in vogue, the drenching of the residuum with beer and gin, but by directly counteracting by diametrically opposing that dangerous tendency to the aggregation of property in fewer hands, which is the great, and, as I believe, the only peril of England ; this is the chief legislative need of the future. I cannot regard it as a 'rock ahead,' because the power to accomplish this end is already in the hands of those who will partake the benefits of such legislation. Indeed, that power which Mr. Greg has named his first 'rock ahead,' is all that is requisite to liberate the industry of England from the trammels of feudalism, and at the same time from a social danger which it is a blunder to regard as insignificant. We must spread a real, not a spurious and delusive Conservatism, by making the many instead of the few personally interested in maintaining the rights of property So long as the agricultural soil of England is mainly held by life tenants, who are but nominal owners, we are not sailing in the race with Belgium, with France, with Germany, with any of our neighbours, under fair conditions. Let us but have this 'diffusion of property' by the reform of our land laws, by affording the artisan class that highest encouragement to thrift in the readiest and safest means of investing their savings, and then we shall pass on over the stream of time in which Mr. Greg fancied he saw these 'rocks ahead,' a nation more united, more wealthy, and more powerful than at any period of our history.

Mr. Greg's third and last 'rock ahead' is one which people will see, or will not see, according to their ideas of Religion. My firm belief is that no two persons can contemplate Mr. Greg's position from precisely the same standpoint, and to those who concur in this opinion it is unnecessary to say more with reference to his fears concerning 'the divorce of the Intelligence of the country from its Religion.' If it be accepted that Religion is, and always has been, and must of necessity be, an exclusively personal affair, 'the Religion of a nation' becomes an inaccurate expression, and the fact is admitted that the truths of Religion are perceived and accepted as the truths of Science are received and accepted in a manner which precisely accords with the mind of the individual. To say that 'the Religion of a nation ought to be the embodiment of its highest Intelligence, in the most solemn moments of that Intelligence,' has a grand sound, but it can only be received as truth with this proviso, that the Religion will be accepted only in some personal or material forms by the many, with an ever-changing vision of its spiritual aspect varying from the lowest to the highest intelligence. This is true even where Religion consists of 'Salvation formulas of Creeds and Churches.' Though both accept the same formulas, yet none of us doubt that between the Religion of Dr. Manning and the Religion of a market-woman of Toledo, there is a difference far wider than that which separates certain members of different Churches. Mr. Greg has put a commonplace truth into the language of culture—that is all. From the foundation

of humanity, what he pleases to call a 'rock' has been dis-
cernible; but no harm has come of it: those who have cared
to learn the truth have known that Religion, whether it be
regarded as of Divine Revelation or of human construction, is
in its acceptance relative to mental condition, and therefore, to
say that the 'highest Intelligence' of a people is not in harmony with the Religion of the mass of the people, is merely to
say that which must be evident in every community to every
thoughtful man. In order to rear his 'rock ahead' out of the
waters of fact, it has pleased Mr. Greg to assume that the
'Christianity of the nations' is one solid uniform body of
thought, severed from its head, which he places in a condition
of timid or blatant (according to culture) negation of all
Religion. There are, in fact, many Churches; and there
are at least four Christianities,—all useful, all progressing,
each attracting members by natural selection. There are
everywhere the Penal Christians, whose rude natures take
delight in the barbarous punishments of Scripture history,
and who find salutary discipline in the fear of hell, the fate of
Ananias, and the cruel sacrifice of Christ. There are everywhere Redemptionist Christians: these are especially the
people of 'Salvation-formulas'; Christ is not only their
Exemplar and Saviour, but their Judge; and this milder
and more humanising creed has made them, and will, beyond
the time of my possible conception, continue to make them
an adornment of any community. Thirdly, there are the
Priestly Christians, including the Catholics and High Churchmen. With these, Christ is the Founder of a system of
theological government, which they claim the sole power
to carry on with the agency of saints and priests. And,
lastly, there are the Christians (and these, I suspect, include
most of Mr. Greg's infidels) who see in Christ's teaching
the highest morality, the truest principles of human government, the ennobling hope of spiritual immortality; they
find all this entangled and overlaid with Eastern metaphor

and interpolated verbiage, which are to them not unintelligible nor misunderstood; and having thus submitted Christianity to the severest rational test, they are pleased to call themselves Christians. If there are any who seem not to be included in these four categories, it is only those of the last, who in revolt from what they regard as the gross and superstitious exaggerations of others, can find satisfaction in nothing but momentary expressions of contempt and abhorrence. I see no 'rock ahead' in this religious progress. We are safe so long as we are free; and not only are we free, but we are becoming, and we must become, more free every day. Mr. Greg looks fearfully to a day when men and women will be still more harshly divided than at present; yet surely this is not the terror of the time when the sexes are usefully co-operating in all directions; and whereas formerly the clergy were the only class of men who sought women's aid, we now find a serious conviction overspreading society that 'it is not good for man to be alone' in other spheres than those of the Church and the family.

With his mechanical idea of the proletariat still in his mind, Mr. Greg supposes that *en masse* they can suddenly be turned from millions who are kept straight by fear of hell into millions bent on the sensual enjoyment of lifelong lust and rapine by the removal of that terror. Does not Mr. Greg perceive that the hope or the fear of immortality being of those things which he says are to the highest Intelligence 'unknowable,' are therefore ineradicable? To talk of a whole people being 'convinced' that there is no 'hereafter' is an absurdity. I cannot think that any man or woman was ever yet held back from any crime by fear of hell, while I fully believe that millions have been led to do good for love of Christ by such virtues as He taught; and as I cannot see how it is possible that the 'highest Intelligence' can ever be divorced from the highest moral principles, I have not the slightest fear that the progress of Religion will bring anything that is hurtful. Mr. Greg will see nothing that tells against his miserable forebodings. Yet is there not every promise, in all we see around us, that every day, more and more, the error, which is made by Mr. Greg and by so many others—that Religion is an affair of nations and not of individuals—is being abandoned? The nation is not less religious, truly; but it grows wonderfully tolerant, except to the law-breakers of the law-established and nationally endowed Church, and they can do exactly what they please when they cease connection with the official service of the State. That inequality of privilege which Mr. Greg says we must remove, is doomed; we have the promise of that in 'the political supremacy of the lower classes.' I do firmly believe with him that the well-being of our community demands 'that no unwise or partial laws favour unequal distribution.' There are such laws touching all departments of our social life; some which are cruel, others which are most strikingly unjust, and some which are exasperating in their inequality. These were our 'rocks ahead'; they were dangerous when we had no power to avoid them. But they are no longer our peril; the people have acquired the political force which will bear us on our course with safety.

XIV.

WOMEN'S SUFFRAGE.

I TASK my memory in vain to recall a time when it did not seem to my humble judgment a self-evident proposition that within the limits of the constitution, as defined by law, the political rights of citizenship were the correlative of the burdens of that condition. Again and again on my way through life I have asked myself the questions: What is the justification of law? Why am I bound by the clearest and most cogent promptings of self-respect to obey and to accept the authority of law? My answer to these self-interrogatories has never varied. I have felt that the authority of law found its supreme and all-sufficient utility in making the weak to be as the strong. When we speak of lawless men or lawless communities, we indicate some who are oppressing others; they are men or communities who know no law but that of might in their dealing with other people; they are brigands who, hardy and well-armed, descend upon the defenceless traveller, or upon the timorous villagers; they are races who, valuing laws for themselves, treat some inferior race with lawless cruelty. Whenever or wherever a law can be found affecting the general welfare of society which places a portion of the fully responsible members of that society under disabilities, denying their equality before the law, we may be sure that statute is imperfect, and will in time give place to a more righteous edict. We know that in this country there are nearly a million more of the weaker than of the stronger sex. We are aware that no dis-

tinction is known in those obligations which are not regarded
as privileges. A woman is equally liable to punishment with a
man. It is not Lady Burdett-Coutts' footman, but herself, upon
whom the tax-gatherer makes his demand. The office of poor-
law guardian has been much and very unwisely degraded ; the
woman householder may vote for him. Town councils and
local boards are not held in very high estimation ; the questions
upon which such elections turn are not of very apparent importance ; they are rarely interesting to the higher mental faculties.
Women may vote at the election of such local officers, and, of
course, when the Education Act was passed, it was obligatory
to concede that franchise. It would have been too absurd
to maintain that women should vote in elections to a body
entrusted to some extent with the administration of justice,
with the regulation of footpaths, roadways, drains, gas-lamps,
and policemen, and yet should have been the only ratepayers
disqualified for voting or taking electoral part in the education
of young children. The political suffrage is still withheld.

Before passing to the grounds on which this denial is supported, I will say that in advocating the political enfranchisement of women, I do not admit the existence of opponents.
There are those who are doing their utmost to retard that
amendment of law which in this world of ours is always going
on—that approach toward the sole justification of its authority,
the equalisation of strength before the law. In this progress there
may be stumbles and faltering, turnings to this side and that ;
but there will be no rest, and every year will find us further on
the road to the goal which, the more successfully we labour to
approach it, appears ever the more distant. As striving to do
justice, to love mercy, and to walk humbly, we get fuller and
fairer views of duty, so before us the horizon of thought and
the perception of right expand in the clearer atmosphere, and
our notion of the fulfilment of duty, which, as we toiled with
faces to the ground in the heavy air of lower life, was narrow
and selfish, becomes ever more wide and more comprehensive, as

the clouds of prejudice and ignorance roll away. I recognise no opponents, only hindrances in the path of progress to that condition of society in which every person shall exercise his or her faculties to the fullest possible extent, and to the utmost advantage of others. I note that the idea which men in general have of the character and position of women may be traced to the earliest historical times. Painters have contributed largely to this idea. I will not speak now of that grievous hindrance to the spread of true Christianity which they, in their ignorance of the realities of Eastern life, have perpetrated in so grossly misrepresenting the life of Christ. How much nearer the hearts of men and women would have been to-day to that glorious example if painters had sketched Him as He was, who shall say? But, blind to reality and truth, they have taught, in their pictures of Eastern women, that grace is compatible with sloth; that suppleness of body comes without training or exercise; that refined beauty can be the natural partner of ignorance and indolence; in short, that every perfection of form and face is consistent with an existence and a diet of which the sure results are obesity and inanity. Let us have done with all such falsehood. Let us believe that figs will sooner grow of thistles than the graces of life of sensual and sordid hours.

I do not care to argue the question of women's possible fitness for enfranchisement, when I recall to mind the venerable figure of one of the greatest mathematicians of this age—Mrs. Somerville. In every sphere of life in which women have been allowed full scope and encouragement they have been admirably successful. For literary brilliance, few men of our time have been the equals of Caroline Norton and George Eliot. And few are the Frenchmen to be compared with Georges Sand, 'whose style,' says Mr. Mill, 'acts upon the nervous system like a symphony of Haydn or Mozart.' The temple of histrionic fame has been fairly open to women, and queens of song have received in this country larger remuneration for their labour than has ever been given by way of payment to any man in the State. I do not argue that women, who are only disqualified by reason of sex, ought to have the political suffrage; for that I regard as a self-evident proposition. I rather propose to remove by solution the hindrances which retard the attainment of their right. I propose to show those who obstruct this measure of justice that their policy is not merely vain, but wasteful; and I have thus glanced from one phase to another of the condition of women with a double intention. I wished to show that the progress of women towards a fuller responsibility is desirable as well as inevitable. I wished to exhibit the disposition of women to accept the force of custom. When I hear it said of any women that they do not desire change; that they would rather 'rest and be thankful'; that the path to which others invite them is unwomanly and 'mannish'—I am not surprised. These are the invariable objections of women all up the gamut of civilisation of which I am striking a few notes. In 1867 I spent a week in a mud-built town upon an oasis in the Great Desert, where every householder walked with the huge key of his house —and of his wives—slung on his girdle. I am quite certain that those women had no desire for English freedom. I have heard a Turkish lady of rank scold her husband because he admitted a strange man to her presence before she had adjusted her face-veil. 'Tis

> 'Custom that makes cowards of us all.'

That women are unfit for enfranchisement, and that all women do not demand enfranchisement, are arguments which we may now set aside. But still I hear that which the Member for Edinburgh University so happily summed up as 'the old "rib" theory' ringing in my ears. The objector to my line of argument says, 'True it is that the progress of women towards fuller responsibility and fuller exercise of mental and moral faculties is inevitable, but your chain of instances only shows her condition relative to that of the man and always in subordi-

nation to the first-born of creation. The English woman is up
to my level as the Bedoueen wife to the standard of her
husband. You assert something more, and that which is unnatural and wholly different from the phases of this equal
progress.' I am prepared to meet such a line of objection.
But I insist upon this : that the measure of that fuller happiness
which this Englishman thinks he has in his married life, the
superior joy which he believes himself to have in the society of
his wife as compared with the Bedoueen, who never regards
women as the intellectual companions of men, is, whether he
knows it or not, the degree of independence which the woman
has gained from the progress of that authority of law which, as
I have said, justifies its claims upon our allegiance only so far
as it tends to equalise the subjection of all to its behests.

Why in so many cases is there a painful contrast between
courtship and marriage—a contrast never to be observed in the
long continuance of the closest and most affectionate friend-
ships? I say that this decline of happiness is at least to some
extent caused by the decline from equality of condition. It is
with me a firm conviction that true love can only co-exist with
sincere respect, and that respect will be very apt to fail
when it is required of one who is independent, for another in a
dependent condition. Remember, I would say, that marriage
is a deliberate act, not of purchase and sale of human rights,
but of partnership ; and just as I believe that an Englishman
would find little happiness in the society of an Arab wife, so I
argue that the nearer the wife's state of legal and political responsibility approaches his own, the greater will be his happiness
and his enjoyment of her society. I know I am at present
occupying low ground ; I might content myself with saying that
this enfranchisement is a right, and therefore should be granted ;
but I will not for that reason forbear from showing men that
their interest and happiness are involved in this progress. I
will not even use an argument so far removed from selfishness
as to speak of children, though it must be clear, I think, that

the education of the young is at present greatly hampered by the illiberality of thought which is so often instilled at the mother's knee, and which leads to so much painful reaction in after-life. I say, then, that if men will strive to place women in a position of equality before the law with themselves, and to promote an education for women equally fitting, they will be in less danger of finding in marriage a disillusion.

But more than this. Many men nowadays groan beneath the burden which the folly and extravagance of their wives brings upon them. To the same cause, let me say in parenthesis, is owing the rapid disappearance of the practice of polygamy in Constantinople. It is in vain that the law of the Prophet allows four wives, when the bills of French milliners and of the vendors of *articles de Paris* permit but one. The allusion is not indeed irrelevant ; for just as the irresponsible extravagance of the women of Stamboul is helping to work out a great moral improvement in their condition, so I believe the frivolity and extravagance of many women among us—the natural but evil fruits of an idle and aimless life—will turn men's minds to the necessity for giving women a more serious training. Whatever tends to inequality in the condition of women relative to men, is favourable to household extravagance. Women who have been accustomed to the expenditure of money and to the observation of wise examples in regard to expenditure, are the most frugal and the most successful in their housekeeping. The objector to my argument says that the progress of women is a menace to his position as head of the family. I say that God only knows who is the 'head' of a family. The true headship of a family can only be determined and is only settled in the same way in which leadership is adjusted among men. Whether the wife be a tyrant or a slave, the hardships of either position will be modified by conceding her equality before the law. It is urged on the other side that women ought not to be troubled with politics ; as if in this London—where probably not one in a thousand of the male population devotes a single hour in the year to his electoral duties—not merely the whole of the female voters, but every woman besides, would give themselves up to political discussion! Finally, driven to his entrenchments, my objector says that the possession of the franchise would be contrary to women's natural position, by which he designs to indicate in a vague and mysterious way, that the Creator specially formed women with reference to their perpetual exclusion from voting at parliamentary elections; and he presumes to think that what has been thus made, he or I can assist in unmaking; for he says that the concession of the suffrage will *unsex* women. Does he suppose, then, that women are *sexed* by these disabilities—these unjust laws—which are continually breaking from their limbs like rotten thongs? Let us get to a more wholesome and intelligent doctrine than this. I would rather argue that because the sex and disposition of men and women are what they are we should not dare to put upon them unequal laws; that we might be quite sure that under a *régime* of equal laws women could not be unsexed. Lately I heard a man—a scholar and a gentleman, the father of children, the husband of a good, virtuous, and intelligent wife—say, in objecting to women's suffrage: 'Why should this talk be made about women? They have nothing to complain of.' I replied to him: 'Put yourself in her place.' I took the liberty of speaking of his wife, with whom I have had the pleasure of long acquaintance. I said: 'She loves your children with an affection that we men can hardly estimate; from early training and conviction of principle, the strongest sentiment of her mind, next to affection for yourself and your children, is towards the Protestant religion. Yet it will not be illegal for you to leave to the sole guardianship of your Irish Roman Catholic footman the education and care of your children, without any regard for her agony of heart and mind. If her uncle were to die to-morrow, and his fortune were by will bequeathed to her, the money would be hers only to the poor extent of £200; she may not attempt to earn her livelihood without your permission; if you strike her, and she flies to my house for shelter, you can force her home again and again; if you starve her, she has no direct claim at law against yourself, and even the Poor Law may refuse her dying appeal for help. A few years ago, and but for agitation of the same sort as that you now condemn, her condition before the law would have been greatly more unequal. If you wished to disgrace her name, you could bring an action for alleged damages sustained by her dishonour; no evidence of vice or profligacy on your part would then have given her claim even to separation; while, on the other hand, you could immediately have obtained a divorce upon proof of her infidelity. Then, her brains and fingers would have been yours; if she earned money, she could not own it; you could take from her any fruit of her labour.' Said I to my friend: 'If you care nothing for your political privileges; if you care nothing for your parental privileges; if you do not value the advantages which, because you are a man, and for no other nor better reason, you have enjoyed through life, in the way of public school or university career, and in all the power to choose for yourself both a career in life and the woman you loved to be your wife—you are a poltroon; and if you cannot promise that those unjust laws which I have indicated as yet existing with regard to women shall, so far as your power extends, be at once set aside, then you are bound, if you wish to escape the suspicion of roguery, to allow and to assist women to help themselves.' If I have expressed any contempt for those who retard the passing of the Women's Disabilities Bill, it is owing to the recollection of their frequent defeat. The Divorce Law may not yet be perfect, but when it was shocking and shameful in its injustice there were scores of lords and gentlemen to assert its excellence. Mr. Gladstone then enunciated a grand doctrine, to which, however, he now seems rather weak-kneed in his allegiance. He said: 'When the Gospel came into the world, woman was elevated to an equality with her stronger com-

panion.' Well might the Hon. Mrs. Norton write bitterly of
this speech : 'The only text on the subject acknowledged by
Parliament is the Old Testament text, " And he shall rule over
her." We keep the doctrine of the Fall, not of the Re-
demption.'

Can women trust their interest to others ? It would seem
not. Were it not for agitation such as that which has now
compelled attention, every employment but the most menial
would be closed to women. The proper education of girls is at
least as important as that of boys, seeing that to women the
education of all is committed, at least during tender years ; but
most of the public endowments have been made or wrested to
the boys. Surely no one who has given fair attention to the
subject would pretend to say that the interests of women receive
even decent regard in the legislature ; and who can measure
the disrespect which their disability entails ? Miss Burdett-
Coutts was a person often referred to as one who had some
claims to the suffrage. I think her present disability is even
more marked. She is a baroness ; she has provided bishops
with endowments ; she has made great gifts, not to London
only, but to other towns ; yet she is far more removed now
from the political privileges of men of the caste into the borders
of which she has consented to step, than before she was made a
peeress. All her virtues, all her wealth, any further accession of
rank, cannot qualify her for the privilege which would come of
right to any peer, were he ever so incapable, drunken, or profligate. See how the unjust principle has ruled even in the
highest places ! The same gifted lady who has written of
Queen Victoria as 'the only woman in England who *cannot*
suffer wrong,' has placed on record in this burning sentence the
different measure which has been meted out'to sinful kings and
erring queens : 'We trace,' she says, 'the incontinence of the
former by successive creations in the peerage ; the faults of the
latter by records of imprisonment and death on the scaffold.'

When men—better than the laws they do not lift their finger

to alter—say : 'Yes ; it is bad that a woman can have no property in her child except it be illegitimate, but then, you know, nobody leaves them to the law;'—we know that the truth is otherwise ; cases are often published which show that women are left to the cruel operation of unjust laws. But indeed men might just as well take credit for the fact that they do not fall under the law against murder. The cardinal fault of many laws relating to women is that they operate precisely in contradiction of the principle which we have said justifies the authority of law ;—they oppress the weak for the benefit of the strong. Do we want more proof ? Look, then, at the law relative to seduction, the punishment for which is usually awarded in an action by one man against another, to determine the charge which he shall make for 'loss of services,' as the seduction is called. See the consequences of the permissive law of primogeniture. It would be *mauvais ton* for them to complain, but I confess that any one in the society of high-born dames may well be penetrated with sympathy for their peculiar difficulties. In the middle class, that which people have is generally their own ; but, although there is scarcely a nobleman who is anything more than the life-tenant of his estate, that is a position of dignity compared with the lot of a dress-loving duchess or countess, whose jewels—like a livery to which she is no longer entitled—will be stripped from her at her husband's death. It is a wonder the dowagers have never yet had the strength of mind to stand upright when their Juggernaut, Primogeniture, passes by !

Women have abundant reason to complain ; and, until much is altered by their own exertions in their favour, they have little means or allurement to qualify themselves for a more independent life. It is to me amazing how, without any of the baits and stimulants which cheer men on in their mental labour, women do in so great numbers display a love for higher education. Many of these ladies study without hope of appreciation or external reward,—a self-sacrifice which no man makes and the extent of which no man can fully conceive. In fact, whether we regard women as weak or strong, their claim to the suffrage is valid. If they are weak, they need representation, for the history of every country and the existing state of our law prove that only those who are directly represented get their rights ; if they are strong, the country cannot afford to legislate with one arm. 'Let male indignation,' writes the Hon. Mrs. Norton, ' be appeased by the thought that for one "strong-minded woman," one woman strong-hearted enough to bear ridicule, and intelligent enough to argue—a hundred at least are sitting, feebly weeping, by lone firesides, or writing quires of letters to brothers and friends, to " see them righted," without the smallest inkling of comprehension of any law whatever except that law of necessity which compels them to suffer !'

The political enfranchisement of women should be demanded in the interest of the community—for the advantage of both sexes. But let us for a moment refer to the position of this claim in America. There is no doubt that its acceptance is retarded in this country to some extent by the slow progress which it makes in the United States. People think that if the go-ahead Republic of the West halts in the political enfranchise-ment of women, how much more should a kingdom of ancient lines and institutions, grown old under a one-sexed suffrage, consider its ways. It is remarked, to the prejudice of this movement in England, that on the other side of the Atlantic no leading statesman has adopted the cause. But it is easy to perceive that the question has a very different aspect in a country governed by universal suffrage, and in a country like our own, where the right of voting is the appanage of residential qualification. In the United States the question is one of more than doubling the electoral body ; here it is a question of adding one-seventh to the electing representatives of the whole people. I am profoundly convinced that the concession may be safely, should be quickly, made. It cannot be for the interest of the community that we should retain disabilities on the Statute

Book which discourage one-half the people from the exercise
of their intellectual faculties, and that half acknowledged to be
the more liberally endowed with some most valuable qualifica-
tions. Mr. Mill asserted that 'with equality of experience and
of general faculties, a woman usually sees much more than a
man of what is immediately before her.' He candidly admitted
the tendency of women 'to build over-hasty generalisations';
but 'the corrective to this defect is access to the experience of
the human race. A woman's mistakes are those of a clever,
self-educated man, who often sees what men trained in routine
do not see, but falls into errors for want of knowing things
which have long been known.' Is it no great loss, no crime,
to relegate to frivolity and fashion, to the unproductive consumption of the world's wealth, such abilities as these? Does
not our legislation show in a thousand ways, and with ever-
increasing force, the waste and injury which the community
sustains for want of female co-operation? Not only is this
country distinguished beneath all the great powers of Europe
for the harsh injustice of its laws in their relation to the rights
of women, as touching their persons, their children, their property, and their homes, but it is the one in which the bulk of
the people have perhaps the least comfort, together with the
largest ability to make themselves comfortable. As compared
with the poor of other countries, the English people know
nothing of economy in their homes. We are famed for a high
rate of infant mortality. Paupers swarm in the streets of the
richest cities in the world; now and then they die of starvation;
the Poor Law frequently breaks down and is set up again by
a peculiar process termed official inquiry; the Marriage Law
is in confusion; the Married Women's Property Law is in a
muddle; we legislate on the drink question without the assistance of those who suffer most in body and soul from the English
plague of drunkenness; the Church and Education are both
questions of the hour. All these, and a hundred other matters
essentially important to women, as well as to men, will before

long be submitted to the ordeal of a general election. I believe
it would be well for the country if women had a voice in the
national verdict. I am not one of those persons who are ready,
as they term it, to trace 'the purpose of God' in every affair ;
but I confess I am unable to comprehend the religion of those
men who, believing that women have equal responsibility in the
sight of God, are resolved to take for their own sex the government of the world, and leave subjection for the other half of the
community. Such stand self-condemned by the law of progress,
which teaches loud and louder to every succeeding generation
that man grows higher and nobler in proportion as he ceases
from violence, and learns to love justice. The pre-eminence of
mere physical strength in man has passed away. The age of
warriors was succeeded by the age of generals, when, as Macaulay
says, 'among the hundred and twenty thousand soldiers who
were marshalled round Neerwinden under all the standards of
Western Europe, the two feeblest in body were the hunchbacked
dwarf who urged forward the fiery onset of France and the
asthmatic skeleton who covered the slow retreat of England.'
Brute force among men has ceased to reign. Men are now
asked to make yet another advance—to be victorious over
themselves. And though, as I have said, I do not profess to a
knowledge of the ways of Providence, yet I will contend with
Mr. Gladstone that much of the teaching of Christ implies the
elevation of woman to legal equality with her stronger com-
panion, and my reason forbids me to doubt that in every duty
of life in which co-operation is possible, the work of the world
will be best accomplished by the united efforts of men and
women.

XV.

THE ENFRANCHISEMENT OF WOMEN.[1]

I AM inclined to envy the insensibility of those who can stand up before educated and accomplished women—their acknowledged superiors in mental attainments, in moral worth and judgment—and refuse the claim even of such to political enfranchisement. For my own part, I find an apology rising to my lips together with the advocacy of women's suffrage. It seemed abasement enough when working men, the humblest, but most numerous class of householders, had to sue the tribunal to which our plea is addressed, with prayers for the legislative right of citizenship. But it is surely shameful that in a country which, for longer than the average period of one generation, has been ruled by a woman—in a country in which against every obstacle, women have won such high place in every path in which their endeavours could be directed—where they are the responsible owners of vast wealth, and where they are exposed to all the rigours of the law—where, though under serious disabilities in regard to earning money, they are yet liable equally with men to the demands of the imperial and local tax-gatherer—it is surely, I say, not without some sense of embarrassment, that a man, who is not the mere slave of precedent, can find himself engaged in advocating the political enfranchisement of women.

Yet I am not disposed to think harshly of men who oppose

[1] An Address to the Members of the Association for the Promotion of Social Science.

their futile resistance to this demand, because I doubt their consciousness of wrong-doing. Half the errors of the world would be cured in an instant if we could inoculate mankind with the idea of progress. The friends of progress must not deceive themselves. There is actually in the minds of a large section of mankind a notion that humanity has from the beginning always wandered far and farther from perfection, though how they reconcile this inverted belief with a loudly proclaimed trust in the providence of God I never could make out. But if the review of progress affords no indictment of the honesty of apathetic objectors to this demand, those can hardly escape the reproach of stupidity if they do not now observe how insecure has become the anchorage of their objections. If any one were to say of the ablest of the many distinguished ladies whom I have the honour of addressing to-night, ' Madam, you and your sex are born in acknowledged inferiority to men ; you are only fit to be classed with reference to political enfranchisement among lunatics, criminals, idiots, and minors '—if he escaped the conviction of more than brutal rudeness it could only be upon the ground of his folly. How much more ridiculous than insulting would such an argument be in our day, when women exercise every suffrage but that of Parliament, and when a woman has sat by right of a larger number of votes than ever were given for a man, in the chief educational council of the kingdom. It is late, far too late, to bring forward ' the old rib theory' ; and though I will not believe that men who oppose the claims of women are directly animated by selfish and unworthy motives, yet sure I am that if they will fairly consider the matter, they will see nothing but the old and dying law of mere might as the foundation of their resistance. Feebly and unworthily as I shall handle a few of the arguments on the side of concession, I have yet so much confidence in the clearness and cogency of these arguments as to have no doubt of the result upon the mind of any one who is open to conviction.

Roughly speaking, we may divide those who withstand the claim of women's suffrage into four classes: those who say that women are unfit for the suffrage ; those who contend that the suffrage is unfit for women ; those who maintain that women do not want the suffrage ; and, lastly, those who assert that women have nothing to gain, no wrongs to redress, by means of the suffrage.

I shall not offend your ears by dealing at great length with the objection that women are unfit to be entrusted with the suffrage. Of course, no man in his senses would deny the eligibility of some women. Among the members of the National Society for Women's Suffrage, is a lady who is nothing less than the most distinguished astronomical mathematician ; there are two others whose acts of philanthropy in Europe, Asia, and America, have made household words of their honoured names ; there are few living writers who do not acknowledge inferiority in her own department of literature to George Eliot ; I know of no man whose services are valued at so high a rate in hard money as those of Adelina Patti. Few would like to deny the claim of Lady Burdett-Coutts to enfranchisement. But do not these blind individuals who are about to fall into the ditch of defeat, do they not see that in admitting the claim of Mary Somerville they concede the whole matter ? It is not to be expected that when by the rule of the strongest, women have through all time been excluded from so many opportunities for intellectual improvement, they should all thus shine before men ; but if, owing to this rude law, which it is the mission of civilisation' to banish, they have been deprived, unjustly deprived, of advantages which, rightly used, tend to make life higher and happier and nobler, they have not had to contend to so great an extent with the vices which together with learning and power, men have done their best to monopolize. Rather than assert that all men were fit for the suffrage, I would contend that all women are as fit as all men for that privilege.

But that is not necessary. Here the right of voting is a
question of property ; and there are very few men who will
venture to argue that if a woman is fit to be entrusted with
the rights and duties of property, she is unfit to vote in
respect of her possessions. If I buy a freehold for £100 it
yields me a vote *plus* the enjoyment of the property, and
any man should be ashamed to confess that such acquirement
of the suffrage is not a valuable consideration. Why then
should any woman have less than I obtain for my money?
Is not this injustice? If not, I know not what is just. Is
it because she is unfit to exercise a right which the most
drunken, and ignorant, and sordid clown may hold as the
appanage of his purchase? This objection that women are
unfit for the franchise, I think, has fallen to the ground.

Let us give our attention now, for a moment, to those
gentler hindrances, who regard the suffrage as unfit for
women. I must confess to you that I always look with
suspicion upon an argument of this sort. When I have
heard people say : ' This is unfit for children,' I have often
found they had no good reason to give in support of such
a limitation. The suffrage is not given to minors, because
minors cannot of themselves hold property—cannot perform
the duties of citizenship, and are not amenable to the full
responsibilities of that condition. It is only on the paternal
theory of government we have a right to say of any privilege :
' This is unfit for them ; let us keep it all to ourselves.'
Such, indeed, is the standpoint of these objectors. They, in
fact, assume a paternal authority over all women. They
assume that women have rights and responsibilities essentially different from those of men. But I never heard that
this difference could be pleaded to bar the operation of a distress warrant issued against the furniture of a woman-
householder ; I never heard that it would excuse her from the
payment of rates and taxes. Surely if the suffrage is unfit
for women, they ought never to be troubled with the cost of

sewers, the wages of policemen, the maintenance of lunatics, the provision for paving. 'Ah! but that is not what I mean,' protests the self-constituted protector of women. 'I mean that women are unfit for scenes in which men are brought together in hot excitement.' Well, I must say, I think it is just then that their influence will be most beneficial. Whether it be so or not does not of course affect in the slightest degree the question of their right. They have in respect of their property a right to the suffrage, and a further right to consider for themselves, whether the circumstances under which they are called upon to exercise it are such as invite them to record their vote, or to repel them from the exercise of the suffrage. But I do maintain that scandals of parliamentary election will be ended most quickly by the adoption of women suffrage. I find no evidence of this stronger than in the very instances which the upholders of the argument that the suffrage is unfit for women bring forward to refute my claim. They have pointed to the presence of disorderly women at the poll in certain municipal elections. Yet the misconduct of those few women produced more solemn and abiding resolution for reform, than the grosser misconduct of men in all the century. What a pity, I say, that we had not years and years ago a few ill-behaved women at the poll, in order that men, shocked at vice to which their eyes were closed in their own case, should so resolve to make the conduct of elections orderly and respectable as the most important act of secular duty! Who indeed can fail to see that just in proportion as we have fewer places of which it can be said that they are unfit for women, so men become more self-respecting, more refined, more virtuous ; in short, more fit for the performance of their own proper share of the duties of life. When I hear it said that something is unfit for women, experience has led me to associate more or less of drunkenness with the forbidden thing. There is riot and revelry, rude license and improper conduct in the things from which fathers, and husbands, and brothers, desire to keep women. But do they lose sight of the fact that the admission of women to functions, the performance of which has been stained with misconduct, is the surest antidote, the most certain way of removing the gross accompaniments of these public assemblies? Why should they doubt this? Let them look to their own dinner-tables, and then ransack their memories for records of the three-bottle men of their grandfathers' day. If men have gained this advance by 'joining the ladies,' with more sense left in their brains than their grandfathers thought necessary for the drawing-room, why should it be questioned that the same result would be produced at the poll? For my own part, I think a further improvement at dinner-tables would be total abolition of the separate system ; the gain would be on the side of temperance and of *esprit ;* for dreary as English dinners not unfrequently are, I confess I always look forward with positive dislike to that most dreary period of the evening, when, in obedience to the nod of the presiding lady, ' one shall be taken and the other left.' I think the argument that the possession of the suffrage would *unsex* women, is one of the most ignorant, shallow, and thoughtless character. Men say that the possession of the suffrage would be contrary to a woman's natural position. This argument is generally put forward by those who are assured that the existence of men and women is the design of a personal Creator. Am I then to suppose this indicates a belief that women are formed with special reference to their perpetual exclusion from voting—not at contested elections to boards of guardians, local boards, town councils, and school boards, but at parliamentary elections? Does the proposer of this objection presume to suggest that he or I can *unsex* women—that we can undo the work of creation—that Parliament can do that which is most impossible? I do not think it necessary to continue argument upon this part of the subject.

I am now prepared to meet the third class of objectors, those who assert that women do not want the franchise. I admit that all women do not demand the franchise ; if they did, there would be little need of such poor efforts as I can make for their enfranchisement. But sure I am that every day and every hour an increasing number of women will join in this demand. Is it a new thing that the suffrage should not be demanded *en masse?* After all, the work of pulling down the park railings, and drawing a tear from the eyes of good Mr. Walpole, were not the achievements of a population. There is far more of real effort represented in the petitions from women which have again and again loaded the tables of the House of Commons. Now, the advocacy of the Women's Disabilities Bill is becoming quite fashionable, but it has been a different matter in years that are but lately passed, and even now, for earnest, sincere women, who feel the injustice of their disabilities deeply in their hearts, it is often a far harder matter to brave the silly prejudices of tyrant custom in the mere signing of a petition than it could be for a man to bear a hand in the removal of any length of Hyde Park railings. When I hear it said that the majority of women do not demand the political suffrage, I am not surprised. Of any unenfranchised class the majority has always been found apathetic. And think what special reason women have for apathy, or seeming apathy! Nine-tenths of them, and probably more, are in some way or other, dependent upon men for the means of subsistence. They are more obedient to custom, more fearful of combating the opinion of the world ; they are much ruled by fashion, and the leaders of fashion—I mean the leaders of fashion in dress and apparel of all sorts—will be slow in demanding for women a life of greater dignity and more equal partnership. But I say this : that whether the woman with whom he talks be frivolous or ignorant, the gay butterfly who regards mere household work as a

chrysalis state, or the poor drudge whose life is almost
breathless in the performance of the vulgar duties of the
most sordid home—no man, be he the bitterest opponent
of this movement to be found within the walls of Parliament,
can fail to arouse in her mind an active demand for
justice, if he will honestly and truthfully set before her
comprehension even those few of the disgraceful anomalies
of our law with which I shall conclude my remarks. For
now, lastly, I am going to do battle with those who assert
that women have nothing to gain, no wrongs to redress,
by the possession of the suffrage, which would produce a
more active interest on the part of the sex in political
affairs. I ought indeed to have put the matter of women's
wrongs before that of their rights. It may perhaps be alleged
against me with some truth that, as a man, I naturally
shrunk from exposing to the discredit of my sex, laws so
outrageous in their injustice, so unkind in their cruelty, so
unparalleled throughout the whole world for their rank injustice.
Let us look at the life of a woman from her cradle as
affected by these laws. We may say of this country that 'all
men and women are born free and equal'; but directly the
educational process begins, then the injustice commences.
The boy finds ample endowments, many of them bequeathed
for the education of poor children, open exclusively to those
of his sex; and in nineteen homes out of twenty, every
effort is made for his advancement as something upon
which the whole well-being of the family depends, while the
sister is often left as it were to feed upon the scanty herbage
which she may find growing by the wayside of the remote
bye-paths of her life. He is encouraged to be 'manly,' which
with many people means skilful at fisticuffs; and rudeness to
those weaker than himself is not regarded as a high crime
and misdemeanour. When the lad is looking through the
pleasant paths of a university career towards that vague world
in which he will some day be an actor, free to try his strength

against the strongest and to win the highest honours in the State, there is settling down upon the mind of the girl a haze of uncertainty. Her common refuge is romance. She is bound by every tie of affection and of interest to be conventional, and to assure herself and her friends that she is very happy. But is she so? Is human nature so very different that an active life can be as it were suspended without emotion? Do not believe this. Even 'girls of the period' set their little wits a-thinking occasionally. And what do they see? Nothing so ennobling as a certain career of active duty inviting every man in a hundred forms. An aimless, idle life, vivifying with the prospect of marriage or fading away towards inferior comfort to that enjoyed in the paternal home —perhaps penury. They find consolation and hope in romance and frivolity, and men find the consequence in the extravagance and want of sympathy of their wives. We have seen to some extent what is the position of women if they inherit property and live unmarried. A million of women in these islands cannot marry because their number is by so many in excess of that of men; but as for those who do marry, they must at the outset of married life accept the imputation from the law, of idiocy, or of a mild and as it were semi-lunatic form of felony. They will not be allowed to retain possession of their property. Either they must commit its custody—with the possibility of utter ruin—to persons called trustees, who ofttimes cannot be trusted, or the husband, who has just vowed to endow them with all his worldly goods, receives by the mere act of marriage a transfer of their property.

> ' Ye who believe in affection that hopes, and endures, and is patient,
> Ye who believe in the beauty and strength of woman's devotion,'

do not make the error of supposing that this lovely fruit grows out of injustice and cruel wrong! As you value this sweetest prize of life, with its clasps, more dear, as an eloquent friend of mine has said, than those of Alma and of Inkerman, as you are zealous for the dignity of true love and for the fidelity of married life, set yourselves to right the wrongs of women !   The time is long past when it was in the power of the strong to force the physically weak to live a life of ignorance and subjection.   All knowledge is open before women ; a really learned woman has long ceased to be a curiosity.   You cannot look for the most conscientious regard for duty and truth and honour from women who live under the thraldom of cruelly unjust laws ; and for yourselves you must make your choice, whether in this matter, you will so act as to receive the respect, the aversion, or the contempt of intelligent women.   If you think I speak too strongly, bear me company a few minutes while I pass but very superficially over some of the iniquities of the laws of this country as they affect women.

Let us take the laws at their best.   Two friends of mine were lately married ; both the man and the woman were possessed of property, which each had managed most admirably and with great success.   The man retains full command over his fortune, but the woman was obliged on entering the portal of marriage to pass her property either to her husband or to trustees : she thought it her duty to choose the latter, and is now thwarted and harassed in regard to every disposition of her fortune.   So much for the good husband.   Now let us look at another everyday picture.   I will repeat the published facts of the case of a woman who is now reduced to selling oranges in the streets of Liverpool.   Her first husband died, leaving her a licensed public-house and £1,000.   She married again.   In the early days of their married life her second husband drew out the £1,000 from the bank in which it was deposited and took ship with his legalized plunder for Australia.   Robbed with the approval of the laws of her country, she made no revolt, but laboured and succeeded in maintaining in comfort and respectability herself and the daughter she had borne to her first husband.   In a few years the unpunishable rogue returned,—miserable, ragged, and destitute. She fed and forgave him. Happy in relieving his distress and in ministering to his comfort, she felt a new pleasure in life. One day he proposed a drive in the country for the hard-working wife and daughter, and they took the unaccustomed luxury of a carriage. On returning they found a stranger in full possession of the bar and the business of the inn. He produced a bill of sale, from the husband, of the house with its contents and goodwill. Imagine the feelings with which this woman found herself and her daughter homeless and penniless, turned out to live a pauper or to die a beggar in the streets of Liverpool! Ladies and gentlemen, I am overwhelmed with shame as I confess that in spite of that legislative abortion, the Married Women's Property Act —such an atrocity as this is to-day possible under the laws of my country.

Mark, too, while on the subject of property, that the law gives a woman no claim whatever to any definite portion of her husband's wealth. He finds her a girl, earning good wages in service, or salary in a shop, or the inmate of a happy home, and makes proposal to her for a life partnership. She accepts. Her part of the work is to increase his time for money-making employment, to be careful of their house, to nurse and educate their infant children, to sustain and improve their status in society by making their home respectable and respected. But the wholesome doctrine that the labourer is worthy of his hire does not apply to her. The law, which is so much a respecter of persons with regard to the man's right to possess himself of his wife's property, that it permits her to receive for her own no sum exceeding £200, coming to her by bequest after marriage, is extremely careless with regard to the main-tenance of women. If a lady of the most delicate health and refined breeding—one whose very existence demanded that which would seem luxurious to women of rustic mould—if such a one were the victim of a secret marriage, of the validity of which she was assured but could not prove, for herself she could not directly obtain, if her husband were the richest man in the State, even a share of such biscuit as he gave his sporting dogs. She, his wife, the deluded unhappy wretch who accepted his vows to love, honour, and cherish her, who was mocked with the endowment at the altar of all his worldly goods—she is the one human being who has no power to enforce her rights against him. But surely justice—? No! Though he may be spending her fortune with harlots, English justice will not listen to her prayer for a mandate compelling the husband to give her food. Some one must feed her, if somebody pleases—for even her claims as a pauper are merely those of perishing humanity, and then he may recover the cost of his bounty from the husband, whom, though she hunger into slow consumption, the law will hardly brand as a criminal, only regarding him as a trivial debtor. But in this condition there is one joy; the famished child she hugs to her poor breast is her own, because its possession is shameful; it is thought to be illegitimate. She may have heard of the case of Lady Helena Newenham, and while she loathes the coarse food the Poor Law gives her, she may bless the injustice which bastardizes her child. This daughter of Lord Mountcashell had two little girls. Separated from her husband,—their father, the Rev. Henry Newenham, made application to the Court of Queen's Bench in Ireland, for their delivery to him. The younger was aged seven, the eldest sixteen; the latter an age at which the law regards the wish of a girl. Both were earnest in their desire to remain with Lady Helena. The Court respected the wish of the elder girl, but decreed that the younger must be delivered to the father. Let me quote a bit from what the reporter called the ' scene in court.' ' An officer came in, bearing a pretty little pet with long fair hair, and intelligent beyond her years.' Can we not fancy an Augustine looking on her, and saying of the sisters—

'Non Angli, sed Angeli.'

If happy! But they were not happy. Something like the horrors of a slave market were to be enacted with the sanction of the Queen's Bench. 'She screamed and struggled violently, exclaiming repeatedly, "Oh! must I, must I? Oh, dear! I won't go to my father! Oh, please, do let me do as I like! Don't send me away! Will mamma *ever* see me again? Grandpa! Grandpa! where are you?"' Then following the wail in childish treble, was heard the sonorous voice of the humane Judge, evidently struggling against deep emotion. 'I shall take care of that, my dear. Your mamma will see you as often as she likes.' A ray of hope overspread the child's face. 'Will it be every day? Tell me—will it be every day?' To which entreaty the Judge replied, 'Oh, yes, every day.' Mr. Justice Fitzgerald must have known this was false; but I dare hope with Sterne, concerning another piece of falsehood, that the tear of the recording angel blotted out his sin. Then the 'grandpa,' himself a peer of Parliament, a member of that House which mutilated Mr. Russell Gurney's Bill,—then Lord Mountcashell, who, the reporter says, 'was much moved,' put in his word: 'Knowing what I know,' he said of the Judge's promise, 'that is impossible.' Finally, the Judge expressed the 'sorrow' with which he administered the law; and the sobbing child, sent from mother and sister, was handed to the father, who carried her out.

You who oppose this claim for the political enfranchisement of women; you who are touched to the heart—for are you not gentlemen and men of honour?—even by my halting and imperfect recital of these wrongs—you ask me, what would I have? I tell you I would have laws which should be distinguished for justice. I would have no legal disabilities. For every employment open to competitive examination women should be permitted to submit their claims. I think men are much better fitted for 'up-country' service in India; while on the other hand the clerical work of many of the public offices, both at home and abroad, might be performed with far greater

advantage to the State by the admission of women. As to
property, the law I hold should give facilities for settlements,
while it should also allow the retention by a married woman
of her property just as though she were a *feme sole.* She
might reasonably be entitled to a moderate share of her
husband's earnings while fulfilling to the best of her ability
the duties of a wife ; and as for the children in legal infancy
—at the death of the father, the mother should be their
guardian by right ; in the case of divorce, I think they should
pass from the care of the criminal parent, who, however,
should be compelled to make due contribution for their
education and maintenance ; when there was a separation,
the children of one sex should go to one parent, and those
of the opposite sex to the other. Such and other needful
reforms in the laws relating to women we should strongly
claim. We cannot trust to lawyers for justice. I lament,
not more the rudeness than the ignorance of men like Mr.
Justice Byles, who, scouting the claim of 1,600 women ratepayers to the political suffrage, exclaimed indignantly, ' I
will not allow that woman can be man, except in a zoological
treatise, or until she is reduced to the condition of fossil
remains ' ; and proceeded from the seat of justice to liken
the position of women to that of the brutes, who, by the way,
are never 'brutal.' Yet he was sitting on what may to-morrow
be the King's Bench ; he had been a Queen's Counsel, when
the accident of a minute might have made him a King's
Counsel ; he spoke every day of mankind inclusive of the
entire race, of the Church inclusive of all worshippers, and of
a kingdom which he dared not say should not be ruled
by a queen. We may hope, however, that when the
English law is nobler, its professors will share the elevation.
And this our hope is based on no uncertain foundation.
For he who runs may read the lesson of the ages. The
decree, stamped upon the face of every people, ordains the
progress of each generation to a fuller exercise of individual

faculties for the greater happiness and responsibility of the individual, and the more complete advantage of all. And with this it is given to men and women, the children of all time, to regard with lasting honour those who labour most successfully to bring human law into harmony with justice ; not those who make themselves the law and dispense justice to the weak as to the strong, but the truer servants of right, who in all their law-making have but one rule of duty, to deal with others as they themselves hope to be dealt with. I humbly advocate these reforms in the English law, not more for the interest of women, than with true and dutiful regard for the interests of my own sex,—for to me nothing is more clear than that the perpetuation of injustice implies the degradation of mankind.

XVI.

THE LEGAL POSITION OF MARRIED WOMEN.

IN the qualities of brilliancy and eloquence, Mrs. Norton was the most distinguished literary woman of her time. As a novelist she was chiefly known; but Mrs. Norton's most brilliant and eloquent compositions were not works of fiction. Her style was not employed in its perfection to protest against other wrongs or to depict other sorrows than those which had pierced her own heart. This is not an imputation of selfishness; it is merely an illustration of the fact that the highest and most successful efforts of genius are those which have their inspiration from the deepest feelings.

Mrs. Norton's finest writings related to her condition as a married woman, and these have been brought but little to the notice of the public; not because she desired privacy— in a letter to the present writer she said, 'I do not shrink from publicity as to a single word I have printed'—but because of the personality with which those writings are pervaded. It is not my intention to revive by any unnecessary allusion the recollection of those wrongs the burden of which forced from Mrs. Norton such passionate eloquence. It is to her legal disabilities as a married woman, illustrated by herself, that the present reference will be confined. No hope is more anxiously urged in those appeals than that the outpouring of her own indignation may, by producing amendment of the laws concerning married women, have a useful result. 'I do not consider this MY cause,' she wrote in her 'Letter to the Queen'—'though it is a cause of which (unfortunately for me) I am an illustration. It is the cause of ALL the women;' and as a knight devotes his sword, so she consecrated her pen first and chiefly to enmity against those laws which still deny legal equality and even legal existence to married women. In some minor points, the laws relating to married women have been amended; but the 'non-existence' against which she protested, and, substantially, the *status* of a married woman, remain unaltered. There has been no change since the time when Mrs. Norton wrote—when Sir Erskine Perry proposed in the House of Commons to give them legal existence in terms very similar to those of the Bill which Mr. Shaw-Lefevre again introduced in a very able speech in 1868, and to those in which Lord Coleridge made an equally ineffective proposal in the Session of 1877.

A husband cannot now confiscate the earnings of his wife, but he can paralyse her power of earning by prohibition. When inquiry was made into the amount of Mrs. Norton's literary earnings, which, as the law then stood, were the property of her husband, she declared the proceeding had made her dream that her

. . . 'gift of writing was meant for a higher and stronger purpose—that gift which came, not from man, but from God. It was meant to enable me to rouse the hearts of others to examine into all the gross injustice of these laws—to ask the " nation of gallant gentlemen " whose countrywoman I am, for once to hear a woman's pleading on the subject. Not because I deserve more at their hands than other women. Well I know, on the contrary, how many hundreds, infinitely better than I—more pious, more patient, less rash under injury—have watered their bread with tears ! My plea to attention is, that in pleading for myself, I am able to plead for all these others. Not that my sufferings or my deserts are greater than theirs ; but that I combine with the fact of having suffered wrong, the power to comment on and explain the cause of that wrong, which few women are able to do.

'For *this*, I believe God gave me the power of writing. To this I devote that power. . . . . I deny that this is my personal cause ; it is the cause of all the women of England. If I could be justified and happy to-morrow, I would still labour in it ; and if I were to die to-morrow it would still be a satisfaction to me that I had so striven.'

Mrs. Norton suffered because she was a woman. Had her case been that of a man, the result could have left no such trouble in the path of life. She had the personal sympathy of the King (William IV.); the friendly aid of the King of the Belgians:

'He who learned perhaps to feel more, having suffered more than others; and who remembered me in my early girlhood, and in my mother's home; he who was husband and father to the heirs of the English Crown; and who in the pride and prime of his own youth saw the sun set one December night on that triumphantly happy position, and saw it rise—a childless widower.'

She had with her—

'Public opinion and the good wishes of good hearts. To what end? Vain, though not valueless, has been this accumulation of kindness, from friends, relatives, and strangers, for want of such laws of protection! They could pity, but they could not help. . . . . It is a glorious thing that the Law should be stronger than the Throne. It is one of dear boastful England's proudest blind boasts. But it is *not* a glorious thing that, being stronger than the Throne, it should be weaker than the subject: and that that which even a king can only do within a certain limit—(oppress or uphold)—may be done with boundless irresponsible power in the one single relation of husband and wife.'

When Mrs. Norton wrote thus in 1855, the Law relating to Husband and Wife was in a somewhat different condition from that which obtains at present. It was different in regard to Divorce, to the Custody of Infants, and to the Property of Married Women. I propose to show, as far as possible in Mrs. Norton's own words, but entirely in harmony, as I believe, with her opinions, what has been the extent of those reforms, and in what directions they have been insufficient. At that time, divorce was a 'luxury for the rich, to be obtained only by special enactment in the House of Lords.' But for women there was neither justice nor divorce. Lord Brougham had lately affirmed in his place in Parliament concerning a case which had come before him as one of the Law Lords: 'In that action the character of the woman was at immediate issue, although she was not prosecuted. The consequence not unfrequently was, that the character of a woman was sworn away; instances were known in which, by collusion between the husband and a pretended paramour, the character of the wife has been destroyed. All this could take place, and yet the wife had no defence; she was excluded from Westminster Hall, and behind her back, by the principles of our jurisprudence, her character was tried.'

No Law Court could then divorce in England. A special Act of Parliament annulling the marriage was passed for each case. The House of Lords granted this almost as a matter of course to the husband who could pay for it, but not to the wife. In only four recorded instances (two of which were cases of incest) did a wife obtain a divorce. Addressing the Queen, Mrs. Norton wrote:

'In an old-fashioned book (written by a favourite of your Majesty's uncle, George IV.) the author says: "If a poor man were to appear in the lobby of the House of Lords, praying to be divorced *gratis* from his wife, it is likely that the Sergeant-at-Arms would take him for some poor lunatic, and send him to Bedlam."'

The law on this great matter has since that time been changed by four statutes. The Divorce and Matrimonial Act, passed shortly after the publication of Mrs. Norton's eloquent pamphlet, established the new Court; and it was provided that either husband or wife might obtain a divorce on the ground of adultery, but the wife can only present a petition for divorce upon allegation that the marital offence has been accompanied by cruelty or desertion. By a subsequent Act the power of decreeing divorce was given to the Judge Ordinary, without reference to colleagues, with the provision that the decree must be 'nisi,' and not final, for at least three months. The third statute relieved the clergy of the Church of England as by law established from obligation to perform the religious office at the marriage of any divorced person. The supplementary provisions of the law are:—as to condonation—that parties who, after the offence charged, have consented to live again as husband and wife, cannot obtain a divorce. Judicial separation may be decreed on the ground of adultery (on the

A A

part of the man without desertion or cruelty), or upon proof of cruelty or desertion.   After such separation a woman is as a single woman in everything except re-marriage; and even prior to a decree of separation, a woman may obtain legal protection for any property which may result from her own industry.   The fourth statute, the Matrimonial Causes Act 1878, empowers the Court or magistrate before whom a husband is convicted of an aggravated assault upon his wife, to issue an order which shall have the effect in all respects of a decree of judicial separation, on the ground of cruelty, and the order may further provide for the payment by the husband to the wife, of such weekly sum as the Court or magistrate may consider to be in accordance with his means, and with any means which the wife may have for her support.

Mrs. Norton's infant children were taken from her under circumstances which could be repeated to-day, the blameless wife having power to reclaim them only by petition.   The natural claim of the mother to the care and guardianship of her infant children is not acknowledged by the law.   But there was no power of petition when she wrote:

'At that time the law was (and I thank God I believe I was greatly instrumental in changing that law) that a man might take children from the mother at any age, and without any fault or offence on her part.   There had been an instance in which the husband seized and carried away a suckling infant, as his wife sat nursing it in her own mother's house.   Another in which the husband, being himself in prison for debt, gave his wife's legitimate child to the woman he cohabited with.   A third (in which the parties were of high rank), where the husband deserted his wife; claimed the babe born after his desertion (having already his other children); and left her to learn its death from the newspapers!   A fourth, in which the husband, living with a mistress, and travelling with her under his wife's name, the latter appealed for a separation to the Ecclesiastical Court; and the adulterous husband, to revenge himself, claimed from her his three infant girls.   In all these cases and in all other cases, the claim of the father was held to be indisputable.   There was no law then to help the mother, as there is no law now to help the wife.   The blamelessness of the mother signifies nothing in those days, as the blamelessness of the wife signifies nothing in the present day.'

It was upon the occurrence of this cruel addition to her

wrongs that the most eminent of the distinguished counsel who had been opposed to Mrs. Norton's claims, stated concerning her, that 'there never was a more deeply injured woman.' She herself wrote of it:

'What I suffered respecting those children God knows, and He only ; what I endured, and yet lived past—of pain, exasperation, helplessness, and despair, under the evil law which suffered any man, for vengeance or for interest, to take baby children from the mother—I shall not even try to explain. I believe *men* have no more notion of what that anguish is than the blind have of colours ; and I bless God that at least mine was one of the cases which called attention to the state of the law as it then existed.'

As it now stands, the English law defining the mother's rights in regard to the care of the children is, as Mrs. Norton has said, far from justice. The Matrimonial Causes Act, 1878, empowers a Court or magistrate to give the legal custody of her children, if they are under ten years of age, to a wife who has obtained an order for judicial separation by reason of her husband's conviction for an aggravated assault upon herself, and by the Custody of Infants Act, 1873, it is provided that in any deed of separation between the father and mother of an infant or infants, the father may by such deed give up the custody of such infant or infants to the mother. But no Court is to enforce any such agreement unless satisfied that compulsion will be for the benefit of the child or children. The natural claim of the mother to guardianship on the death of the father is still denied by Parliament ; and in case of separation or divorce, a blameless, virtuous woman, the only proper and efficient guardian of the children of a vicious and profligate father, is mocked by processes of law which, being complied with, enable her to obtain possession of her children, but only to the age of sixteen. To get even this measure of justice she must exhibit the fact that it is not hers by law; she must petition a Judge of the Chancery Division, who ' *may*' thereupon order that her claim, founded on natural right, upon most obvious equity, and fraught with nothing but the clearest benefit to the infant children, shall be acknowledged. When this claim is again urged in Parliament, the following appeal by Mrs. Norton will surely be remembered :

'Ah ! how often in the course of this Session—in the course of this year—will the same men who read this appeal with a strong adverse prejudice, be roused by some thought in a favourite author ; struck by some noble anecdote ; touched by some beautiful pageant of human feeling, seen among glittering lights from a side box, chanted, perhaps, in a foreign tongue ! And yet I have an advantage over these—for *my* history is *real.* I know there is no poetry in it to attract you. . . . There was none of the "pomp and circumstance" of those woes that affect you, when some faultless and impossible heroine makes you dream of righting all the wrongs in the world ! But faulty as I may be—and prosaic and unsympathised with as my position might then be—it was UNJUST, and unjust *because your laws prevent justice.* Let that thought haunt you, through the music of your Sonnambulas and Desdemonas, and be with you in your readings of histories and romances, and your criticisms on the jurisprudence of countries less free than our own. I *really* wept and suffered in my early youth—for wrong done, not *by* me, but *to* me, and the ghost of whose scandal is raised against me this day. I *really* suffered the extremity of earthly shame without deserving it (whatever chastisement my other faults may have deserved from Heaven). I *really* lost my young children—craved for them, struggled for them, was barred from them—and came too late to see one who had died a painful and convulsive death, except in his coffin. I *really* have gone through much that, if it were invented, would move you ; but being of your every-day world, you are willing it should sweep pass like a heap of dead leaves on the stream of time, and take its place with other things that have gone drifting down—

> " Où va la feuille de Rose
> Et la feuille du Laurier !"'

The third matter is that of the Property of Married Women. When Mrs. Norton first wrote on this subject, a married woman had no property, she could have no property as the result of her own endeavours. Mrs. Norton said : 'the power of earning by literature—which fund (though it be the grant of Heaven and not the legacy of earth) is no more legally mine than my family property . . . the copyrights of my works, my very soul and brains are not my own.'

In concluding her 'Letter to the Queen' she wrote :

' Let the Lord Chancellor, whose office is thus described in Chamberlayne's *State of England*—" To judge, not according to the Common Law, as other Civil Courts do, but to moderate the rigour of the Law, and to judge according to Equity, Conscience, and Reason ; and his Oath is to do right to all manner of people, poor and rich, after the Laws and Customs of this Realm, and truly counsel the King "—let the Lord Chancellor, I say, the " Summus Cancellarius " of Great Britain, cancel, according to the laws and customs of this realm of England, my right to the labour of my own brain and pen ; and docket it, among forgotten Chancery Papers, with a parody of Swift's contemptuous labelling—

" Only a Woman's Pamphlet."

But let the recollection of what I write remain with those who read ; and above all, let the recollection remain with your Majesty, the one woman in England who *cannot* suffer wrong, and whose Royal assent will be formally necessary to any Marriage Reform Bill, which the Lord Chancellor, assembled Peers, and assembled Commons may think fit to pass, in the Parliament of this free nation, where, with a Queen on the throne, all other married women are legally " NON-EXISTENT." '

That plea for 'existence,' thus put forward in 1855, Mrs. Norton renewed in 1874. But since 1873 no change whatever has been made in the Law affecting the Property of Married Women. In 1874, she distributed a few copies of a pamphlet entitled *Taxation by an Irresponsible Taxpayer*, which bears neither a date nor the name of any publisher. The *brochure* deals with the grievances of the London ratepayer ; for humour, it might have been written by her grandfather.[1] Still she was 'non-existent as a married woman. Non-existent for protection, but not non-existent for extortion. . . . Liable as a "female occupier" to pay taxes, but not able as a "female occupier" to hold my house except through trustees, or to compel by any process of law the payment of an agreed income.' She had been libelled and 'informed that being a married woman, I could not prosecute of myself, that my husband must prosecute. There could be no prosecution, and I was left to study the grotesque anomaly in law of having my defence made *necessary*—and made *impossible*—by the same person.' She was overcharged in respect of her house, and the condition of the street in which she lived was neglected. She set herself to work upon the local authorities, and soon discovered that ' the ways of vestries (one

---

[1] Mrs. Norton was granddaughter to R. B. Sheridan.

of those corporate bodies without a conscience of whom Sydney
Smith speaks) are past finding out.'   At last, 'beginning to feel
that curly irritation attributed proverbially to "the worm that
is trodden upon,"' she insisted 'on knowing whose business it
was to survey.'   In the endeavour to compel attention to the
second head of the complaint, she says : 'I tried the simple and
useful experiment of placing some waste sand, birdseed, withered
chickweed, and refuse from a cage in the centre of the street
opposite my door, where I had the satisfaction of seeing that it
remained for more than ten days without being swept away.'
She proposed to the Vestry 'that the elegant title of Chester-
field Street should be changed to Rumble Row, Oozy Lane,
Parish Passage, or some other appropriate title.'   She asked to
be informed 'why *music* should be hawked without a licence
more than any other commodity ? '   She complained that while
the '"place of settlement" of any one of the dirty loungers who
slouch along with greasy leather straps supporting discordant
organs on their shoulders is "no affair of the parish," another
man is incarcerated for spouting passages from Shakespeare's
Richard III. and bidding a policeman (in that esteemed dra-
matist's words) "take any form but that," while English children
"found begging" or "sleeping under archways" are (very
properly) packed off to schools and reformatories to learn
more regular habits of life.'   She declared that 'the vigorous
grasp of justice which squeezes pence from penny earnings for
the compulsory education of the little truant who prefers the
furrows of the plough to the path of knowledge—grows delicately
helpless and relaxed when dealing with aristocratic neglect :' and
cited 'Lord Justice James, who in deciding a Chancery suit this
spring, observed : "A man may leave a good wife and deserving
children penniless, and bestow the whole of his fortune upon
the vilest companions of his profligacy and most wicked accom-
plices of his crimes, and the law cannot gainsay him."'
     The Law relating to the Property of Married Women has
been amended, not in the spirit of justice, but with a grudging

sense of expediency which has left it more full of anomalies than before. It is doubtful if the power of a married woman to engage in any remunerative occupation is not dependent on the will of her husband ; it is certain he may prohibit her from earning anything. But if her occupation bring profits, those profits are now unquestionably her own. The payment due for her brain-work or handicraft has, since 1870, ceased to be legally due and payable to her husband. If she inherit property by intestacy of the late owner, that is her own, but no bequest above £200 can belong to a married woman. No amendment of the law has touched her *status ;* she is now non-existent as she was before Mrs. Norton was born : she may be libelled with impunity ; she cannot sue or be sued ; all her personal property passes to her husband at the day of marriage, and his by the same process is the rental of her real property. When the Married Women's Property Bill was passed to the House of Lords in 1870, it contained two harmonious and inter-dependent provisions. One provided that a wife might retain as her own the property she possessed before marriage ; the other, that a husband should no longer be liable for debts which his wife had contracted before marriage. The House of Lords held the former to be revolutionary, and struck it out ; but their lordships, in their wisdom, retained the latter, and so left un-married female traders with injured credit, and tradesmen generally with no remedy against a defaulting bride. The Act of 1870 thus provided women—it has been suggested by way of dowry—with a mode of cheating creditors. Women who could obtain goods on credit before marriage could avoid payment by matrimony ; and one case is on record in which a costly pianoforte was obtained in this way. The Act of 1870 absolved the husband from liability ; and the wife, remaining non-existent, could not be sued. But this legislative blunder had cruel consequences for women traders, who could obtain no credit when there was ground for suspicion that by accepting the non-existence of married women they might defraud a creditor. That tradesmen—electors and fathers—should be cheated, was to Parliament intolerable, and haste was made, upon discovery of the defect in 1874, to put a patch upon this loose place in the Act of 1870. It was enacted—*not* that a wife should be responsible for her debts incurred before marriage, which would have implied the legal existence of a married woman—but that a husband should be liable for such debts to the extent of the property acquired through the marriage, the confusion being well preserved by the fact that a wife's property in her husband's hands is not at present liable for debts contracted by her before marriage in regard to marriages which took place between 1870 and 1874.

When it was proposed, in 1870, that by contracting marriage a woman should not forfeit her property, Lord Penzance, then Judge Ordinary in the Divorce Court, made a speech, of which the *rechauffée* was again served up in the last Session of Parliament. His lordship suggested that if a married woman could hold property, she would go into partnership with some cousin 'who need not be a woman.' Lord Westbury had a fear that if some one left her £20,000 she would spend it on a diamond necklace. The *Times*, in a most liberal article, ridiculed these absurd alarms, suggested that Lord Penzance's judgment had been 'warped by the nature of his duties'; that being 'accustomed to see nothing but the ugly side of matrimonial nature,' he might 'be excused for taking a sort of Old Bailey view of the marriage state, and particularly for looking upon wives as a set of extravagant queans, with whom flirtation is only kept short of adultery by the fear of himself and the machinery he directs.' And with regard to all such arguments the *Times* asked, 'Is there any reason to suppose that she will be the less faithful to the marriage relation when she has the responsibility of property, and when society looks to her to advance the interests of her children, than when she is dependent for everything upon her husband; and, on his failing her, must look to some friend who, to use Lord Penzance's phrase, "need not be a woman"? We believe that the case of a married woman does not differ from that of all other human beings, in the fact that a certain degree of pecuniary independence tends to the promotion of morality and the proper fulfilment of the duties of life.'

Lord Coleridge, in the past year (1877), introduced a Bill which would have given effect to these sentiments, and full legal existence to a married woman. But it was hustled out of the House of Peers by the Lord Chancellor, who for the occasion reproduced the 'Old Bailey view' of Lord Penzance. Lord Coleridge has the support in this matter of another very distinguished Judge. The Master of the Rolls has declared that to him 'it is not intelligible upon what principle a woman should be considered incapable of contracting, immediately after she has, with the sanction of the law, entered into the most important contract conceivable.' Sir George Jessel has further pointed to the fact that 'the slavery laws of antiquity are the origin of the Common Law upon this subject,' and has expressed his astonishment 'that a law founded upon such principles should have survived to the nineteenth century.' 'The rule in this matter'—I am quoting the words of Mr. Mill—'is simple; whatever would be the wife's or husband's, if they were not married, should be under their exclusive control during marriage; which need not interfere with the power to tie up property by settlement, in order to preserve it for children. Some people are sentimentally shocked at the idea of a separate interest in money matters, as inconsistent with the fusion of two lives into one. For my own part, I am one of the strongest supporters of community of goods, when resulting from entire unity of feeling in the owners, which makes all things common between them. But I have no relish for a community of goods resting on the doctrine that what is mine is yours, but what is yours is not mine; and I should prefer to decline entering into such a compact with any one, though I were myself the person to profit by it.'

In no point did Mrs. Norton find the Law relating to the Property of Married Women more galling than in the nullity of a contract, securing her income during separation, which was ' repudiated on the legal technicality that " man and wife being one, a man could not contract with his own wife." ' But at all points she was met and injured by the laws.

When Englishmen beat General Haynau in rude recompense for his alleged flogging of Hungarian women, a charge which the General denied, Mrs. Norton asked : ' Is there no pain and degradation except *physical* pain and degradation ? Is there no indecency but in ideas of nudity ? No barbarity but in stripes and blows ? The Haynaus of England are they who will not help to change such laws ! Had I been a man, I would have worked out their revision and reform ; but I am only a woman —and, in the land which my Queen governs, women count for nothing in important matters.' Then, with reviving eloquence, she resolved, ' woman though I be,' she would do what she could ; and saying, ' This is not a day to smile at *any* boast of what accidental circumstances or individual energy may bring about,' drew this beautiful illustration :

' Sixty-eight years ago, on the deck of a vessel struggling through a stormy passage to the Isle of Martinique, sat the mournful mother of a little girl only three years old. This mother was young, beautiful, forsaken. Her husband, being weary of her, had become " a little profligate "—and the wife yearning—as many a broken-hearted girl has yearned before, under such circumstances of neglect and disappointment—for the old dear home of her childhood, was returning to her parents and friends. There was no fierceness in that woman's heart. Her grief was the gentle grief of Faust's Margaret :—

" Ich wein'—ich wein'—ich weine ! "

In love and generous devotion through life, she had scarcely her equal ; and she had through life the fate those women who seem to deserve it least oftenest obtain. For that mournful Creole weeping alone on the stormy seas —helplessly returning to her own family—was Josephine de Beauharnais, the neglected wife of the Comte de Beauharnais, afterwards the repudiated Empress of Napoleon I., and that little child—who sat trembling in the storm by its mother's side—was Hortense, afterwards Queen of Holland, and mother of Napoleon III.

' If, as that Creole mother wept, some voice had whispered, Your lot is grief—grief now, and grief in spite of splendour in the years to come—but you shall be Empress of France ; the little girl by your side shall be a Queen, her son an Emperor, and the music of a chance love-song which that child shall compose in after-years shall become the great solemn march and national hymn of France ; for ever making melody of triumph in her son's ears, whether sounding on his native shores among millions of electing sub-jects, or played in the royal palaces of a rival nation, proud of reckoning upon his friendship and alliance—I say, if such a whisper had come in the wild wind and mingled with the dash of the stormy spray, would not the fervent-hearted Creole have shuddered with fear lest delirium—not hope—had taken possession of her mind ? God only sets the measure of *what may be ;* and I say my son or grandson may be Lord Chancellor, and may alter these laws in favour of the lawless, at present in force in England.'

'The greater part of what women write about women is mere sycophancy to men.' That was Mr. Mill's opinion, and it is true to a certain extent even of Mrs. Norton. She resembled Madame de Staël in this amiable weakness. 'Un homme peut braver l'opinion ; une femme doit s'y soumettre,' is the motto of *Delphine.* The title-page of Mrs. Norton's boldest and best work, 'A Letter to the Queen,' from which some of my quo-tations have been made, has for a motto, 'Only a woman's hair.' Injustice called from her eloquent and passionate protest ; she claimed 'protection' from the law. The true right of women— that of equality before the law—she never put forward ; she was apt to confuse that claim with a plea for natural equality, which can be no creation of Parliament, and has nothing whatever to do with law. She declared her 'honest conviction to be' that 'women have one RIGHT (perhaps that only one). They have a right, founded on nature, equity, and religion, to the protection of man.' She was bitterly conscious that in her own case even this pitiful claim had been denied. Had she been less unhappy, less conscious of her personal petition, she would have been more stubborn ; her claim would have been a larger petition of right. She was over-weighted with the burden of her own sorrows. She was the victim of bad laws. But her hope that her sufferings would be the seed of reform, was a well-grounded hope. Her belief that such examples are 'the little hinges on which the great doors of justice are made to turn,' had a sure foundation ; and the only prophecy on which she ventured has been verified, and will be further verified.   It was this: ' In our little corner of the earth—where so much besides is busy and fermenting for change—the time is ripely come for alteration in the laws for women.   *And they will be changed.'*

Hazell, Watson, and Viney, Printers, London and Aylesbury

www.ingramcontent.com/pod-product-compliance
Lightning Source LLC
Chambersburg PA
CBHW030912270326
41929CB00008B/667